ACCELERATING

THE

GLOBALIZATION

OF

AMERICA

THE ROLE FOR INFORMATION TECHNOLOGY

INSTITUTE FOR INTERNATIONAL ECONOMICS

ACCELERATING

THE

GLOBALIZATION

OF

AMERICA

THE ROLE FOR INFORMATION TECHNOLOGY

CATHERINE L. MANN

WITH JACOB FUNK KIRKEGAARD

WASHINGTON, DC • JUNE 2006

Catherine L. Mann has been a senior fellow at the Institute since 1997. She served as assistant director of the International Finance Division at the Federal Reserve Board of Governors, senior international economist on the President's Council of Economic Advisers at the White House, and adviser to the chief economist at the World Bank. She directed the Ford Foundation–funded project Latin-Asian Dialogue to support collaborative research comparing Asian and Latin American countries on how technology affects entrepreneurship, government, education and skills, and financial intermediation. She has also engaged in projects on technology and policy in China, Thailand, Vietnam, Taiwan, Sri Lanka, Mexico, Morocco, Tunisia, South Africa, Australia, Canada, Finland, Germany, and New Zealand. She is the author or coauthor of *APEC and the New Economy* (2002), *Global Electronic Commerce: A Policy Primer* (2000), and *Is the US Trade Deficit Sustainable?* (1999). Her current work focuses on the economic and policy issues of global information, communications, and technology, particularly with reference to the US economy, labor market, and international trade.

Jacob Funk Kirkegaard has been a research associate at the Institute since 2002. Before joining the Institute, he worked with the Danish Ministry of Defense, the United Nations in Iraq, and in the private financial sector. He is a graduate of the Danish Army's Special School of Intelligence and Linguistics with the rank of first lieutenant; the University of Aarhus in Aarhus, Denmark; and Columbia University in New York. He is the coauthor of *Transforming the European Economy* (2004). His current research focuses on European economies and reform, pension systems and accounting rules, demographics, offshoring, high-skilled immigration, and the impact of information technology.

INSTITUTE FOR INTERNATIONAL ECONOMICS
1750 Massachusetts Avenue, NW
Washington, DC 20036-1903
(202) 328-9000   FAX: (202) 659-3225
www.iie.com

C. Fred Bergsten, *Director*
Valerie Norville, *Director of Publications and Web Development*
Edward Tureen, *Director of Marketing*

Typesetting by BMWW
Printing by United Book Press, Inc.
Cover photo: Getty Images

Printed in the United States of America
08 07 06   5 4 3 2 1

Library of Congress Cataloging-in-Publication Data

Mann, Catherine L.
   Accelerating the globalization of America : the role for information technology / Catherine L. Mann, assisted by Jacob F. Kirkegaard.
       p. cm.
   Includes bibliographical references and index.
   ISBN 0-88132-390-X (978-0-88132-390-0 : alk. paper)
   1. Computer industry—United States. 2. Information technology—Economic aspects—United States.   3. Globalization—United States.   I. Kirkegaard, Jacob F. II. Title.

HD9696.2.U62M35 2006
303.48'330973—dc22   2006015561

Contents

Figures

Boxes

Preface

Throughout the latter half of the 1990s, the expanded importance of information technology (IT) clearly raised productivity growth in the United States. But did globalization of IT also play an important role? On the one hand, cross-border trade in IT products moved from trade surplus into deficit. On the other hand, IT companies pursuing a globally integrated strategy reaped huge rewards. Subsequent to the technology bust in 2000, white-collar employment of US technology professionals fell even as immigration of technology professionals expanded. During the 2004 political campaign, "outsourcing" and "offshoring" of US jobs became a hot topic. With the increased emphasis on national security after 9/11, the potential for doing more research and development abroad also raised eyebrows. The objective of this book is to analyze all these issues and to answer a central question facing US policy and US business: how the globalization of the IT sector is affecting the overall globalization of America.

The book examines the pattern of globalization of the IT sector and how globalization reduces the prices of these products. It notes that foreign markets are becoming increasingly important as both producers and buyers of these products, a fact that encourages companies to go global. At home, the lower prices afforded by globalization promote greater adoption and diffusion of IT throughout the economy. The subsequent transformation of business processes generates the productivity growth that continues to be enjoyed by the overall US economy, as reflected in high economic growth rates and low inflation. There is clearly room for the continued globalization of IT, particularly in software and services, to contribute to further US productivity growth, as leading nontechnology sectors deepen their use of IT and lagging nontechnology sectors start to adopt it.

However, these forces have not been evenly distributed throughout the economy. The flip side of business transformation and productivity growth is pressure for labor market adjustment. As IT is taken up by more sectors, including nontechnology service activities, the requirements for such adjustment are felt more widely. At the same time, with other countries also embracing IT, more pervasive globalization forces are reaching into sectors and occupations that have never before faced international competition. This deeper global engagement appears to increase job churn and differential returns to job skills and to widen wage disparities throughout the economy. The demands for labor adjustment are as unprecedented as the productivity growth that we all enjoy, and they are likely to increase with even wider diffusion of IT.

The Institute for International Economics has for some time noted that the gains to the United States from globalization, while very large, are not equitably shared. We have repeatedly argued for clear and close linkages between domestic and international policies, suggesting how such linkages need to be central to US foreign economic policy (especially in *The United States and the World Economy: Foreign Economic Policy for the Next Decade*, 2005) and proposing new approaches, such as wage insurance, to support positive adjustment. This book examines these tensions against the backdrop of an industry that is both global and innovative. In the context of IT, globalization goes hand in hand with technological change and requires analysis of what domestic policies are needed to facilitate adjustment so that resources remain fully employed, thereby ensuring that the benefits of both globalization and technological change are widely shared. The book's policy proposals focus on further promoting the business transformation that is key to productivity growth, facilitating the needed labor market adjustment—in particular, rectifying skill depreciation within the current technological working class and ensuring an adequate pipeline of both research workers and funding to support technological leadership.

The Institute for International Economics is a private, nonprofit institution for the study and discussion of international economic policy. Its purpose is to analyze important issues in that area and to develop and communicate practical new approaches for dealing with them. The Institute is completely nonpartisan.

The Institute is funded by a highly diversified group of philanthropic foundations, private corporations, and interested individuals. Major institutional grants are now being received from the William M. Keck, Jr. Foundation and the Starr Foundation. About 33 percent of the Institute's resources in its latest fiscal year were provided by contributors outside the United States, including about 16 percent from Japan. Specific support for this project was provided by the Toyota Motor Corporation, the Ewing Marion Kauffman Foundation, and the Japan Foundation–Center for Global Partnership.

The Institute's Board of Directors bears overall responsibilities for the Institute and gives general guidance and approval to its research program, including the identification of topics that are likely to become important over the medium run (one to three years) and that should be addressed by the Institute. The director, working closely with the staff and outside Advisory Committee, is responsible for the development of particular projects and makes the final decision to publish an individual study.

The Institute hopes that its studies and other activities will contribute to building a stronger foundation for international economic policy around the world. We invite readers of these publications to let us know how they think we can best accomplish this objective.

C. FRED BERGSTEN
Director
May 2006

Executive Summary

Beyond the hyperbole of the technology boom of the 1990s, a strong and steady undercurrent of transformation is sweeping through firms, workplaces, and markets in the United States and, to a lesser degree, the global economy. Technological innovation lies at the heart of these changes, but they are enhanced by the policy and business environment, and by globalization, particularly of information technology (IT) and communications networks. The forces of innovation and globalization affect more than just the technologically advanced sectors. The globalization of IT and innovation promotes increased investment in, and the pervasive use of, networked IT throughout the US economy. This widespread use of IT and communications in the United States, along with the embrace by other countries of the possibilities created by these technologies, have accelerated America's overall global engagement, economic growth, and consequent labor adjustments.

Limiting or otherwise slowing down technological change and globalization means forgoing real and large gains such as productivity growth, job creation, and higher living standards. The absence of innovation and globalization constrains a country's economic potential. On the other hand, failure to address the adjustment costs that can be a consequence of such globalized technological change also hampers efforts to achieve those potential gains, to the extent that business capital and workers are not well matched to rapidly evolving economic needs. These mismatches generate macroeconomic sluggishness, as well as anxiety for the people affected, thus shrinking the economic pie inside a country's potential frontier. Therefore, policy must promote innovation and technological change while also facilitating adjustment to that change, rather than limiting or avoiding change or ignoring redistribution. Such policies will ensure that all resources of the economy are used efficiently and effectively.

IT is an uncommon product—it is called a "general-purpose technology." Given the right economic and institutional environments, it generates broad-based investment demand throughout the economy. Investment in IT and communications products is price elastic, so lower prices induce a more than one-for-one increase in investment demand. The resulting investment in IT and communications by nontechnology sectors raises productivity growth through two channels: first, the investment itself, through capital deepening; and second (particularly evident in the United States), by boosting total factor productivity (TFP), which increases when firms network together and use IT and communications effectively to change their business strategies and workplace practices. IT and communications in the workplace yield key changes in the demand for skills: The return to cognitive and problem-solving skills rises, but the return to step-by-step routine activities falls. The ensuing labor restructuring also is part of TFP.

All told, IT and communications are productivity-enhancing tools and intermediate activities that change the nature of what a business does, how it does it, and whom it employs. Regarding the US economy, against a backdrop of higher productivity growth at the macroeconomic level, there is substantial variation in the impact of IT and communications on individual sectors and occupations. This variation may point to areas for future productivity gains and occupational changes as technological innovation and globalization proceed.

What is the role for globalization in this process? IT and communications constitute a rapidly changing global industry. While the United States is the leader in the use and diffusion of IT products into the economy, other countries are rapidly increasing production, and a growing number are using the tools of IT and communications networks to engage in global trade as well as to induce domestic transformation. Fragmented and globalized production by both US and foreign IT firms—through cross-border investment, production, and sales—reduce IT and communications prices further. Given the linkage between prices and widespread investment and organizational transformation, the globalization of the IT industry accelerates, broadens, and deepens the globalization of America.

Globalization and technological change are altering the business strategy of US IT firms, with implications for the balance of payments. The United States remains the largest market for spending on IT products (hardware, software, and services). However, foreign markets are growing more quickly, particularly for commodity hardware, which can be produced more cheaply in those markets both for those markets and for the home market as well. At the same time, around the world but particularly in industrial countries, there is a shift toward relatively more spending on IT services and software—tools that make the hardware work for the customer. These two factors—faster global demand growth and the shift toward IT services and software—are reflected in the production, hiring, and trade patterns of US multinational IT firms. These firms buy cheaper intermediate products and develop high-value-added hardware for sale to global markets. They increasingly emphasize IT services and software, which are developed and delivered in the destination markets.

Globalization of IT and communications networks goes beyond firms in the IT sector to facilitate more tradable business and professional services. Nontechnology sectors (such as finance) that are leaders in investment in IT and networks as well as in productivity performance are also leaders in international trade in business and professional services. Going forward, enhanced use of globalized IT by more service sectors could usher in a new wave of productivity growth as this globalization reduces the prices of IT services and software, enabling IT adoption by more service activities, as well as more two-way trade in services.

These gains from IT could accrue more widely throughout the world, but various policy, business, environmental, and international factors hamper the domestic uptake of IT abroad. It is crucial that other countries ultimately use IT to promote domestic economic development, rather than focus only on producing IT products for export. First, this technology applied to local needs promotes domestic development and productivity gains, which encourages more balanced domestic growth. Second, the liberalization of services and sectors that have newly opened to the possibility of international trade because of IT creates the possibility of two-way trade in services. This trade benefits both the US and foreign economies and facilitates more balanced global and domestic growth patterns.

As technology becomes more integral to all facets of business organization and activity, and as more foreign countries embrace its possibilities, a greater share of the US and global economies becomes exposed to international economic forces. This expansion and deepening of globalization on the back of increased use of networked IT highlights long-standing policy challenges and creates new challenges as well.

First, to maintain technological leadership, the United States must keep the engine of innovation stoked. Some innovation is keyed to local market needs, some comes from globally integrated teams, and some is "blue-sky." Maintaining a pipeline of new products, services, and ideas that meet the known (and unknown) needs of US businesses, consumers, and government requires sufficient home-grown researchers, discerning buyers, and adequate public and private funding for innovation.

The second policy challenge involves the domestic and global diffusion of this productivity-enhancing, general-purpose technology. To keep the prices of technology and technology-enabled activities declining, and to facilitate an even greater uptake of IT in the domestic economy, the United States needs to work harder to negotiate deeper global engagement, particularly in newly created international markets for services. Enhanced productivity growth through the use and diffusion of IT abroad comes in part from more liberalized trade in services.

Finally, as a consequence of both faster technological change and deeper global engagement, a larger segment of the economy will have global opportunities and face global competition, which raises the stakes for incumbent as well as new workers. A new policy agenda and compact is needed for workforce preparation and participation.

Maximizing the benefits of technological innovation and transformation, which go hand-in-hand with deeper globalization, is key to ensuring the continued positive impact of IT on the US economy and beyond. But so too is ensuring that the benefits of those innovations are more widely obtainable and shared. Innovations not implemented because resources cannot adjust forfeit some of the potential of the economy.

These changes are appearing fast and furiously. Agile businesses respond to the opportunities and challenges, and workers feel the effects. So policymakers also must respond to the new environment of globalization and technological change. The United States needs to develop optimal policies to prepare new workers and support current ones as they face the joint challenges of technological change and globalization.

If the United States fails in this policy leadership, the greater promise of globalization and technological change will be muted not only here but also around the world as other countries similarly may be unable to galvanize the policy changes they need to reap the gains. As the world's technological and market leader the United States stands to gain more, or lose more, if other countries limit the internal changes to their economies that technology entails. The pace and economywide scope of technological change and globalization are quickening and broadening. Urgent attention to policy leadership is crucial.

Chapter Overviews

Chapter 1 of this book discusses why an analysis of accelerating globalization starts with the more narrow focus on IT products and the IT and communications industries. Investment in IT, and its pervasive use throughout the economy, is probably the most important single factor precipitating dramatic and rapid changes that are affecting firms and workers economywide. Just as scientists use the petri dish to accelerate the production of bacteria for study, so too does a study that starts with IT inform how technological and global forces accelerate change in the US economy. The chapter's findings include the following:

- IT is income and price elastic. Income elastic means that as GDP grows, the demand for IT products increases more than one-for-one with it. Price elastic means that as prices decline, the investment demand for IT products increases more than one-for-one with the declines in price.

These elasticities are a reflection of the general-purpose nature of IT and are crucial factors underlying the role that IT has played in enhancing economywide productivity growth, particularly in the United States.

- Data for foreign markets reflect the income elasticity. In markets with rapidly growing income—regardless of the level of that income—expenditures on IT products increase even faster. For example, during the 1990s, real GDP growth for Singapore, Korea, Poland, Malaysia, China, and India—countries with very disparate levels of GDP per capita—was greater than 4 percent, while the increase in IT spending was more than double that.

- Responsiveness to price changes—that is, price elasticity—is a second important ingredient in considering how the globalization of IT accelerates US productivity growth. To the extent that the globalization of IT production reduces the price of the IT product below what it otherwise would have been in the absence of globalization, then price declines are greater, and demand for IT products increases further, which feeds into higher productivity growth. Considered another way, relatively lower prices for IT products due to the globalization of production raises the rate of return to IT investment, and more projects achieve internal benchmarks that firms use to decide whether to invest.

Chapter 2 presents data and analysis on the linkages between US firms and global marketplaces for IT production and demand. The US market for IT products is, by far, the largest in the world. However, both production and demand for these products are expanding rapidly abroad, particularly in the developing world. In addition, spending is shifting from hardware to software and IT services—tools that make the hardware work—particularly in the industrial economies. These patterns of global demand, along with the technological capabilities to increasingly fragment IT production, influence US producers' business strategies. The chapter's findings include the following:

- IT spending can be decomposed into spending on hardware, software, and IT services. Although spending on all categories has risen in all countries, the composition has changed over time and differs in a systematic way across the level of economic development. The growth rate of global spending on IT hardware, which is fastest in the developing world, is now exceeded by the growth rates of spending on IT services and software.

- Within the global market, the US market is still the largest, accounting for 40 percent of global spending in 2003. But new markets and producers have emerged, particularly in the developing world, which did not, in general, experience the technology crash of 2001. Global exports of IT hardware have become less concentrated among producers in industrial countries.

- Trends within the US marketplace and for US multinational firms are a microcosm of what is happening in the overall global marketplace. US multinational IT firms are expanding sales abroad and shifting toward production of IT services and software. Increasing global competition in the hardware industry has accelerated the trend that sees US firms increasingly producing IT services (including software). IT services sales and employment increased from less than 10 percent of total global activities of US IT firms in 1989 to 42 percent of sales and 57 percent of employment in 2003.

- Patterns of production and sales of US multinationals reflect technology, cost, and demand patterns. Hardware production is more globally integrated with significant cross-border sales of intermediate products (both from the US parents and from their foreign affiliates to other foreign affiliates). IT services are almost exclusively final sales in the destination market. As a result, US hardware multinationals have production facilities around the world, increasingly in low-wage countries where labor-cost differentials are 2.7 to 1. In contrast, IT service production facilities are principally in the industrial markets where labor costs are similar to the United States.

- As US multinationals have focused on producing high-value-added hardware for export and have emphasized IT services and software, foreign firms have played an increasingly important role in the US marketplace as producers, and particularly as importers, of IT hardware, particularly commodity hardware. The resulting overall trade deficit in IT hardware, which contributes through lower prices to higher productivity growth overall in the US economy, comes from imports from unaffiliated foreign producers.

Chapter 3 traces how the globalization of the IT industry and the widespread diffusion of IT products have affected the US economy. Even taking the results of innovation as the most important factor, the globalization of IT production has large, specific, and quantifiable effects on the US economy because lower prices increase the diffusion of IT investment and promote a broader transformation of business and the workplace. This broad transformation of business and the workplace underpins the acceleration of productivity enjoyed by the US economy. The chapter's findings include the following:

- There are two categories of IT hardware for which there is sufficient information to do a structured analysis of the impact of globalization on IT prices: dynamic random access memory chips (DRAMs) and personal computers (PCs). These products are a paradigm for understanding more generally the forces linking the globalization of IT production and the prices of IT products for US buyers. The bulk of the overall trend decline in DRAM prices is almost surely due to innovation in production technology. But new global production facilities and changes in global production and demand as reflected in price-cost margins also significantly affect the prices of DRAMs for US buyers. For PCs, an increase in net imports of computers, peripherals, and parts accelerates the decline in prices due to an increased net supply of PCs in the US market. New foreign producers and importers of PCs and laptops play a large role in these price dynamics.

- Globalization of IT services and software is just beginning and has taken hold only in certain segments of commodity- or network-oriented products. In the more competitive and globalized market for computer games and prepackaged software, price declines are significant, although still less than for IT hardware. For the more tailored custom software, less globalization has taken place, and prices have not fallen.

- Trends in the use of IT in the US economy can be measured via input-output tables. The share of IT hardware in total intermediates fell from 3.4 to 2.4 percent between 1998 and 2004, but the share of IT services in total intermediates rose from 1.5 to 2 percent. The drop in hardware is consistent with its lower prices, and the two trends together are consistent with the movement away from hardware as well as with the growing importance of IT services (including software) for making IT useful to firms.

- The first key aspect of the relationship between IT capital and productivity growth is the complementary relationships between IT investments within the plant, IT investments to network plants, and IT use by workers. To the extent that globalization of IT reduces the price of investments and aids or hinders IT uptake (including the training needed by workers to use it effectively), productivity growth likely is enhanced or dampened. Two additional links between productivity and international trade are that trade in technologically sophisticated products is associated with higher productivity and that industries that have invested heavily in IT have a greater propensity to export.

- Substantial sectoral variation underlies the macroeconomic relationship between productivity growth and IT investment. Service sectors both lead and lag in the use of IT and in contributions to productivity acceleration. The leading service sectors account for 31 percent of GDP and include wholesale trade, securities and commodity brokers, depository institutions, and communications. These activities evidence strong network externalities from forward linkages to customers. Lagging sectors, such as health care, construction, and some business services, exhibit low IT intensity and a below-average contribution to productivity acceleration. These may lag because of the less "codifiable" information content of the activities of the sector, the lesser degree to which firms in the sector are organized in or around IT networks, the greater number of small and medium-sized enterprises in the sector, the greater extent of sector-specific regulation, and less exposure to international market forces.

- Widespread use of IT and the ensuing productivity experience of the United States are relatively rare. Research on industrial countries suggests that differences in outcomes relate to differences in patterns of investment and responsiveness of domestic markets to economic signals, as well as to patterns of international trade. In particular, detailed data comparing the United States and Europe point to differential productivity growth in service activities as the source of differential overall performance. Analysis of developing countries reveals that the emphasis on production and export of IT products, rather than domestic investment and use, does not fully exploit the potential gains from IT. This is because the declining prices for IT products in global markets mean that the terms of trade (export prices compared with prices of imported products) are moving against these producers.

Chapter 4 first considers international trade in IT products and then examines how deeper globalization of IT, as well as policy reforms and the development of strategies in key countries, means that a wide range of services—heretofore "nontraded" business and professional services ranging from finance to back-office accounting—may now be traded internationally or have the potential to be internationally tradable in the near future. The chapter's findings include the following:

- International trade in IT products comprises both intrafirm trade by multinationals and what is called arm's-length trade between unaffiliated firms. The behavior of such relationships differs across IT hardware and software and IT services. For hardware, intrafirm trade of US-parent IT hardware multinationals is a positive contributor to the balance of payments, but it is becoming a smaller proportion of IT hardware trade. Imports of intermediate products from affiliates appear to support increases in foreign sales of higher-value-added hardware products. But these foreign affiliates of US parents increasingly meet foreign demand from their own production facilities abroad. So the overall balance of payments deficit in IT hardware comes from growing imports from unaffiliated firms, as well as from foreign producers (the new global entrants). In contrast, in IT services (including software), the overall trade balance is positive, but the figures for intrafirm trade are negative. The higher (and increasing) affiliated import share as well as the rising pace of two-way trade may be evidence of increased fragmentation of the software and IT service production process to new affiliates abroad.

- International trade in a wide range of business and professional services is an increasingly important part of the global economic landscape. Increased use of IT and international communications networks both in the United States and abroad are key factors underpinning the globalization of this broad range of services. Technological change, as well as changes in customer and business attitudes over time, has eroded the attributes of services—transactions costs and functional integration—that heretofore made them "nontradable."

- The United States is the global leader in international trade in services, but there is also substantial two-way trade. For the United States, international trade in services such as finance and many components of business, professional, and technical services is growing despite relatively lackluster GDP growth in the major industrial markets for these exports, and the US services trade balance remains solidly in surplus. The competitive advantage of the US environment in business and professional and technical services is corroborated by data on where multinational corporations conduct their "headquarters" services. US multinationals expanding overseas and integrating their operations globally has not been associated with a deterioration of the US services trade balance. In addition, foreign multinationals with subsidiaries in the United States also are increasingly doing their internal service transactions in this country.

- There are "natural" as well as policy-induced limits on the globalization of services. Natural limits come from the interface between the global marketplace and the local jurisdiction with regard to policy and regulation, as well as heterogeneity with regard to "face-to-face" needs for some buyers and sellers of services. For example, professional licensure and regulatory standards vary across domestic as well as international jurisdictions, and mutual recognition agreements do not yet exist. Policy-induced limits include the fact that international trade negotiations have made little headway in agreeing on a more liberalized trade regime for many of the services that can be done internationally. Much greater attention to such negotiations is warranted. Trade liberalization scenarios find that for many economies, the gains from service-sector liberalization alone could be about one-half of the total gain from liberalizing agriculture, manufacturing, and services together. This is because services are an input to the international trade of all other products.

Chapter 5 discusses the implications of the synergies between trade and technological change for US workers. Data point to greater volatility in job prospects and to particular risks facing some low- and middle-income workers from this combination of technology and increased tradability of services. On the other hand, workers with a combination of skills flourish in the new environment. The chapter's findings include the following:

■ During the boom years when IT was being incorporated widely through-out the economy, job churn increased. The very transformation and net-working of businesses that generate productivity growth and macro-economic gain have, at the same time, contributed significantly to the restructuring of labor activities.

■ As IT becomes more deeply integrated throughout the economy, work-ers with IT skills will be more exposed to the general business cycle because they are not necessarily working in the IT sector but rather in IT occupations throughout the economy. Indeed, two-thirds of those employed in IT occupations are not in the IT-producing industries (hardware, services, and software).

■ Not only do workers in IT occupations now face business-cycle risk but also some rungs on the occupation ladder face explicit technology risk. Certain occupations (such as computer programmers) face risks consistent with an increased "commoditization" of these skills. Other workers (such as computer operators) are replaced as PC use domi-nates mainframe computers. In addition, the fragmentation of the pro-duction process of software in conjunction with the cheaper interna-tional communications linkages changes the skills demanded in the United States and allows some of these skills to be purchased abroad.

■ Factors that have reduced the price of IT and thus facilitated more investment in IT differentially affect US workers with different levels of educational attainment and who do different tasks in different sec-tors. Greater investment in IT in some industries has yielded higher returns to those workers with educational attainment beyond high school. Industries whose business processes have favored investment in IT have moved the task mix in favor of workers with higher skills. IT appears to play a role in the rising earnings dispersion observed in the wage data. To the extent that the globalization of IT reduces its price and promotes its diffusion, globalization and IT go hand-in-hand to exacerbate earnings inequality in America.

■ Determining what service occupations might be at greater risk for international tradability is challenging. One approach considers the geographic concentration of occupations, with the most concentrated potentially more tradable. Some 30 percent of the US labor force falls into this category, and the number of jobs in these occupations is increasing. On the one hand, workers in these occupations earn about 17 percent more than similar workers in nontradable service occupations. On the other hand, these workers also face a more volatile job environment, with higher rates of job loss. These highest-earning yet volatile occupations appear to be in the same sectors that have the highest IT intensity and make the greatest contribution to productivity growth, and where there is comparative advantage in international trade.

■ Detailed data on IT-related professions are a microcosm of broader trends. Low-wage workers who use IT (telemarketers, switchboard operators, telephone operators, computer operators, and data entry keyers) appear to be particularly hurt by the combined effect of technology and international trade, with 711,000 jobs, representing some 30 percent of these jobs, disappearing during 1999–2004. On the other hand, the number of jobs held by high-skilled, judgment-oriented, and problem-solving IT workers—such as researchers, applications and systems software engineers, database administrators, and network systems engineers and administrators (but excluding programmers)—increased by 513,000 jobs, or by about 23 percent, over the same period. However, the data also show the rising skill "bar" against which domestic and foreign workers compete in the global marketplace. Between 1999 and November 2004, the number of high-wage "programming" jobs fell by 133,000, or almost 25 percent of the number of these jobs held in 1999.

■ The increased globalization of services includes the cross-border movement of skilled workers via skilled-worker visa programs (L-1 and H-1B visas). Countries with close economic relations in terms of direct investments in and cross-ownership of companies, such as the United Kingdom, Japan, and Germany, top the list of countries whose citizens are admitted on L-1 visas. With regard to H1-B visas, "computer-related occupations" is by far the biggest occupational category of H-1B recipients. Indian citizens accounted for about half of all H-1B visa petitions granted in 1999–2001, but they also accounted for about 70 percent of the total decline in numbers of H-1B visa petitions granted for initial employment in 2001–02.

■ Corporate users of H-1B workers include Motorola, Oracle, Cisco, Intel, Microsoft, and IBM but also the US finance industry and major educational institutions. Some large employers of H-1B workers are Indian IT service companies in the United States. The average wage paid appears to exceed the average prevailing wage for similar jobs, but with caveats. US firms show a much wider dispersion of wages offered, as well as a higher average wage, which suggests that US firms consider a wider diversity of candidates in terms of skills and specialized knowledge.

Chapter 6 looks at the next phase of global integration—innovation itself, including research and development (R&D), venture capital funding, and the pipeline of research professionals. Data suggest both positive and sobering views on continued US technological leadership. The chapter's findings include the following:

- R&D plays an important role in US productivity performance and economic growth, accounting for between 5 and 9 percent of growth in GDP over 1996–2000 and between 3 and 10 percent over 1961–2000. However, R&D can come through several channels, including from abroad. US productivity growth is about 30 percent higher in industry sectors where there is inward foreign direct investment and high R&D intensity, suggesting positive spillovers between global and domestic technological innovation.

- Data point to a rising research intensity for the US economy overall, a much higher and rising research intensity in the IT sectors, and a dramatically lower research intensity at US IT affiliates abroad compared with their parents in the United States. The computer and electronic products sector has 2.8 times more research workers than the economy overall, while software has 5.3 times more. Within the IT sector, research-worker intensity is shifting from IT hardware to IT software and services, consistent with previous patterns noted.

- With regard to patenting activities, the US share of US Patent and Trademark Office patents granted to US-located, first-named inventors has remained relatively stable, albeit with a bit of a decline in recent years. Despite these aggregate data, individual US firms continue to lead patenting, and US IT firms are increasingly represented in the top ranks of patenting firms. No other country comes close, not Japan nor Europe as a whole.

- The intellectual property surplus in the balance of payments has continued to rise. The bulk of the increase in intellectual property receipts comes from rising net intellectual property in services, whereas net intellectual property for manufacturing has stagnated. In addition, R&D and testing services run a consistent trade surplus.

- The picture of the US workforce, which needs to be able to create, work with, and buy innovative products, is less salutary. The heart of the current US workforce (aged 45 to 64) remains the best-educated workforce among the member countries of the Organization for Economic Cooperation and Development. The younger workforce in the United States faces more rapid technological change and deeper global integration, with resulting higher stakes. Yet the generation of Americans entering the workforce today (25- to 34-year-olds) barely makes the top-10 ranking in terms of educational levels of OECD member workforces, although those educated at the tertiary level fare substantially better against this global standard.

- Given the importance of research workers for research-intensive IT and related activities, both the "incumbent stock" as well as the "pipeline flow" of science and technology talent are important. About 40 percent of all graduate students and all science and engineering PhDs awarded at US universities (rising to more than half in mathematics/computer sciences and engineering) are non-US citizens and nonpermanent residents. With rapidly improving career and business opportunities in the home countries of many foreign students (notably India and China), an increasing proportion of these students appear to be returning home. These science and technology demographics, in conjunction with the locus of demand for technology products shifting to rapidly growing economies abroad, encourage US firms to open R&D facilities in foreign countries.

- The number of foreign countries receiving venture capital finance has increased, particularly in the last 15 years, with firms in more than 50 countries currently receiving funds. The percentage of venture funding going abroad remains quite small, although there is a rising trend in small-value seed money going abroad. There is growing interest in funding portfolio companies both in the developing world as well as in countries with key skills. The top countries and regions receiving US venture finance are the EU countries, the United Kingdom, and Canada. However, the next largest total recipient over 1999–2005 was China, with India and Israel ranked after Korea and the Nordic countries and Switzerland.

Chapter 7 puts forth a policy agenda to ensure that the benefits of technology-enhanced globalization continue and are widely shared. A proactive policy agenda will promote innovation in the United States and encourage and enable US workers and businesses to embrace and use IT to make the most of global opportunities in production, sales, and trade in both the manufacturing and service arenas. The US policy agenda can be the model for other countries. To have no policy agenda or strategy has both short- and long-term consequences. In the short term, a slowdown in productivity growth or poor matching of labor skills to evolving labor demands implies lackluster job creation and a US economy operating below its potential. In the longer term, if innovation flags and skill-building is inadequate, the United States will relinquish its technological and economic leadership.

A proactive agenda must meet global challenges as well as the challenges of innovation and transformation. Innovation creates a technological frontier, which pushes out the potential of the economy. Innovation increasingly will be global, so how will the United States retain its leadership? Transformation means that businesses must be able to change products and production techniques, and workers must have the desire and skills to welcome new job opportunities. But transformation also means business turbulence and job restructuring and losses, even as there is greater growth overall, so what policies promote transformation and adjustment? Global competition comes as more countries use IT domestically for growth, rather than only as a source of export revenues. This, in turn, means that more countries could be customers and partners, if markets are open. What should the United States do to promote effective use of IT around the world? A proactive agenda by firms and policymakers centered on these themes can meet the specific challenges of new ideas, new jobs, and new competition, which can deepen the benefits of globalization of IT for the overall US economy.

Acknowledgments

This book has been in preparation for quite some time as the "target" kept moving. Early versions focused on understanding relationships among the productivity and technology booms and the IT hardware international trade deficit. The take-off of offshore outsourcing of IT services, software, and other white-collar jobs demanded that the book address this new phenomenon, so the draft was expanded accordingly. Finally, we added sections on the nascent globalization of R&D and venture capital financing and its significance for how IT accelerates the globalization of America.

Sacha Wunsch-Vincent, now at the Organization for Economic Cooperation and Development, and Daniel Gould, now at Morgan Stanley, assisted with the research at various stages while they were at the Institute. Jacob Funk Kirkegaard, who started at the Institute as a research assistant, has through his work on this book developed into a researcher in his own right and is pursuing a PhD in political science.

The Institute has a well-developed strategy for obtaining outside insights and evaluations of its work in progress. Study group participants who read and commented on an intermediate version include Moreno Bertoldi, Jan Boyer, Lael Brainard, Al Fitzpayne, Michael Gadbaw, Markus Haacker, Harry Holzer, Kent Hughes, Ralph Koslow, Vin O'Neill, Steve Stewart, and Tim Wedding as well as my Institute colleagues Mac Destler, Monty Graham, Nick Lardy, Michael Mussa, and Ted Truman. In addition, a number of reviewers read the final manuscript, offered detailed comments, and helped improve the final product. The reviewers include Bart van Ark, Christopher Caine, Dale W. Jorgenson, J. Steven Landefeld, David McCurdy, Harris Miller, Pamela Passman, and Lee Price. The Institute's publications staff ensures that the final product reaches the marketplace in good time and in good shape; my thanks to Madona Devasahayam and Marla Banov in particular.

This book presents puzzles, research questions, and policy issues. It starts but does not finish analyzing the sources and implications of accelerating globalization in America. It offers one very important lens, that of the role for IT. I hope that my structured approach to investigation and multiple sources of data will elicit further research and analysis, which will improve our understanding of the United States in the global economy and the accompanying policy challenges.

Accelerating Globalization: Why Focus on Information Technology?

The US economy is experiencing accelerating globalization. Yet this book starts much more narrowly with a look at information technology (IT). Why focus on IT first? How does IT relate to globalization and the acceleration of change that is its consequence?

First, IT is the most robust growth sector in the global economy, with demand in the world marketplace that outpaces investment and trade growth for any other product. Chapters 2 and 3 will discuss these patterns in much more detail. Second, IT ushers in a dramatic and accelerating pace of change in industries and the workplace, as examined in chapters 4 and 5.

If IT is a global phenomenon, why focus on the United States? The answer is because the United States is not only a leading IT producer and buyer but also the leading IT user, as evidenced by the broad-based diffusion of this technology throughout the economy. Through foreign direct investment and offshore affiliate relationships, US firms are leading forces in globalizing the use of IT. As will be discussed in chapters 5 through 7, the effects of IT—globalization and the acceleration of change— are most apparent in the US economy, as are the consequent policy issues. More broadly, the US experience is a useful harbinger of what may be in store for other countries as they become increasingly exposed to rapid globalization through the pervasive use of networked IT.

Why does IT accelerate change? IT is a special kind of general-purpose technology with significant network effects and a high measured rate of economy-wide return from investment. It is not surprising that demand for IT is so robust. But IT also is becoming a force pushing for more globalization of many nontechnology industries. The technology itself enables an ever-widening range of production of all sorts of goods and services that can be fragmented and carried out in far-flung locations. Since trade and technology demonstrate this complementary dynamic, the globalization of IT by both the United States and other countries feeds on itself to increase investment in and diffusion of IT throughout the US economy. This, in turn, accelerates the overall globalization of America.

Globalization in a Petri Dish

The story of the accelerating pace of globalization of the US economy starts with IT. The sector has seen dramatic and rapid innovation, as evidenced by unprecedented declines in quality-adjusted prices of computer hardware. Recognition of the globalization of production and demand came with the Information Technology Agreement in 1997, when 44 economies accounting for more than 90 percent of trade agreed to eliminate all tariffs on six categories of key products related to IT and communications by 2000. The communications network of the Internet burst on the global scene only in 1995 and now encircles the world, enhancing the globalization of business and professional services.

Investment in and pervasive use of IT throughout the economy is probably the most important single factor precipitating dramatic and rapid changes that affect firms and workers. Just as scientists use the Petri dish to accelerate the production of bacteria for study, so too does a study that starts with IT inform how technological and global forces accelerate change in the US economy.

IT also has an enormous effect on the US economy because of the strong synergies it creates between global and technological forces. IT and global networks reduce the transaction costs of global production of many kinds of goods, allowing for greater fragmentation of the production process to different locations. Computers, software, and communications networks enhance the digitization and codification of services, which allows them to be functionally separated from the main activities of a firm. Globalization of technology tools and networks facilitates production fragmentation and functional separation along a wider and wider spectrum of goods and services, resulting in innovation-driven and globalization-enhanced change that affects an increasingly larger segment of the US business community and workforce.

Examining the US experience yields insights into the role that IT and networks play in accelerating change not only in the United States but also in other countries. The United States is the worldwide leader in almost every key area of the IT experience, including

- the fragmentation of the production of IT goods and the functional separation of services activities;

- global sourcing for the production of goods and, increasingly, services;

- research and development that advances innovation further in the IT sector, with implications more broadly throughout the economy; and

- most importantly, the pervasive use of IT outside technologically advanced sectors to enhance economic performance and promote broad economic change.

Thus, understanding the globalization of IT is a prerequisite for understanding both the historical and potential future path of the performance of the US economy.

Defining Information Technology

The IT package used throughout the world has numerous components: hardware, software, services, and communications equipment and networks, just to name a few. IT and communications are often analyzed as a joint sector, but this book disaggregates the two sectors, not only addressing them separately but also making even further distinctions. Much of the first half of the book focuses on IT hardware—where it is produced, who buys it, and how it is used throughout the US economy. In part, this focus is because the data are available and superior for a sufficiently long time series for analysis. However, IT services and software as components of the IT package are becoming more important in terms of marketplace size and growth. Finally, communications equipment and networks are extremely important as well, since it is the networked nature of the IT package that makes it particularly valuable for economic performance. Moreover, the changes around the globe in terms of access to communications networks and their price are the key to greater international tradability of business and professional services that goes beyond just IT services to include, for example, call centers and financial analysis. Along with the globalization of IT hardware, software, and services, this increased international tradability of business and professional services is a particular accelerant for the globalization of America (box 1.1).

Why treat IT and communications differently? First, the institutional, regulatory, and ownership structure of communications networks are quite mixed across countries, some partially or wholly government owned, others with limited domestic and cross-border competition in services delivery and investment. Thus, it is difficult to compare data on communications networks across countries. In contrast, virtually all IT hardware, software, and services firms are private-sector companies affected by domestic and global competitive forces.

Related to these market structure differences, technological change can be more easily seen and quantified in the prices of IT products than in the

Box 1.1   Technology definitions

Communications. The total value of voice and data communications services, such as local and long distance wire-line telecommunications, wireless telecommunications, paging, satellite communications, Internet access, private line services, and other data communications services. It also includes communications equipment, such as wire-line and wireless telephone handsets, personal digital assistants (PDAs), wired and wireless local (LAN) and wide area network (WAN) equipment, modems, multiplexers, and telephone answering machines and systems.

Internal company IT spending. A company's own IT staff salaries, software development, and customization expenditure.

IT hardware. The total value of purchased and leased computers, semiconductors, storage devices, memory upgrades, printers, monitors, scanners, input-output devices, terminals, mainframes, and other peripherals.

IT sector. Generally considered to include IT hardware, services, and software.

IT services. The total value of purchased services, such as IT consulting, computer systems integration, network systems integration, office automation, IT facilities management, equipment maintenance, web hosting, computer disaster recovery, and data processing services.

Semiconductors. Considered IT hardware rather than part of the IT services category, these components include printed circuits, semiconductors, memory chips, capacitors, electron tubes, and other miscellaneous electronic components.

Software. The total value of purchased or leased packaged software, such as operating systems, programming tools, utilities, applications, games, and outsourced software development. The last group would include computer programming, World Wide Web page design, and application development.

For additional definitions and information on technology definitions, see WITSA (2002, 2004). See also definitions specific to US statistical agencies in appendix A.

overall communications sector. To be sure, communications prices do change over the time period of analysis, particularly with respect to communications equipment and connection costs in some markets. But it is regulatory change, not technological change, that is the predominant factor affecting the price of communications services.

While the data do not always allow for optimal separation of information and communications technology into these two components, this book will always endeavor to do so, and when not possible, will clearly explain why and how the interpretation of the data might be affected by the commingling of communications with IT.

Economic Characteristics of IT

What is it about IT that leads to such strong growth in demand? IT is an uncommon product—a general-purpose technology characterized by elastic investment. First, investment in IT rises more than one-for-one as an economy becomes wealthier, and as that IT is networked and used more pervasively throughout such economies. IT products generate important spillover effects in the industries that use them and between the firms that are networked using IT.

Moreover, investment in IT is price elastic, so that as prices decline, investment increases more than one-for-one with the declines in prices. These features are consistent with relatively high rates of return on IT investment as compared with investment in other types of plant and equipment or structures. All these characteristics are related to and promote widespread investment in IT by nontechnology industries.

It is also the case, however, as will be discussed in the chapters that follow, that these special characteristics of IT and their implications for generalized economic performance are augmented or tempered by the nature of business, product, and labor markets. Reaping the benefits of this general-purpose technology requires that the forces of change being generated by the IT investments be allowed to percolate through those markets.

Price Elasticity and Income Elasticity Properties of IT Investment

IT is income and price elastic. Income elastic means that as a measure of GDP grows, the demand for IT products increases more than one-for-one with it. Price elastic means that as prices decline, the investment demand for IT products increases more than one-for-one with the declines in price.

GDP elasticity is consistent with a situation where spending on IT products pervades an economy, extending beyond the confines of the IT sector itself. Such is the case in the United States to a great degree and in other countries to some extent. This extension of IT investment and spending is a crucial factor underlying the role that IT has played in enhancing economy-wide productivity growth in the United States.

Data for foreign markets reflect the superior GDP elasticity. In markets with fast-growing income—regardless of the level of that income—expenditures on IT products increase even faster. For example, as ranked by the World Bank's Human Development Index, real annual average GDP growth over the 1990s for Singapore, Korea, Poland, Malaysia, China, and India was above 4 percent, while the increase in IT spending (measured in nominal terms) was more than double that, and in several countries, IT spending increased by more than 15 percent annually during the decade. Data for US producers reveal the same phenomenon. European sales by US IT firms in the 1990s rose 5.1 percent, while GDP in those countries grew by only about 2.5 percent. Asian sales by US IT firms increased by 12 percent, while GDP growth in those countries was 7 percent. A "pull" factor that promotes globalization for US firms is the relatively more rapid growth in GDP in many emerging markets.

Responsiveness to price changes—that is, price elasticity—is a second important ingredient in considering how the globalization of IT accelerates US productivity growth. As will be explored in chapter 2, to the extent that the globalization of IT production reduces the price of the IT product below what it otherwise would have been in the absence of globalization, then price declines are greater and demand for IT products increases. To the extent that investment demand is particularly responsive to price changes, the relatively greater decline in price associated with globalization is associated with more than a one-for-one increase in demand for IT products, which feeds into higher productivity growth. Considered another way, relatively lower prices for IT products due to the globalization of production raises the rate of return to IT investment, and more projects achieve internal benchmarks that firms use to decide whether to invest. Based on econometric estimates, it appears that IT investment is particularly responsive to price changes, meaning that the lower price due to globalization has a magnified effect on demand for these productivity-enhancing products.

Econometric analysis of the demand for IT products yields the key parameters of income and price responsiveness. Surprisingly, there are relatively few estimates of these key parameters. However, several researchers—using different countries, demand variables, time periods, and regression methods—find similar results that confirm that IT demand is particularly responsive to price and income changes. The price elasticity is at least −1.0 for IT hardware and often more elastic (a larger negative number in absolute value), and income elasticities are often well over 1.0.

Using sample ranges from 1975 or 1979 to 1994, Kenneth Flamm (1997) provides data for semiconductors. Aggregating all sectors that use semiconductors, he finds a price elasticity ranging from −1.22 to −1.48 and an income elasticity of about 1.0, which is not precisely estimated. When the income coefficient is constrained to 1.0, the price elasticities range from −1.12 to −1.25, depending on the choice of income variable. Flamm then decomposes the aggregate demand data into sectors that use semiconductors—consumer electronics, auto electronics, computer equipment, industrial electronics, communications equipment, and the government sector. For this disaggregated analysis he has to shorten the sample period to 1988–95. He finds price elasticities ranging from −0.6 (industrial equipment) to −1.1

(communications). On the other hand, the income elasticities of demand for semiconductors are large, ranging from 5 to 10.

Tamim Bayoumi and Markus Haacker (2002) use data for IT hardware, software, and communications equipment for 1992–99 from a sample of 41 countries (as well as subsamples of countries). They include time and country dummies in their econometric specification. They find price elasticities ranging from –0.9 (communications equipment) to –1.3 (IT hardware). The income elasticities range from 1.2 (communications) to 1.8 (IT software). As a robustness check, they examine a subsample of 18 countries (including the 12 largest consuming and 12 largest producing countries) and find price elasticities ranging from –0.6 (communications) to –1.1 (IT hardware) and income elasticities ranging from 0.7 (communications) to 1.6 (IT software). Finally, they use national income accounts data for the United States and France for 1980–98. For the United States, they find price elasticities ranging from –2.6 (communications) to –1.5 (IT hardware) and income elasticities ranging from 4.1 (communications) to 3.2 (IT hardware). The figures for France are similar.

In sum, IT products are GDP elastic throughout the world, and are price elastic in many subsectors. In the aggregate both characteristics are true for the United States as well. These elasticities are important underpinnings for the analysis to follow on how the globalization of IT enhances investment in the sector and thus accelerates productivity growth in the United States.

IT Network Externalities and the Rate of Return to IT Investment

Other approaches to estimating the special characteristics of IT products include examining externalities or spillovers and cost of capital or rate of return. These approaches confirm the findings of the econometric evidence on income and price elasticity of IT demand.

First, IT investment exhibits particularly strong network effects; that is, as more businesses use IT products, the value of using them rises. "Metcalfe's Law," named for Robert Metcalfe of Xerox's Palo Alto Research Center, is a formal enunciation of this observation, which states that the value of an IT product increases with the square of the number of users of the product. For example, a situation in which five people are using interconnected personal computers (PCs) is assigned a network value of 5 squared, or 25. Add another person using a connected PC and the value of the network leaps to 6 squared, or 36. Because IT products often involve information exchange, the benefit of investing in and using the product is greater when multiple parties invest in the same, or at least an interoperable, product, because now that information can be shared among more users. Adding this up in a macroeconomic setting, these network effects at the product and business level suggest that a rise in the stock of IT capital within a sector or country is disproportionately beneficial to growth.

A number of researchers have found these network externalities in both micro and macro data. For example, for individual IT software application products (such as spreadsheets), the product purchased and used by a greater number of users is priced higher than the one used by fewer people—there is a "network premium" embodied in the price of that product (Brynjolffsson and Kemerer 1996, Shapiro and Varian 1999). Using data on IT investment and capital stock by industry sector, other researchers have found that spillovers or externalities, as measured by the reduction in costs and increase in marginal products, are greater in sectors that have larger stocks of IT capital and more extensive forward and backward transactional linkages with sectors that also have a high stock of IT capital in place (Mun and Nadiri 2002).[1] Chapter 3 will discuss the macroeconomics of network effects and the implication of the differences in investment in IT capital across sectors in the United States.

Because network connectivity augments the value of IT capital, the communications sector takes on added importance in supporting economic growth. The sector comprises the communications equipment, the presence of a network, and regulations on the use and pricing of the network. These factors show up in cross-country research. For example, when researchers segment a sample of countries into industrial countries and two groups of developing countries (divided between those with faster and slower increases in IT and communications technology relative to GDP), they find that the industrial countries and the developing-country group with the larger increase in domestic investment in these technologies have faster productivity growth (Lee and Wan 2001). Developing countries with lower rates of domestic investment in technology have muted productivity gains because they did not invest much themselves, but they did get some productivity gain just from being networked into the global communications network. Other research, particularly of emerging markets, finds that, controlling for the level of development, trade protection (particularly tariffs on PCs and communications equipment) and high-priced communications negatively impact the adoption of the Internet (Knight 2003). Policies that raise the price of IT and communications equipment through tariffs and raise the costs of transmission through regulated pricing reduce both domestic investment in IT and the networking gains from that investment.

Another manifestation of the special characteristics of IT capital is its relatively higher estimated marginal product compared with other kinds of capital. The marginal product of a type of capital is the additional value added in business output from investing in an additional unit of that type

---

1. See also Wilson (2004, 27) for a discussion of the fixed effects regressions suggesting a permanent component to the stock of IT capital.

Figure 1.1   Implied marginal products and Bureau of Labor Statistics rental prices, by asset type

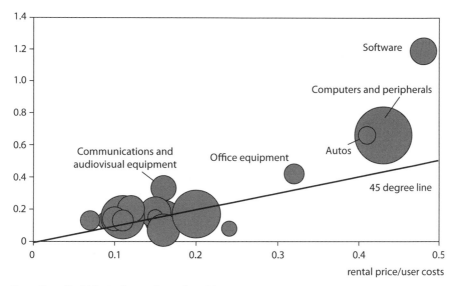

marginal product estimate

Note: Size of bubbles indicates share of total investments.

Source: Wilson (2004).

of capital. This higher marginal product of IT capital can come from the network externalities just discussed, from being more technologically advanced than other kinds of capital, and from being positively related to changes in the organization of the workplace.

Using a very detailed dataset, Daniel Wilson (2004) finds that the marginal product of IT capital (which in principle equals what businesses are willing to pay for the product) exceeds that of other kinds of capital by several times over (figure 1.1).[2] Moreover, the estimated marginal product relative to rental price (the cost of a unit of capital services) is greater than 1 for IT products. Overall, the return to a dollar of IT capital service is more than the $1 that one would have to pay for it.

In this regard, the relative return-to-rent ratio is particularly great for software. There are a number of possible reasons why software might be particularly special, including its rapid rate of depreciation, its network benefits, and the extent to which it requires associated changes in the organizational structure of the workplace. These results may also be consequences of tax differences for IT equipment and software. Nevertheless,

---

2. The bubbles for IT products in figure 1.1 lie above the 45 degree line.

these results with respect to the higher relative return to software use are consistent with the higher estimated price elasticities reported earlier.

Going forward, as globalization of IT products expands from hardware into software, there is the potential for declines in the price of software. These price declines portend additional gains to IT investment and the associated acceleration of productivity and economic growth through channels similar to those to be analyzed more explicitly in the context of IT hardware in chapter 3.

2

Linkages Between
US Firms and Global Markets
for IT Products

The US market for IT products is by far the largest in the world. However, the demand for these products is expanding rapidly abroad, particularly in the developing world. There is increased production abroad as well, particularly of IT hardware. And finally there is a dramatic move toward greater spending on software and IT services, particularly in the industrial economies. These patterns of global demand, along with the technological capabilities to increasingly fragment IT production, are what determine decisions by US producers as to which components of final demand to produce and where to locate production.

US multinational IT firms go abroad for cheaper components, particularly hardware components, which they can then recombine with domestic resources to produce competitively priced and higher value-added products for the domestic and global marketplace. In addition, US multinational IT firms go abroad to serve the local marketplace for IT services, in particular. The data show a dramatic pattern of US firms producing software and providing services through affiliates located in the country of sale.

The integration of globalized production and the movement of US IT firms toward producing software and services have implications for prices of IT products in the United States and for investment in IT throughout US industries, with follow-on consequences for sectoral and overall US productivity and growth. This chapter examines the foundations of globalized production. It looks at how the global marketplace is expanding, examines the integration of global production of US multinational IT firms, considers the role for foreign IT firms in the US marketplace, and identifies the multinational firms that are players in the IT sector.

An Expanding Global Marketplace

Because there are many ways to measure IT and communications networks, it may be hard to accurately assess the growing importance of spending on technology around the world. But there is no question that the global IT and communications marketplaces are large and expanding.

These markets can be measured through production, expenditure, cross-border investment, and trade. However measured, the global markets for information and communications technology products has expanded much faster than global GDP, global merchandise trade, or global foreign direct investment (FDI) flows. As a benchmark, the annual growth of global real GDP averaged around 3 percent from 1993–2004; growth in the volume of trade in goods and services for the period was slightly more than 7 percent, and growth in current dollar FDI averaged 14 percent.[1]

Consider various measures of the global IT and communications markets:

- The value of global shipments of semiconductors, a fundamental input for both computers and communications equipment, quadrupled from about $50 billion in 1990 to about $213 billion in 2004, surpassing the technology-cycle high of $204 billion in 2000 and representing compound annual growth of 11 percent.[2]

- Worldwide spending on IT reached $1.2 trillion in 2003, for the first time surpassing the 2000 level (inflated by Internet/Y2K expenditure) and growing almost 10 percent per year as it emerged from the slowdown after 2001. Communications equipment in 2003 also surpassed its 2000 level for the first time, with global spending totaling roughly $1.2 trillion.[3]

- Global exports of IT goods increased from about 5.6 percent of global exports in 1990 to 9.1 percent in 2003, while the share of communications equipment rose from 1.8 to 3.1 percent.[4]

---

1. IMF's *World Economic Outlook* database, September 2005, and UNCTAD's *World Investment Report 2005*.

2. See Semiconductor Industry Association, www.sia-online.org/pre_statistics.cfm (accessed March 15, 2006).

3. See WITSA (2004, 23 and 27). Expenditure data exclude spending internal to a company for development and customization.

4. UN ComTrade database, http://unstats.un.org/unsd/comtrade (accessed September 30, 2005). IT goods defined as Standard International Trade Classification (SITC) revision 3 categories 751, 752, 759, and 776, while communications equipment defined at SITC revision 3 category 764.

- Worldwide FDI in electrical and electronic equipment manufacturing almost tripled from 1990 to 2003 to a stock of $279.8 billion, or 9.7 percent of the 2003 inward stocks of FDI in manufacturing (UNCTAD 2005, table A.I.4).

- International merger and acquisition activity in the IT and communications sectors experienced rapid increases in the late 1990s, declined somewhat after 2000, but remained high through 2003 compared to the mid-1990s.

Global Spending on IT and Communications Technology Products

This expenditure can be broken down into spending on IT (hardware, software, and services) and on networked communications-related hardware and transmission services. Although spending on all categories rose in all countries from 1993 to 2003, the composition changed over time and differs in a systematic way across the level of economic development. Appendix 2A examines the case of semiconductors, which highlights many of these trends.

First, consider global spending on IT versus communications. Each of these markets is huge, with spending of about $1.2 trillion in each category. In both markets, the United States accounts for about 45 percent of global spending. However, the patterns of growth through the technology cycle differ somewhat. Global spending on communications exhibits a greater boom and bust than global spending on IT, although for the United States, just the opposite is true. One rationale for the globalization of US producers of IT and communications equipment could be market diversification and the smoothing of the technology cycle (table 2.1).

Second, focus on global spending on IT products—hardware, software, and services. Although the industrial-country markets remain largest and therefore greatly influence global growth rates, there has been an evolution of rapid growth in IT spending from the industrial-country to the developing-country markets. From 1993 to 2003, the share of developing countries (defined here as countries that are not members of the Organization for Economic Cooperation and Development) in global expenditures on IT rose from 5.7 to 9.1 percent.[5] In addition to the shifting expenditure share toward the developing world, it is also apparent that these countries did not experience the "technology bubble." For example, there was a marked decline in the US growth rate of IT expenditure from 7.6 percent annually during the 1990s to only 2 percent during the

---

5. See WITSA (2002, 29; 2004, 23, 27). The methods of expenditure compilation in the two WITSA publications do not match completely, but for the purposes of this ratio comparison this methodological issue is not significant.

Table 2.1 Large and growing markets for IT

Rank	Country	2003 expenditure (billions of US dollars)	CAGR, 1993–2001 (percent)	CAGR, 2001–03 (percent)
IT spending[a]				
1	United States	472.9	7.6	1.2
2	Japan	136.3	2.8	−2.4
3	Germany	88.0	5.9	13.2
4	United Kingdom	77.0	8.4	7.8
5	France	69.6	6.4	14.5
6	Italy	35.8	29.1	13.1
7	China	30.5	6.2	24.5
8	Canada	29.3	5.9	10.1
9	Brazil	20.1	7.4	24.7
10	Netherlands	18.9	9.3	13.2
11	Australia	17.3	11.6	16.4
12	Korea	15.3	5.5	14.8
17	India	8.4	7.5	34.8
20	Mexico	7.0	18.7	11.9
21	South Africa	6.5	11.7	31.3
23	Taiwan	5.8	7.1	14.1
25	Russia	5.3	1.8	23.0
34	Ireland	2.6	9.2	11.2
35	Malaysia	2.4	12.3	13.1
39	Thailand	1.7	2.7	19.0
World total (70 countries)		1,182.2	6.9	6.5
Communications spending[b]				
1	United States	459.1	4.9	2.1
2	Japan	187.4	14.5	0.6
3	Germany	58.8	2.9	6.2
4	United Kingdom	55.4	9.1	4.3
5	France	43.8	4.9	6.9
6	China	40.4	26.0	4.7
7	Italy	30.0	7.5	5.8
8	South Korea	23.8	8.7	4.3
9	Canada	21.9	6.6	3.4
10	Spain	19.6	5.0	7.9
11	Brazil	18.4	19.0	0.8
13	Netherlands	16.0	7.4	6.5
14	India	15.4	19.6	4.7
16	Mexico	13.3	2.2	1.0
18	Taiwan	12.5	9.3	2.5
20	Russia	10.8	6.5	7.6
22	South Africa	8.8	5.8	8.4

(table continues next page)

Table 2.1 *(continued)*

Rank	Country	2003 expenditure (billions of US dollars)	CAGR, 1993–2001 (percent)	CAGR, 2001–03 (percent)
35	Malaysia	4.9	9.3	4.9
41	Ireland	3.7	12.0	2.1
42	Thailand	3.7	5.4	4.8
World total (70 countries)		1,232.0	8.5	3.1
IT hardware[b]				
1	United States	119.0	6.7	–2
2	Japan	53.2	2.4	–9
3	Germany	32.0	7.5	7
4	China	24.2	29.2	21
5	United Kingdom	23.1	9.2	1
6	France	17.9	5.6	7
7	Italy	12.2	7.6	7
8	Canada	11.0	7.5	10
9	Brazil	10.1	10.2	26
10	Korea	10.1	13.5	10
11	Australia	6.5	5.0	12
13	Netherlands	5.6	9.5	6
14	India	5.0	8.8	35
17	Mexico	4.4	20.1	15
18	Taiwan	3.7	12.5	14
20	Russia	3.1	–2.2	21
27	South Africa	2.8	5.2	27
31	Malaysia	1.5	11.9	9
34	Ireland	1.3	16.6	7
37	Thailand	1.0	6.0	14
World total (70 countries)		402.7	13.4	4
IT services[b]				
1	United States	248.9	11.7	1.7
2	Japan	68.5	7.9	2.5
3	France	38.6	14.8	16.9
4	United Kingdom	38.3	5.3	10.5
5	Germany	37.6	9.7	16.5
6	Italy	16.9	7.9	16.1
7	Canada	13.2	7.7	9.4
8	Netherlands	8.1	10.4	15.9
10	Brazil	7.4	39.2	24.5
11	Australia	7.2	11.0	17.6
15	Korea	3.9	13.2	27.1
17	China	3.3	9.6	53.9
20	India	2.5	10.9	34.9

(table continues next page)

Table 2.1   Large and growing markets for IT   *(continued)*

Rank	Country	2003 expenditure (billions of US dollars)	CAGR, 1993–2001 (percent)	CAGR, 2001–03 (percent)
21	South Africa	2.4	8.9	34.1
23	Mexico	2.0	19.0	8.0
24	Russia	1.6	7.9	26.9
28	Taiwan	1.2	0.8	13.6
34	Ireland	.8	10.8	15.6
41	Malaysia	.5	10.6	24.2
47	Thailand	.3	–4.0	20.6
World total (70 countries)		554.3	10.2	7.2
IT software[b]				
1	United States	105.0	14.4	3
2	Germany	18.5	7.7	19
3	United Kingdom	15.6	15.3	12
4	Japan	14.6	14.4	4
5	France	13.0	12.6	19
6	Italy	6.6	7.1	18
7	Netherlands	5.2	14.2	17
8	Canada	5.2	14.6	11
9	Australia	3.6	11.7	22
10	China	3.1	18.9	36
14	Brazil	2.5	19.4	21
18	Korea	1.3	48.5	21
19	South Africa	1.3	30.7	35
22	Taiwan	.8	6.2	16
23	India	.8	14.8	35
26	Mexico	.6	6.6	7
28	Russia	.6	19.4	22
31	Ireland	.5	19.3	17
35	Malaysia	.4	14.4	16
38	Thailand	.4	15.9	34
World total (70 countries)		225.2	13.4	10

CAGR = compound annual growth rate

a. Includes IT hardware, services, and software spending but excludes communications and internal spending. For 1993–2001, CAGR also includes office equipment and internal spending, and the world total consists of only 55 countries. China data do not include Hong Kong.

b. For 1993–2001, CAGR also includes internal spending, and the world total consists of only 55 countries. Software spending includes purchased or leased packaged software, as well as outsourced software development. Internal software development and customization are excluded. China data do not include Hong Kong.

Note: Cells may not add up due to rounding.

Source: WITSA (2002, 28–29, 33–34; 2004, 7–12).

postbubble recovery period (2000–2003). The large weight of the United States and other industrial economies lowered the average annual global growth rate of IT spending from 6.9 percent over 1993–2001 to only 3.7 percent from 2001–03—not much higher than average world GDP growth of 3.1 percent for this recovery period.[6] But, for the developing world, growth in IT spending continued unabated. IT spending in China and India, for example, grew 20 percent or more per year throughout the period, with China at $31 billion (totaling $75 billion including communications spending) rising to become the sixth largest IT market in the world by 2003, ahead of Italy and Canada. From the standpoint of incentives facing US companies, some of these developing-country markets are not only big, they are also growing fast, and more rapidly than industrial-country markets.

Third, consider global spending patterns on IT goods versus software and services (table 2.1). The US market dominates the global totals, accounting for more than 30 percent of global spending on IT hardware and an even more dominant near 50 percent of global spending for IT services and software. Global expenditure patterns on the different components of the IT package (hardware, services, and software) suggest a trend toward increased spending in the future on IT services and software. This pattern of spending on the various parts of the IT package is exhibited by almost all countries (figure 2.1), with the trend most notable in the industrial countries. But even for many developing countries, spending on IT hardware is now exceeded by spending on software and services that operate on the installed base, as can be seen in the "other non-US world" category in figure 2.1.

The US market, where the penetration of IT into business has been the most pervasive, is not only the largest market but also the "front-runner," that is, the one where software and services as a ratio to IT hardware spending is the highest. Three times as much money is spent (data in nominal dollars) on IT services and software in the United States as on IT hardware, with other large industrialized economies approaching similar multiples. While the demand for hardware is growing fastest in the developing countries, software and services expenditure in those nations has been a bit delayed (albeit exhibiting rapid growth from very modest bases), as these locations wait for hardware and communications infrastructure to be put into place. For developing economies, there is still much to do to create an installed based of IT hardware, so the ratio of services and software to hardware is much lower. In addition, IT software

---

6. IMF's *World Economic Outlook* database, September 2004, www.imf.org (accessed September 30, 2005). It must be emphasized that these expenditures are denominated in market exchange rate current dollars, so for some countries there may be an exchange rate factor affecting the growth in expenditure in dollars as opposed to the growth rate in local currencies or on a purchasing power parity (PPP) basis.

Figure 2.1 Ratio of software and services to hardware spending, 1993 and 2003

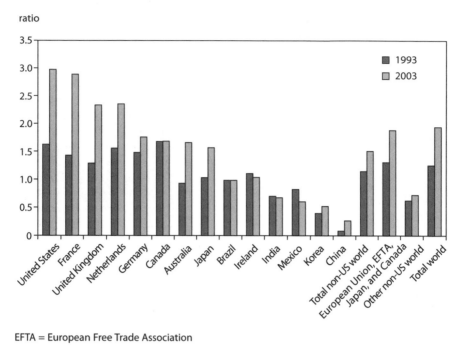

EFTA = European Free Trade Association

Source: WITSA (2002, 32–34; 2004, 8–10).

and especially services must be tailored to local needs, at the very least in the local language and suited to the local business milieu. Going forward, once the hardware penetration rates reach those of the industrial countries, the demand for software and services likely will explode, particularly once domestic and foreign (including US) firms can locate and serve the domestic market.

Behind these ratios the data reveal dramatic growth rates both in IT hardware and in services and software. IT hardware spending in large emerging markets—including China, India, and Mexico, but not Brazil or Russia—posted double-digit growth rates for the post–tech bubble period, even as industrial-country spending slowed. China rose to be the world's fourth largest IT hardware market in 2003, poised to overtake Germany, while Brazil was in the global top 10 for IT hardware market size. In the market for IT services and software as well, growth was at double-digit rates even during the recovery period after the technology bust. In particular, China and India stand out with spending on IT services increasing from small bases by annual average growth rates, respectively, of 37 and 22 percent since 2001. Developing countries have seen continued double-digit growth rates in IT software, albeit from small bases, throughout the period from 1993 to 2003. An important issue, particularly relevant for emerging markets, is to what extent the spending on IT in these countries is destined for domestic use. It appears to vary considerably across the developing world, with consequences for economic well-being (see chapter 3).

In sum, the United States is still the biggest market overall and has experienced the biggest boom-bust technology cycle. Expenditures on software and services exceed that for IT hardware in the United States, which is also the case for other industrial countries. Growth abroad did not experience the boom and bust, and is growing much more rapidly, although from a smaller base, particularly in developing countries. In those countries, growth is more balanced in that it is quite rapid for all IT categories (hardware, services, and software) as well as for communications equipment. This trend in global markets toward more rapid growth in demand abroad and increasing demand for services and software is the environment in which US firms operate, and it creates the incentives to which they respond in terms of choosing locations for production and sale.

Fragmentation of Global Production Patterns

As global markets have grown, new players in global trade have emerged and trade in IT goods and communications equipment has become less concentrated in a few producers in the industrial countries (tables 2.2a and 2.2b). In terms of concentration of IT exports, the top five countries in global IT exports accounted for 49 percent of global exports in 2004, down from 62 percent in 1990. (The numbers are almost identical for communications equipment.) From 1990 to 2004, the US share shrank from 19 to 11 percent of global IT exports, and Japan's share dropped from 20 to 8 percent. Powerhouse exporters in China, Malaysia, Mexico, Taiwan, and Korea vaulted in the ranks of IT exporters. On the import side for both IT and communications, there has been less change in the top five, but nations have changed within that group. The US share of global imports of IT slipped from the number one ranking at 21 percent to number two (if China and Hong Kong are taken together) at 15 percent. One reason for the new entrants is the Information Technology Agreement (box 2.1).

Comparing country rankings for imports and exports points to the importance of two-way trade in IT and communications products, which is a sign of the globalization of production. For some countries, two-way trade goes along with domestic IT and communications spending, while for others that trade is divorced from domestic spending patterns. The most striking example of the latter situation is Singapore, which is such a small market for IT spending that it does not even appear in table 2.1. But Singapore is a huge importer and exporter of IT goods. Similarly, Malaysia is ranked relatively low in the table on IT hardware spending (table 2.1), even though it is an important two-way trader. On the other hand, Korea is the ninth

Table 2.2a Country ranking and concentration of global IT exports and imports, 1990, 2000, and 2004[a] (percent)

	1990			2000			2004		
Rank	Country	Share of world total	Cumulative	Country	Share of world total	Cumulative	Country	Share of world total	Cumulative
Exports									
1	Japan	20.40	20.40	United States	16.97	16.97	China	14.31	14.31
2	United States	19.28	39.68	Japan	14.05	31.01	United States	11.01	25.32
3	United Kingdom	7.71	47.39	Singapore	9.80	40.81	Singapore	8.72	34.04
4	Former West Germany	7.35	54.74	Korea	6.55	47.36	Japan	7.91	41.95
5	Singapore	6.87	61.61	Taiwan	6.41	53.77	Germany	6.89	48.84
6	Taiwan	5.90	67.51	United Kingdom	5.64	59.41	Taiwan	6.40	55.23
7	France	4.39	71.90	Malaysia	5.56	64.97	Netherlands	5.89	61.13
8	Korea	4.30	76.21	Netherlands	4.71	69.68	Malaysia	5.44	66.56
9	Netherlands	4.20	80.40	Germany	3.66	73.34	Korea	5.17	71.73
10	Italy	3.14	83.54	Ireland	3.38	76.72	United Kingdom	4.08	75.82
11	Malaysia	2.67	86.21	France	3.24	79.95	Mexico	2.77	78.58
12	Ireland	2.58	88.80	Philippines	3.05	83.00	France	2.69	81.28
13	Canada	2.12	90.92	China	3.05	86.06	Ireland	2.36	83.64
14	Hong Kong	1.41	92.33	Thailand	2.14	88.20	Philippines	2.29	85.93
15	Thailand	1.31	93.64	Mexico	1.92	90.12	Canada	1.40	87.33
16	Sweden	0.88	94.52	Canada	1.62	91.74	Italy	1.34	88.67
17	Belgium-Luxembourg	0.74	95.25	Italy	1.50	93.24	Belgium	1.09	89.76
18	Austria	0.67	95.93	Hong Kong	1.12	94.36	Hong Kong	0.87	90.63
19	Spain	0.62	96.54	Belgium	0.70	95.06	Spain	0.79	91.42
20	Switzerland	0.45	96.99	Hungary	0.51	95.57	Hungary	0.78	92.20
21	Mexico	0.32	97.32	Indonesia	0.48	96.05	Czech Republic	0.72	92.92
22	Israel	0.30	97.62	Spain	0.44	96.49	Australia	0.55	93.47
23	Denmark	0.29	97.91	Austria	0.41	96.90	Austria	0.54	94.01
24	China	0.27	98.18	Israel	0.41	97.30	Sweden	0.53	94.54
25	Philippines	0.23	98.41	Sweden	0.38	97.68	Switzerland	0.46	95.00

Imports

	1990			2000			2004		
1	United States	20.56	20.56	United States	20.26	20.26	United States	14.79	14.79
2	Former West Germany	9.74	30.30	Japan	6.68	26.93	China	12.47	27.25
3	United Kingdom	8.99	39.29	Singapore	6.66	33.59	Hong Kong	7.61	34.86
4	France	6.54	45.83	Germany	5.92	39.50	Germany	6.47	41.32
5	Italy	4.48	50.31	United Kingdom	5.91	45.41	Singapore	6.20	47.52
6	Singapore	4.47	54.78	Hong Kong	5.44	50.85	Japan	5.77	53.29
7	Netherlands	4.46	59.24	Taiwan	4.80	55.65	Netherlands	5.03	58.32
8	Japan	4.38	63.62	China	4.51	60.16	United Kingdom	4.30	62.63
9	Canada	3.80	67.42	Netherlands	4.33	64.49	Malaysia	4.21	66.83
10	Taiwan	3.64	71.06	Malaysia	4.08	68.57	Taiwan	3.93	70.76
11	Korea	3.22	74.28	Korea	3.97	72.54	Korea	3.47	74.23
12	Hong Kong	3.03	77.31	France	3.47	76.01	France	2.89	77.12
13	Malaysia	2.28	79.58	Canada	2.87	78.88	Mexico	2.84	79.95
14	Spain	2.12	81.70	Mexico	2.76	81.64	Philippines	2.43	82.38
15	Switzerland	1.62	83.32	Ireland	1.89	83.53	Canada	1.76	84.14
16	Sweden	1.59	84.92	Italy	1.75	85.28	Italy	1.58	85.72
17	Belgium-Luxembourg	1.53	86.44	Thailand	1.72	87.00	Ireland	1.54	87.27
18	Australia	1.50	87.94	Philippines	1.41	88.41	Belgium	1.07	88.34
19	Austria	1.28	89.22	Belgium	1.02	89.44	Spain	1.03	89.36
20	Ireland	1.23	90.45	Spain	0.87	90.30	Australia	0.83	90.20
21	Thailand	1.23	91.68	Australia	0.83	91.13	Hungary	0.83	91.03
22	Denmark	0.80	92.48	Switzerland	0.80	91.93	Czech Republic	0.66	91.69
23	China	0.77	93.24	Sweden	0.70	92.63	Sweden	0.66	92.34
24	Finland	0.72	93.97	Brazil	0.66	93.29	Switzerland	0.63	92.98
25	Norway	0.59	94.55	Hungary	0.55	93.84	Brazil	0.54	93.51

a. Information and communications technologies defined as the sum of Standard International Trade Classification (SITC) categories 751, 752, 759, and 776.

Note: Data for Taiwan are from the OECD ITCS database and include all exports as no data for reexports are available; 1991 data are shown for 1990.

Source: UN ComTrade database, SITC, rev. 2. For 1990, 109 reporting countries; for 2000, 163 reporting countries; and for 2004, 123 reporting countries. As all major world trading nations have reported, the differences in number of reporting countries do not materially affect the results. Data show domestic exports only, i.e., reexports have been subtracted.

21

Table 2.2b Country ranking and concentration of global communications exports and imports, 1990, 2000, and 2004[a]
(percent)

		1990			2000			2004	
Rank	Country	Share of world total	Cumulative	Country	Share of world total	Cumulative	Country	Share of world total	Cumulative
Exports									
1	Japan	26.71	26.71	United States	12.37	12.37	China	17.09	17.09
2	United States	13.92	40.63	United Kingdom	7.98	20.35	Korea	12.05	29.14
3	Former West Germany	7.40	48.04	Japan	7.81	28.16	Germany	8.89	38.03
4	United Kingdom	5.35	53.39	Germany	6.76	34.92	United States	7.02	45.04
5	Taiwan	5.04	58.43	China	5.99	40.91	Japan	6.95	52.00
6	France	4.88	63.31	Sweden	5.64	46.55	United Kingdom	4.25	56.24
7	Sweden	4.27	67.58	France	5.60	52.15	Sweden	4.15	60.39
8	Singapore	4.13	71.70	Canada	5.57	57.72	Mexico	3.88	64.26
9	Korea	3.50	75.20	Mexico	5.49	63.21	France	3.78	68.04
10	Hong Kong	2.87	78.07	Korea	5.09	68.30	Singapore	3.60	71.64
11	Netherlands	2.71	80.79	Finland	4.69	72.99	Finland	3.52	75.17
12	Canada	2.64	83.42	Malaysia	2.90	75.89	Hungary	3.29	78.45
13	Italy	2.44	85.87	Singapore	2.84	78.73	Taiwan	3.08	81.53
14	Malaysia	2.05	87.92	Taiwan	2.61	81.34	Netherlands	2.63	84.16
15	Belgium-Luxembourg	1.75	89.67	Netherlands	2.59	83.93	Malaysia	2.58	86.74
16	Finland	1.54	91.21	Israel	1.94	85.87	Canada	2.18	88.92
17	Denmark	1.11	92.33	Italy	1.86	87.74	Italy	1.75	90.67
18	Switzerland	0.97	93.30	Ireland	1.54	89.28	Israel	1.05	91.72
19	China	0.92	94.22	Belgium	1.53	90.80	Belgium	0.88	92.60
20	Thailand	0.88	95.10	Thailand	1.05	91.85	Denmark	0.85	93.45
21	Israel	0.73	95.83	Denmark	0.89	92.74	Spain	0.72	94.17
22	Austria	0.69	96.53	Indonesia	0.85	93.59	Czech Republic	0.57	94.74
23	Ireland	0.51	97.03	Spain	0.74	94.33	Ireland	0.55	95.29
24	Norway	0.48	97.52	Hungary	0.70	95.02	Austria	0.54	95.82
25	Spain	0.48	97.99	Brazil	0.60	95.62	Brazil	0.48	96.31

Imports

#	1990			2000			2004		
1	United States	21.46	21.46	United States	20.42	20.42	United States	20.54	20.54
2	Former West Germany	7.93	29.40	United Kingdom	7.02	27.44	China	9.27	29.80
3	United Kingdom	6.43	35.82	Hong Kong	6.92	34.36	Hong Kong	9.24	39.04
4	Hong Kong	4.90	40.72	China	5.54	39.90	Germany	7.61	46.65
5	France	4.58	45.31	Germany	4.84	44.74	United Kingdom	6.50	53.15
6	Singapore	4.25	49.56	Japan	4.02	48.76	Japan	3.87	57.02
7	Italy	3.74	53.29	Mexico	3.40	52.16	Italy	3.61	60.63
8	Japan	3.60	56.89	France	3.36	55.53	Singapore	3.47	64.10
9	Canada	3.28	60.16	Canada	3.35	58.88	Mexico	3.46	67.56
10	Netherlands	3.06	63.23	Netherlands	3.09	61.97	France	3.38	70.94
11	China	3.01	66.24	Italy	2.79	64.76	Netherlands	3.26	74.20
12	Spain	2.97	69.21	Korea	2.32	67.07	Canada	2.58	76.78
13	Taiwan	2.10	71.31	Spain	2.27	69.34	Spain	2.43	79.21
14	Korea	1.98	73.29	Singapore	2.19	71.53	Korea	1.98	81.18
15	Malaysia	1.97	75.26	Taiwan	1.87	73.40	Hungary	1.80	82.99
16	Sweden	1.88	77.15	Australia	1.62	75.02	Sweden	1.71	84.69
17	Belgium-Luxembourg	1.65	78.79	Sweden	1.55	76.57	India	1.61	86.31
18	Switzerland	1.62	80.41	Malaysia	1.48	78.04	Malaysia	1.50	87.81
19	Thailand	1.46	81.87	Brazil	1.38	79.42	Australia	1.45	89.26
20	Austria	1.46	83.33	Belgium	1.28	80.70	Taiwan	1.24	90.50
21	Mexico	1.45	84.78	Turkey	1.20	81.90	Belgium	1.07	91.57
22	Australia	1.40	86.17	Ireland	1.03	82.93	Denmark	1.01	92.58
23	Finland	0.91	87.08	Finland	0.97	83.90	Russia	0.99	93.57
24	Indonesia	0.84	87.92	Austria	0.92	84.82	Austria	0.96	94.53
25	Denmark	0.81	88.73	Denmark	0.91	85.73	Finland	0.94	95.47

a. Communications defined as Standard International Trade Classification (SITC) category 764.

Note: Data for Taiwan are from the OECD ITCS database and include all exports, as no data for reexports are available; 1991 data are shown for 1990.

Source: UN ComTrade database, SITC, rev. 2. For 1990, 109 reporting countries; for 2000, 163 reporting countries, and for 2004, 123 reporting countries. As all major world trading nations have reported, the differences in number of reporting countries do not materially affect the results. Data show domestic exports only, i.e., reexports have been subtracted.

Box 2.1 The Information Technology Agreement

The Information Technology Agreement (ITA) was formally concluded at the Singapore Ministerial Conference of the World Trade Organization (WTO) in December 1996.

The ITA is notable for both economic and political economy reasons. It represents a departure from the standard WTO negotiating approach even as it espouses the key WTO principle—most favored nation status. From the perspective of average tariffs, the ITA makes a difference: the average tariff rate on covered products is 3.6 percent for ITA members and 11.2 percent for nonmembers (Bora 2004). Its impact on trade in information technology and communications products has been hard to judge for a number of reasons, but on balance it appears to have enhanced trade in these products, particularly exports for the signatories.

Under the ITA, countries agreed to bring tariffs on trade in covered products in six categories (computers, software, telecom equipment, semiconductors, semiconductor manufacturing equipment, and scientific instruments) to zero by 2000, either immediately or by equally staged tariff reductions in four tranches from July 1997 to January 2000. Provision for extending the final phase to 2005 was agreed to at the initial signing, and some countries did avail themselves of the extensions for some products, including, for example, India, Malaysia, and Indonesia. China joined in 2003, but its implementation schedule has not been derestricted to public view. Brazil, Mexico, and South Africa are among the nonacceding countries. Under WTO auspices, the Committee of Participants on the Expansion of Trade in Information Technology Products was organized upon inception of the agreement. This committee is addressing issues of product classification and nontariff measures, as well as calls to broaden the product coverage under a so-called ITA II.

The runup to and negotiation of the ITA departed in several ways from the more standard approach in a multilateral trade negotiation. First, it was a sectoral agreement that was negotiated in isolation from a multilateral trade round, rather than being part of a single undertaking. The broad outlines of the agreement were broached by the business advisory group and interested country partners—including the United States, Japan, Canada, and Mexico (although the latter has not signed on)—in the context of the 1996 summit year of the Asia Pacific Economic Cooperation (APEC) forum, headed that year by the Philippines. The November 1996 meeting of APEC ministers in Subic Bay provided both explicit tariff-cutting formulas and product coverage for an agreement, as well as the momentum for the actual ITA, which was agreed upon by a set of WTO mem-

(box continues next page)

Box 2.1 *(continued)*

bers at the Singapore Ministerial Conference the following December. Not all WTO members signed on at Singapore, however, and this too is a way in which the ITA differs.

A third way in which the ITA differed from a standard WTO agreement was that one of the provisions of the Declaration on Trade in Information Technology Products—the official term for the agreement made in Singapore—was that the declaration would not come into effect unless participants representing approximately 90 percent of world trade in the covered products notified their acceptance of the ITA by April 1, 1997. At the signing in Singapore, only 29 countries or economic regions accounting for about 83 percent of global trade in IT products acceded to the agreement. These included Australia, Canada, 15 European Community members, Hong Kong, Iceland, Indonesia, Japan, Korea, Norway, Singapore, Switzerland (including Liechtenstein), Taiwan, Turkey, and the United States. However, before the April 1 deadline, 15 more countries or economic entities joined, bringing the coverage of trade up to the required 90 percent, and the declaration came into force. ITA members now account for 95.5 percent of trade.

Has the ITA made a difference for global trade in technology products and for countries that are members? Theory and practical experience tell us that reducing tariffs leads to more trade, and that trade should grow more for the countries that cut tariffs the most. In fact, empirical evidence of the ITA has been difficult to ascertain. First, many of these tariff reductions took place in the context of dramatic increases in global trade in IT products associated with the technology boom up to 2000 and subsequent crash. It is difficult to parse out the changes in trade due to changes in tariffs alone. Second, the product coverage of the ITA does not match the tariff-line classification system. Therefore it is not possible to perfectly assess ITA commitments across countries.

Bijit Bora and Xinpeng Liu (2004) undertake a comprehensive research effort using the very detailed data available and gravity-model analysis. Their results suggest that two trading partners, both ITA members, trade 7 percent more with each other than if neither of them were a WTO (or ITA) member. If two countries are trading partners—the exporter a member of the ITA and the importer not—then the importer imports 6 percent less than if neither of the trading partners were members of the WTO (or ITA). Therefore, a non-ITA WTO member would import about 14 percent more if it joined the ITA.

An alternative econometric approach by the author finds that being a member of the ITA is statistically associated with imports of IT products, controlling for do-

(box continues next page)

largest exporter, the eleventh largest importer, and twelfth largest in expenditure on IT hardware, indicative of a more balanced trade and domestic spending pattern. Imbalances in trade patterns also show up in tables 2.2a and 2.2b.

Finally, China and India are both fast-growing markets for IT hardware spending, but their integration with globalized production of IT is quite different. China is the major two-way trader, but India does not appear in the top 25 traders (it is ranked below 40th).

Despite its high rank as an exporter, China may not gain the most from its participation in globalized production. That is, even though China probably is the world's most important production assembly platform for IT and consumer electronics products, it is not necessarily the one with the highest value added on domestic content. China had a very modest trade surplus in technology products of $14 billion in 2003. Chinese domestic value added may account for as little as 15 percent of the value of Chinese technology exports, with the remainder being import content.[7]

India probably is harmed by its lack of participation in global production to the extent that its domestic IT prices exceed the global prices for these products. India, for example, delayed full implementation of the Information Technology Agreement. Some implications of an imbalance between production for exports versus for domestic spending will be addressed in more depth in chapter 3.

───────────────

7. Technology product trade surplus and domestic value added based on Chinese data inclusive of consumer electronics, office equipment, computers, and communications equipment from Lardy (2005, 132).

Integrating US Firms into the Global Marketplace

Even as the production and use of IT hardware continue to increase and spread around the globe, and even as US producers maintain an importance presence in these products, the key trend in the market is toward production of and demand for IT software and database and network management services.[8] How are US IT firms responding to these trends both in the US market and abroad?[9]

US firms continue to supply the high value-added IT hardware market for both domestic production and production abroad, but increasingly are relinquishing commodity hardware production to imports or to foreign-owned firms in the United States. At the same time, the fragmentation of production, well established for IT hardware, is beginning to take place on the "soft" side of IT, thus increasing domestic and foreign assets, employment, sales, and two-way international trade in components of IT services and software activities.

There are several perspectives from which to analyze the global integration of US IT firms. First, the product perspective: What do these firms sell in the global marketplace, particularly comparing the relative size of hardware versus software and services activities in the global marketplace? Second, the geographical perspective: What does the global production and sales strategy look like for a US multinational IT firm?

Sales by US Multinational IT Firms in the Global Marketplace

The first perspective on US multinational IT firms is how they produce and sell in the global marketplace. As noted above, global spending on IT totaled more than $1 trillion in 2003, with both the dollar value and rate of growth of global spending on services and software exceeding those for hardware. Recall that table 2.1 showed that the technology bubble was more apparent in spending on IT in the United States, whereas for other countries, particularly developing ones, expenditures on IT products continued to rise rapidly. How have US firms reacted to this trend in product and service type and geographical location of spending in the US and global marketplaces?

---

8. IT services are a specific subset of what are called information technology–enabled services (ITES). ITES is a much larger set of services that can be digitized and outsourced from the internal operations of the firm to which they are related. These include call centers for financial firms or insurance claim processing. The potential for international trade in these services will be discussed in chapter 4.

9. For a historical perspective, see Mann (1994, 1997).

Figure 2.2 US firms' global sales and employment in hardware and services, by industry of parent, selected years

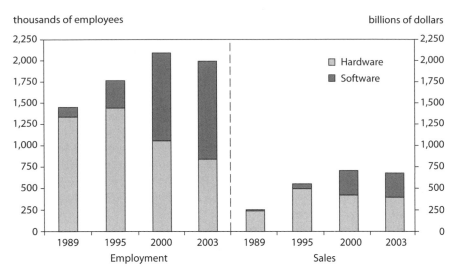

Source: Bureau of Economic Analysis financial and operating data for US multinational companies.

The US Commerce Department's Bureau of Economic Analysis (BEA) conducts a large annual survey of US multinational IT firms.[10] These data indicate that global sales by these firms—including sales in the US market and sales in foreign markets—rose dramatically during the 1990s, but then stabilized at the 2000 peak until 2003 (last available data). Similarly, the number of employees around the world rose throughout the period before falling from the technology peak in 2000. Most notable is the shift in the composition of global sales and employment from hardware to services and software, following the pattern already observed in global IT spending. US multinationals' global services and software sales now are on par with global hardware sales. US multinationals' employment in hardware has fallen absolutely and global employment in services and software has continued to rise and exceeds global hardware employment (figure 2.2).

In sum, growing global competition in the hardware industry (as seen in new exporters) and growing demand for services and software in

10. The BEA defines US multinational IT firms for data prior to 1999 as those primarily conducting business in US Standard Industrial Classification (SIC) categories 357 (computer and office equipment), 367 (electronic components and accessories), and 737 (computer programming, data processing, and other computer-related services). From 1999 to the most recent data from 2003, the companies are defined as those primarily in North American Industry Classification System (NAICS) categories 3341 (computer and peripheral equipment manufacturing), 3344 (semiconductor and other electronic components manufacturing), 514 (information services and data processing services), and 5414 (computer systems design and related services). See appendix A for elaboration of methodological issues related to classification systems.

global spending have both pushed and pulled US firms toward producing IT services and software and away from producing IT hardware. Services sales and employment increased from less than 10 percent of total global activities of US IT firms in 1989 to 42 percent of sales and 57 percent of employment in 2003.

How US Multinationals Meet Domestic and Foreign Demand

The second perspective on the operation of US multinationals considers the importance of the US marketplace. The data on global IT expenditure show that the US marketplace has been by far the largest in the world, accounting for 32 percent of total expenditure on IT hardware and 48 percent of global spending on IT services and software (WITSA 2004, 24–26). Considering just US-parent multinational firms, how important is the US market to them? Does the US market dominate for them as much as it dominates in terms of global spending?

The US (i.e., domestic) share of US-parent firms' global IT hardware sales declined from 35 percent in 1989 to just below 30 percent in 2003 (figure 2.3). US multinationals' sales of IT services in the United States as a share of their total global IT services sales fell dramatically over this period from nearly 100 percent to around 55 percent by 2003. So the US market represents about the same share of hardware sales for US multinationals as the United States accounts for in the global marketplace for IT hardware spending. For services (including software), the domestic share of US multinationals' global sales is a bit higher than the US share in global spending on IT services. In sum, data indicate that the US market continues to be an important part of US IT firms' business strategy, but that to an increasing extent US firms are expanding sales abroad because that is where the fastest growth is. The trend in the US marketplace and for US multinationals is a microcosm of what is happening in the global marketplace. Moreover, the rapid expansion of US firms' IT services abroad is consistent with the US "frontrunner" status.

A third perspective on the operation of US multinationals analyzes the trends in terms of how US firms can meet domestic and global market demand. US multinationals can meet US domestic demand in two ways: through domestic production, or by importing from affiliates located abroad (known as majority-owned foreign affiliates, or MOFAs). The multinationals can serve the foreign market by exporting US-based production or by producing abroad at MOFAs and selling to that market or to third markets. What do the data show in terms of how US multinationals serve the domestic and foreign markets? It may be surprising to learn that the picture is one of stability: the multinationals show neither a reduction in export share to meet global demand nor much of an increase in import share to meet US domestic demand. To the extent that global production and out-

Figure 2.3   US multinational companies' sales in US and global markets, by industry of parent, selected years

billions of dollars

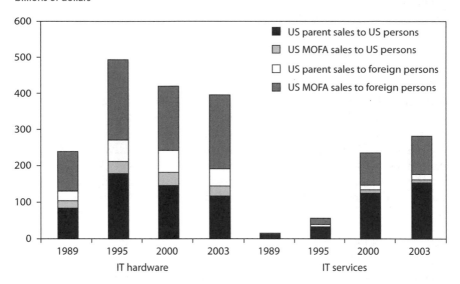

MOFA = majority-owned foreign affiliate

Source: Bureau of Economic Analysis financial and operating data for US multinational companies.

sourcing abroad of parts of the production process are an important feature of the business strategy of US multinationals, these data indicate that a stable global production strategy has been in place for some time (figure 2.3).

The data are more complete for US multinationals that produce IT hardware. Consider first the decision to produce in the United States and export versus producing abroad and selling from that affiliate to the foreign market. In IT hardware, the share of foreign demand met by exporting IT hardware—using US parent sales to foreign "persons" as a proxy for US exports—has been about 30 percent of total foreign sales (sum of US parent sales to foreign persons and US MOFA sales to foreign persons in figure 2.3). With regard to the decision to produce IT hardware abroad and import or to sell in the US market from domestic production facilities, the share of US domestic sales met by foreign affiliates of the US parent (that is, imports) has been stable at roughly 15 percent. So the foreign market is a more important destination for US domestic production facilities than is the US domestic market for the foreign production affiliates of US multinationals.

This stability in the shares of exports and imports of US multinationals belies a significant change in to whom the US multinational sells abroad (to an affiliate or a direct sale to an unrelated foreign buyer), or how US demand is met (from a US affiliate or from an unrelated foreign firm).

These changes will be addressed in the next two sections, first by examining the globally integrated production platform of US multinationals and the cost drivers of that platform, and second by looking at foreign firms' participation in the US market. The bottom line is that foreign firms—that is, those with no ownership relationship to US multinationals—are playing an increasingly important role in the US marketplace as producers in the United States, and particularly in terms of selling into the United States from abroad (that is, as the source of imports of IT hardware). This is consistent with the pattern already noted, that US multinational IT companies are reducing their emphasis on producing IT hardware so as to shift into IT software and services.

The picture is murkier for IT services. The share of foreign demand met by sales from US parent companies (that is, exports) was about 20 percent.[11] The data indicate that more than 90 percent of US domestic demand has been met through domestic sales by the US parent, and that that share has risen. These data therefore do not show an increase in the share of US IT services demand through imports of IT services by affiliates of US multinationals (so-called offshoring or offshore outsourcing).[12] The limited data cannot establish whether US IT multinationals' services increasingly rely on third-party providers rather than on affiliated firms, as was the case for US IT hardware multinationals and for which there is some evidence from the international trade data. Looking forward, technological changes that support further fragmentation of the production process of services and software, as well as remote purchase and sale, certainly will increase the two-way trade in services. It remains to be seen to what extent that trade will be at "arm's length" or between related parties of a US multinational, and whether it will be in surplus or deficit on an overall or affiliated international trade basis. These issues will be discussed further in chapter 4.

Integrated Global Production Platform of US Multinational IT Firms

This section drills down into the structure of globalized production by US multinational IT firms. US IT hardware firms have well-established global production networks with cross-border flows of intermediate products to

---

11. See appendix A for more detail on the way in which data are collected on multinational companies—"industry of parent versus industry of affiliate." The main classification issue is whether to consider affiliates by their own industry sector or by the industry sector of the parent firm. For affiliates of computer hardware companies whose primary line of business is wholesale trade (rather than hardware production), the distinction can be quite significant. On the other hand, whereas the dollar value of sales is different with the alternative classification, the shares and trends are generally the same.

12. Recall, however, that the data only cover the IT services industry and hence would not include, for example, a US airline offshoring its back-office transactions to India.

Table 2.3   Sales by US IT hardware majority-owned foreign affiliates, by destination and industry of parent, selected years (percent)

Sales to	1989	1995	2000	2003
1 Parent	15	12	14	11
2 Other local foreign affiliates	4	2	3	1
3 Foreign affiliates in other foreign countries	16	26	25	20
4 Unaffiliated US persons	0	1	3	1
5 Unaffiliated local persons	61	53	40	57
6 Unaffiliated persons in other foreign countries	3	6	15	11

Source: Bureau of Economic Analysis, US Direct Investment Abroad: Financial and Operating Data for US Multinational Companies (table III.F.9), www.bea.gov (accessed September 30, 2005).

serve their markets both in the United States and abroad. In contrast, US IT services firms have used a strategy based on production and sale in the same market—domestic production sites for domestic sales and foreign production sites for foreign sales. In the future, fragmentation and globalized production of software and services may well yield integrated global production for services and software similar to the one used for IT hardware. However, as that fragmentation process is just beginning, current data reveal little. Hence, this section will focus primarily on the evolving integrated and globalized production platform for IT hardware and its implications for companies' assets and employment.

Because the global production network for IT hardware has been in place for some time, it makes sense to look at it in more detail (table 2.3). The global production networks for IT hardware start with the 30 percent or so of US production that is sold abroad (exported), of which 75 percent goes to affiliates, according to 2003 data.

Benchmark year surveys indicate that 84 percent of the sales (exports) from the parent go to the affiliates for "further manufacturing," that is, it represents intermediate products entering the integrated global production network. So about 20 percent of total sales by the US parent go to affiliates for "further manufacturing." Therefore, a minority of US parent total sales, but the vast bulk of exports of these US IT hardware firms, is slated for further manufacturing. What happens to these intermediate products once they arrive at the foreign affiliate?

More than half of the affiliate production is sold in the same country (line 5 in table 2.3). About a third goes to other affiliates—some back to the US parent, but relatively more to other affiliates in other countries. Even as affiliates' sales have climbed dramatically, the relative distribution of sales has not moved significantly over the period shown in table 2.3, indicating that this integrated global production network for US IT hardware developed well before that. Over this time period as well, the US content (that is, the export percentage value) in the final sales of affiliates has held relatively constant at about 25 percent.[13] On the other hand, there is some evidence that affiliate operations are being consolidated in fewer foreign locations, perhaps to maximize economies of scale at the most technologically advanced or lowest-cost locations.[14] (Line 6 in table 2.3 notes the rising share of sales to unaffiliated persons in other foreign countries.)

Since the US-produced content of affiliate operations has remained stable, increased production and sales abroad should yield a complementary increase in US exports. That is, if the consolidation of production in some affiliates yields more cost-effective production that is passed on to lower prices, then these lower prices would tend to increase global sales, and US exports to the integrated global production network also should increase. In fact, the trade data just for US multinationals does reveal this response.[15]

Costs and Technology: Drivers of the Integrated Global Production Network

In a world with a growing number of competitors, cost-efficient production and the use of cutting-edge technology are the keys to maintaining and increasing market presence. How have US multinationals responded? For IT hardware, aggregate data show that US firms have significantly reduced average labor costs by locating production facilities abroad. But labor cost is not the only issue—increased capital intensity in IT hardware production, regardless of ownership or location, is also a factor. For IT services, labor costs in affiliates abroad are about the same as in the United States. Employment abroad appears driven not by cost differentials but by the need to be in the market where the service is delivered.

For IT hardware, cost savings and technology drive the structure of global production. Integrated global production of IT hardware goes hand-in-hand with cost differentials and changes in capital intensity. First, trends in the capital intensity of IT hardware firms suggest that technological change is an important factor driving employment in the production structure. An increase in capital intensity in production facilities is widely observed at US-located facilities of different ownership. While the increase in capital intensity is less intense in US-owned facilities in low-wage locations, it is still apparent (figure 2.4).

---

13. This figure is derived from detailed data on destination of parent and MOFA sales: US parent sales to affiliates divided by MOFA sales (excluding sales back to parent or unaffiliated US buyers).

14. Insufficient publicly available geographic detail makes it impossible to determine in which countries these facilities are located.

15. See chapter 4 for a discussion on intrafirm trade.

Figure 2.4   Trends in capital intensity in IT hardware, 1989–2003
(total assets in US dollar terms per employee)

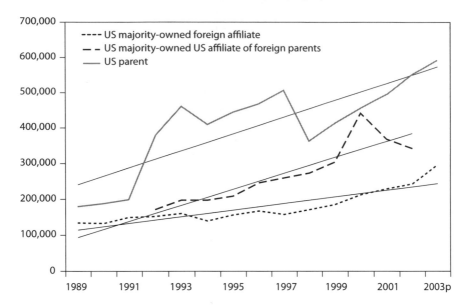

Source: Bureau of Economic Analysis financial and operating data for US multinational companies.

Even with the overall increase in capital intensity, wage-cost differentials are substantial, and do influence the location of production as well as the decision to produce at all (figure 2.5). In 1989, average wages at US IT hardware facilities were 1.8 times greater than average wages at US affiliates. By 2003, the cost differential was 3.4. (Both the starting and the ending wage differentials are larger than for manufacturing as a whole, although the trend in increasing wage differentials is the same for both IT and manufacturing and slowed after 2000.) Over this period, average wages at US IT hardware facilities increased about 43 percent, while average wages at affiliate operations dropped about 20 percent. The widening gap between wages at the affiliates and those at domestic production locations suggests a geographical shift of production to low-wage locations. But this wage pattern also implies a widening differentiation in what workers do and the skills they have at the foreign versus domestic locations. The highest skills and highest wages are paid to workers in US production facilities.

Pulling together the earlier discussion of the operations of US firms and the (limited) geographic detail regarding the location of US facilities suggests several trends. First, operations by US IT hardware companies in what are generally considered "low-wage" countries (in US dollar terms) increased in the 1990s. However, a substantial portion of the adjustment

Figure 2.5 Average total annual compensation for US majority-owned foreign affiliates (MOFAs) and US parents, by industry, selected years

US dollars

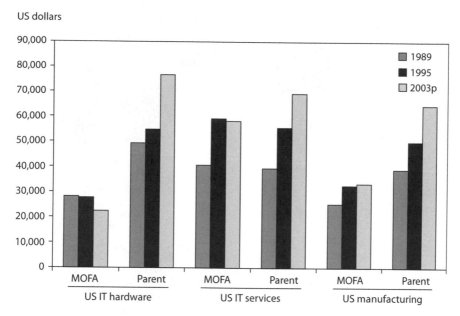

p = preliminary

Source: Bureau of Economic Analysis financial and operating data for US multinational companies.

came from high-cost affiliates outside the United States, which is confirmed by data on global employment. Whereas employment by US multinational ITs in the United States dropped 48 percent from 1992 to 2003, employment in affiliates in other industrial countries with similarly high wages fell even more (56 percent) over the same period (figure 2.6). Moreover, the increase in capital intensity at all plants means that even as employment fell at US and other high-wage locations, these workers were not replaced one-for-one with low-wage workers.

The timing of changes in employment location and in capital intensity is an important indicator of what products continue to be produced in the United States. The more significant change in capital intensity in IT hardware came in the first half of the 1990s, while more dramatic growth in wages occurred in the second half of that decade. (This is not the pattern observed for manufacturing as a whole.) The increasing wage premium in the second half of the 1990s for skilled workers at US-based IT hardware facilities is consistent with these plants producing the highest-value IT hardware for US and global markets.

IT services present a different picture of how technology and local market demand drive the location of production. How do costs, technology,

Figure 2.6   Regional employment by US multinational IT hardware companies, 1992, 2000, and 2003 (thousands of employees)

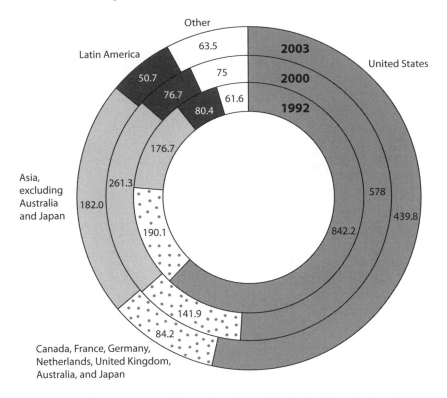

Source: Bureau of Economic Analysis financial and operating data for US multinational companies.

and localization affect IT services in the global marketplace? First, as discussed, the global demand for IT services, while growing quickly, is not yet as diversified in production or in demand around the world as it is for hardware. The services market is better developed in the advanced industrial economies, where there is a more significant installed base of IT hardware and higher spending on IT services and software.

Second, the dramatic increase in average wages at US IT services multinationals from 1989 to 2003 was greater than the increase in average wages in US IT hardware firms. The average wage is much higher for services affiliates abroad than in hardware affiliates abroad (figure 2.5). This suggests that the services produced and the skills necessary at both US and foreign locations have increased, and that the markets in which the services are delivered are similar in terms of wage costs. Employment data in figure 2.7 confirm these observations. US IT services affiliates tend to be located in other advanced industrial economies. Because labor costs in the industrial economies more closely mirror US labor costs, there is

Figure 2.7 Regional employment by US multinational IT services companies, 2000 and 2003 (thousands of employees)

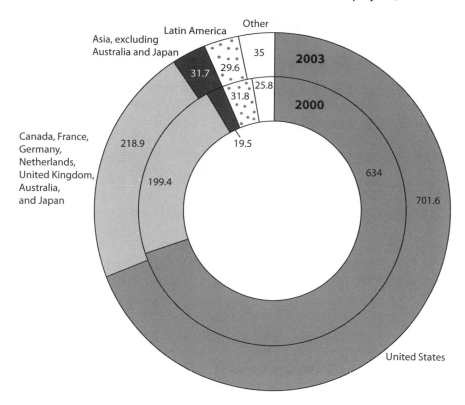

Source: Bureau of Economic Analysis financial and operating data for US multinational companies.

less of a cost advantage to creating a globally integrated production network for services. These data, along with the data on IT spending, are consistent with the observation that services tend to be produced and sold in the same market.

On the other hand, the fragmentation of the production process for services to lower-wage locations may be starting to show in the data. From a very small base of 45,000 employees, employment in developing countries outside Latin America rose nearly 50 percent between 2000 and 2003. But with only 67,000 employed there, developing countries outside Latin America account for only 7 percent of total global employment. While this may represent the early stage of the fragmentation and globalization of the production of IT services and software, overall employment in affiliates abroad increased some 39,000 (about 14 percent) during 2000–2003, and employment in the United States by the parent firms increased by 68,000 (11 percent) over the same period—a much higher absolute number of employees than in the low-wage locations abroad. So even as fragmentation and globalization of IT services have increased, the expansion into lower-wage locations is well outweighed by expansion in hiring at home and in other industrial-country markets with similar wage structures. This pattern of expanding sales and employment is consistent with the investment and price elasticities discussed earlier.

In sum, the trend of the integrated global production platform looks different for IT hardware versus software and services. IT hardware employment in the United States and high-wage countries has fallen dramatically, but has only been partially replaced by low-wage labor. Increased capital intensity has also played a role in the domestic employment trends, and the wages earned at home have increased, commensurate with the higher valued-added production that remains in the United States. IT services and software employment and wages have increased dramatically in the United States, even as there have been modest increases in employment in both high- and low-wage affiliates abroad.

Foreign-Owned IT and Communications Firms in the US Marketplace

US multinational IT firms are not the only players in the US marketplace. Foreign firms with no ownership affiliation with US firms are playing an increasingly important role in the US marketplace. Foreign firms can participate in the United States through new "greenfield" direct investment—i.e., by establishing new plants and facilities. But the data suggest that what is taking place even more is mergers and acquisitions. That is, when US firms sell US-located assets that no longer fit with their business strategy, foreign firms purchase some of those assets, hire some of the employees, and continue to serve the US market. "Contract" firms such as electronics manufacturing services are important examples. Does this ownership transformation affect the US IT marketplace, US firms, or US workers?

Mergers and Acquisitions in the IT and Communications Sectors

Data on assets and employment of IT multinationals operating in the United States—including multinationals of both US and foreign ownership—reveal one way that foreign firms can participate in the US marketplace, namely through merger and acquisition activity among US and foreign owners of IT hardware firms. Aggregated data from the BEA on the IT sector alone show the total value of assets owned in the United States by US-parent multinationals and the value of assets owned in the United States by foreign-parent multinationals above a cut-off value of assets.

**Figure 2.8   Acquisition and establishment of US IT companies
by foreigners, 1987–2002**

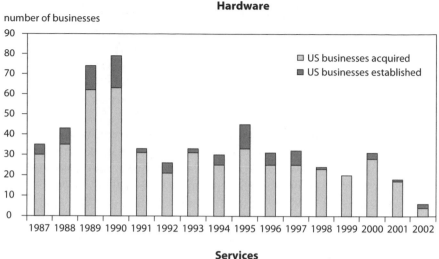

Notes: Threshold for inclusion in these data is 10 percent foreign ownership. Key is the same for both figures.

Source: Bureau of Economic Analysis, Foreign Direct Investment in the United States: Financial and Operating Data for US Affiliates of Foreign Multinational Companies, www.bea.gov (accessed September 30, 2005).

Changes in these two values may not be directly due to merger and acquisition deals. But to the extent that greenfield direct investment is unimportant, merger and acquisition is what is going on. A second source of data on mergers and acquisitions, from the Organization for Economic Cooperation and Development (OECD), which incorporates both IT and

Box 2.2   Adapting to change and seeking markets: IBM versus Bull

Two trends characterize the global IT marketplace: the large shift from hardware toward software and IT services, and the rising importance of foreign demand for IT products. With such a massive market shift, it is noteworthy that IBM has remained the world's biggest IT company. IBM has accomplished this by meeting the market as it has shifted, that is, by trending toward IT services and by going abroad. By seeking the growing markets, the firm has maintained its leadership position.

IBM's services revenues grew from 9 to 48 percent of total revenues from 1991 to 2004, while hardware revenues declined from 57 percent to less than a third of the total. Meanwhile, the share of software revenues in IBM's total has remained fairly stable at about 15 percent. Throughout the 1990s, IBM sought new markets outside the United States for its new services products and has maintained a roughly one-third/two-thirds US/non-US geographic revenue distribution from 1991 to 2004. IBM—the company that invented the personal computer—is now an IT services and software company more than it is an IT hardware company.[1] Indeed, with the sale in December 2004 of its personal computing division to the Chinese company Lenovo (while becoming that company's preferred IT services provider), IBM continued in 2005 the trend away from hardware toward IT services.[2]

Why did IBM move toward services? Was it forced by declining profitability to abandon hardware? Has it grown profitably by providing IT services? Through the 1990s, IBM's gross margins in hardware were significantly higher than in IT services. By 1999, however, gross margins on the two product groups converged, with a decline in hardware margins and a rise in IT services margins.[3] The fact that IBM's IT services margins improved as the company moved into this sector points

(box continues next page)

communications, is built on a deal-by-deal basis, but there are fewer details on employment and asset value. Finally, Thomson VentureXpert details the cross-border flows of venture financing, a subset of the total cross-border financial activities. It makes sense to take a look at these three data sources.

On the matter of new establishments versus acquisitions, figure 2.8 shows two trends. First, in both hardware and services, new establishments are far less important than are foreign acquisitions of US assets. Second, the time series of data on foreign acquisitions of US assets corroborate the evolution away from hardware and toward services.

According to the BEA, US parent companies in the IT sector reduced assets by almost 30 percent (from $363 billion to $259 billion) between 1995

Box 2.2   *(continued)*

to the likely "pull" from opportunities for profitable growth in IT services. And, consistent with the aggregated sector data presented in the main text, the declining hardware margin is consistent with a "push" out of the increasingly competitive marketplace. IBM's story shows the importance of adapting to change.

What happens in the competitive global IT markets to companies that do not adapt to change and market signals? The French computer company Bull was created through the nationalization of the French computer industry in 1982 as a "national computer champion." Bull has attempted to establish itself as an important player in the high-value server market as well as in the market for specialized computer engineering services. In contrast to IBM's restructuring and redirection to support profitability in new market segments and locations, Bull's strategy has been financed by subsidies, including €517 million in December 2004.[4] In 2002, Bull lost €548 million on revenues of €1,514 million and has barely broken even since. By 2004, Bull was still shrinking, with revenues of only slightly over €1 billion and 7,500 employees.[5] Bull demonstrates that simply financing IT companies does not yield global players.

———————————

1. This change also has significant data classification implications. See appendix 2B.

2. See IBM press release, "Lenovo Completes Acquisition of IBM's Personal Computing Division," May 1, 2005.

3. Only gross margins are available by company segment, and therefore these data do not account for selling, general and administrative, research and development, interest, tax, and other expenses. They are consequently indicative only of the net profitability of each segment.

4. European Commission press release IP/04/1424, December 1, 2004.

5. See Bull S.A. annual reports for 2003 and 2004, Paris, www.bull.com (accessed March 15, 2006).

and 2003. The expression "reduced assets" is important, as these data aggregate both company exits as well as mark-to-market valuation of company assets. (Unfortunately, the data do not distinguish between these two fundamentally different economic outcomes.) One can infer that some companies either exited the industry, diversified out of it (such as IBM, as discussed in box 2.2), or were taken over by rivals, since the number of US IT parent companies declined by roughly the same 23 percent from 1995 to 2003. The reduction in US IT hardware assets occurred at a time when foreign competition via imports to the US market heated up and the market for IT services started to emerge, both of which tended to push the leading US businesses away from producing IT hardware, particularly standardized hardware, in the United States.

Foreign investment in the United States behaved quite differently during the 1995–2000 technology boom and bust that followed. During the boom, foreign investment in US IT hardware firms increased from $14 billion to $46 billion. Even as US hardware firms reduced assets, the reported value of assets owned by foreigners increased by an amount equal to about 40 percent of the decline in the value of the assets sold by US owners. After the bust (2002), foreign-owned assets declined, but this could be due to fewer survey respondents, as well as to lower stock market value of those assets.

Data on specific merger and acquisition activity trend in broadly similar ways to the BEA aggregated data.[16] Against the backdrop of the overall technology boom and bust, the United States as a target for global mergers and acquisitions stands out for having even higher volatility than the global market as a whole. For the United States as a target country, about $2 billion in 1995 in foreign-source mergers and acquisitions rose to $103 billion in 1999, before falling back to about $11 billion in 2003 (table 2.4).[17]

Target countries outside the OECD in 2002 and 2003 had mergers and acquisitions comparable in magnitude to those of the United States, which may indicate the increasing attractiveness of IT and communications assets in low-wage but increasingly high-skill countries, such as India and China.

From these data it is not possible to tell whether US bidders increasingly target non-OECD markets. On the other hand, data from Thomson Venture-Xpert on venture capital investments and buyouts in the IT sector (discussed in more detail in chapter 6) indicate that between 1999 and 2005 (November 11) about 30 percent of the venture finance abroad went to non-OECD countries (totaling about $33 million), of which 25 percent went to China, 12 percent each went to India and Israel, 8 percent to Hong Kong, and 3 percent to Taiwan. Notably over the period, the share of overseas finance to the China, Hong Kong, and Taiwan production areas shifted dramatically to China, with in fact no deals recorded in Taiwan and Hong Kong in 2005.

---

16. Most of the preceding discussion has used the narrower definition of IT that excludes communications companies. Here we use the broader definition of IT and communications, in part because of limitations of the source data that do not allow us to break out the strict communications companies. Differences in merger and acquisition activity where the sector of communications appears to be most relevant are addressed in the text.

17. The fact that the European Union has a perhaps surprisingly large share of the "targets" is an indication of the ongoing gradual integration and cross-border consolidation of the EU telecommunications sector following the liberalization of the sector in Europe during the 1990s. The increase over 1999–2001 may also be due to the restructuring of telecommunications firms in the European Union. Developed countries other than those in Europe and not including the United States did not have significant foreign investment in their IT and communications sectors during this period.

Table 2.4 IT and communications sector cross-border mergers and acquisitions, by country, 1995–2003

Country	1995	1996	1997	1998	1999	2000	2001	2002	2003	Total, 1995–2003
By target country										
United States										
Billions of dollars	2.1	11.9	11.3	27.7	103.2	57.6	77.6	13.3	10.8	315.6
Percent	8	25	13	19	33	10	33	13	13	
European Union[a]										
Billions of dollars	16.9	27.7	47.7	125.6	301.1	79.8	49.2	n.a.	n.a.	n.a.
Percent	62	57	53	40	52	34	48	0	0	
United Kingdom										
Billions of dollars	6.7	3.0	3.0	5.6	67.5	104.4	25.1	5.5	6.0	226.7
Percent	25	6	3	4	22	18	11	5	7	
Germany										
Billions of dollars	1.0	14.2	2.0	3.4	6.7	97.2	22.5	6.8	13.3	167.1
Percent	4	29	2	2	2	17	10	7	16	
France										
Billions of dollars	1.0	1.0	13.3	9.3	6.5	8.2	11.9	1.8	5.7	58.9
Italy										
Billions of dollars	1.9	2.0	11.4	2.2	9.4	6.4	.4	1.7	1.1	36.6
Canada										
Billions of dollars	2.0	.3	.4	2.0	13.5	75.6	5.4	2.3	2.0	103.5
Japan										
Billions of dollars	.3	.7	.6	18.4	17.8	15.0	13.2	.65	7.0	73.7
Percent	1	2	1	13	6	3	6	1	9	
Australia										
Billions of dollars	2.5	.5	12.0	.7	14.7	1.9	9.1	1.3	1.2	43.9

(table continues next page)

Table 2.4 IT and communications sector cross-border mergers and acquisitions, by country, 1995–2003
(continued)

Country	1995	1996	1997	1998	1999	2000	2001	2002	2003	Total, 1995–2003
Korea										
Billions of dollars	n.a.	n.a.	n.a.	2.3	1.5	3.0	7.7	9.9	.6	25.0
Total OECD										
Billions of dollars	24.0	41.3	73.8	108.3	278.5	490.0	203.1	79.6	67.8	1,366.0
Percent share of world total	89	85	82	75	89	84	87	78	83	
Total non-OECD										
Billions of dollars	3.1	6.9	15.3	34.6	31.2	86.4	27.8	19.6	10.6	235.4
Percent share of world total	11	14	17	24	10	15	12	19	13	
Unspecified (billions of dollars)[b]	.04	.3	.8	1.4	2.2	5.9	2.7	3.1	2.9	19.3
Total world	27.2	48.4	89.9	144.3	311.9	582.3	233.6	102.3	81.3	1,621.1
By country of bidder										
United States										
Billions of dollars	7.7	4.1	12.0	21.3	33.1	57.1	35.0	16.6	11.8	198.9
Percent	28	9	13	15	11	10	15	16	15	
European Union[a]										
Billions of dollars	6.9	11.4	23.4	45.1	169.6	245.2	116.0	34.3	21.4	673.3
Percent	25	24	26	31	54	42	50	33	26	
United Kingdom										
Billions of dollars	1.7	6.8	7.1	7.6	76.4	57.3	40.3	5.2	8.9	211.3
Percent	6	14	8	5	24	10	17	5	11	
Germany										
Billions of dollars	3.1	.8	3.6	1.8	59.2	22.1	41.3	4.4	.1	136.4
Percent	12	2	4	1	19	4	18	4	0	
France										
Billions of dollars	.2	.3	3.1	9.5	13.3	78.3	8.9	8.2	9.3	131.1

										Total
Italy	Billions of dollars	.1	.7	2.8	8.5	5.8	10.5	3.8	.5	.8	33.2
Canada	Billions of dollars	.9	4.1	.9	23.8	3.0	26.5	5.3	.6	1.7	67.0
Japan	Billions of dollars	1.1	1.9	1.4	1.5	1.5	12.9	12.4	2.3	.1	35.0
	Percent	4	4	2	1	0	2	5	2	0	
Australia	Billions of dollars	.4	.4	3.1	.8	2.4	.7	13.6	1.5	8.0	31.3
Korea	Billions of dollars	.2	.3	.2	.3	.2	n.a.	.2	.2	.2	1.8
Total OECD	Billions of dollars	18.4	22.6	41.4	92.8	215.4	347.7	184.2	57.2	44.7	1,024.6
	Percent share of world total	68	47	46	64	69	60	79	56	55	
	Percent share of world specified total	97	93	93	91	90	86	93	81	91	
Total non-OECD	Billions of dollars	.5	1.7	3.3	9.0	24.9	57.7	14.3	13.2	4.6	129.1
	Percent share of world total	2	4	4	6	8	10	6	13	6	
Unspecified[b]	Billions of dollars	8.2	24.0	45.1	42.5	71.6	176.9	35.0	32.0	32.0	467.2
	Percent share of world total	30	50	50	29	23	30	15	31	39	
Total world		27.2	48.4	89.8	144.3	311.9	582.3	233.6	102.3	81.3	1,621.1

n.a. = not available

a. Includes the 19 members of the European Union that are also members of the Organization for Economic Cooperation and Development (OECD), excluding Latvia, Estonia, Lithuania, Malta, Cyprus, and Slovenia.

b. Unspecified refers to cases where there is no individual specified country bidder.

Source: OECD (2004a, annex table C.2.9, 2.10).

Global Mergers and Acquisitions

It is often assumed that an increase in global production of any kind of product is associated with new investment in a production facility in that country. However, direct investment through mergers and acquisitions is another way to create a global production platform without necessarily adding to global productive capacity.

Table 2.4 lists cross-border merger and acquisition activity in the IT and communications sectors for the world's major economies. Not surprisingly, the main international acquirers of IT and communications assets are found among the OECD countries.[18] More surprising perhaps is that US companies account for a relatively small share of acquirers, about 15 to 20 percent of the total, which is significantly below the roughly 50 percent share of US equity markets in global market capitalization and the roughly 50 percent US share in global expenditure on IT goods and services (table 2.1). This may reflect a US strategy of organic international growth through direct investment in newly created foreign-owned subsidiaries. Or it may mean that leading US IT firms have found relatively few inviting takeover targets outside the United States. Or it may be, as explained in box 2.3, that US and European IT and communications companies have different approaches to global expansion. European companies appear to rely more on large foreign acquisitions to enter a telecommunications market, whereas US companies have focused on buying smaller, but numerous, foreign technology companies. The large Asian economies have been virtually absent from the international merger and acquisition stage.

The Role for "Contract" Manufacturers of IT Hardware

Global IT hardware producers face three realities: IT product prices continue to decline through exponentially increasing processing power; the infrastructure costs of building production facilities continue to rise exponentially; and product cycles are shortening. In this business environment, cutting costs is imperative, but at the same time companies must in-

---

18. The relatively large share of all merger and acquisition activity listed in table 2.4 as unspecified might warrant some caution in making such a statement. However, this uncertainty comes from the original source of the data (Dealogic) and is caused by financial disclosure rules and the fact that "bidders" are often existing (international) shareholders. There is no reason to believe that the OECD share among the "unspecified" is less than the OECD share of the world specified total, i.e., 83 percent or above. Another cause of concern with respect to overinterpreting these data lies in the risk that "one-off events," such as the international purchases of countries' auctioned 3-G licenses in 2000, are included in the aggregate numbers. This may serve to particularly inflate the European data.

Box 2.3 Mergers and acquisitions: Build it or buy it

US and European information technology and communications companies, particularly large telecommunications firms, appear to pursue very different globalization strategies. US IT and communications firms are generally much more likely either to buy smaller foreign companies and integrate them into their global business and leverage the technology acquired. Such was the case of Hewlett-Packard's purchase of the Dutch company Indigo N.V., as described in box 6.1, or through the global business strategy of IBM (box 2.2).

European IT and communications companies, on the other hand, have tended to buy their way into new markets through acquisitions of, in many cases, large foreign companies. This strategy is exemplified by Deutsche Telecom's $22.5 billion takeover of the US carrier VoiceStream in 2001, or Vodafone's $62 billion acquisition of the US carrier AirTouch in 1999 and $183 billion acquisition of the German carrier Mannesmann in 2000.

It is premature, however, to jump to conclude that the United States "builds" and Europe "buys." First, most of the European "mega-deals" occurred at the height of the boom in the late 1990s, when executive "animal spirits" were certainly stirred by rocketing share prices. Second, much cross-border consolidation took place within the European Union as telecommunications markets were rapidly liberalized, and purchases of large market shares may have been necessary in order to compete with dominant, formerly state-owned incumbents. Third, similar consolidation in telecommunications has subsequently occurred (indeed, it is still in progress) in the US market—with the obvious difference that none of these deals has been "international." Last but perhaps most important for the US IT companies operating within the broader definition of IT and communications, many large US firms have for decades been building an extensive overseas subsidiary network, in part as a reaction to domestic regulations in those markets. In this respect, the US firms' international growth strategy operates as a "first mover" relative to their European competitors, so the Europeans may therefore have fewer strategic options for growth other than through large acquisitions.

crease research and development budgets in order to stay at the technological frontier.

An increasingly popular cost-cutting strategy adopted by US IT hardware producers is to turn to contract manufacturers, in which selected parts of or even the entire IT hardware manufacturing process is outsourced by the name-brand firm to specialized electronics manufacturing services (EMS) companies, such as Flextronics International or Solectron. The EMS industry experienced very rapid market growth throughout the

1990s, expanding to an estimated $115 billion in 2000, before experiencing a postbubble contraction. In 2004, the EMS industry nearly reached the levels seen in 2000, but has gone through a considerable consolidation, with the top 50 companies in the industry now accounting for as much as $94 billion of the total market.[19] Industry observers are predicting continued rapid growth and a world market of $245 billion by 2008 (Electronic Trend Publications 2004).

By outsourcing to an unaffiliated EMS company, US IT hardware manufacturers with household names can reduce overall production costs through lower capital investment requirements, improved inventory management and purchasing power (by tapping into the EMS firms' economies of scale), and access to advanced EMS manufacturing facilities strategically located in low-cost countries. In particular, manufacturing of high-volume "commoditized" products (those with well-established engineering technologies and standards) can be outsourced and produced in low-cost countries, which improves the price competitiveness of the overall product that carries the brand name of the US multinationals. Hence, EMS outsourcing can complement the US IT hardware companies' own global supply network of foreign affiliates. The relative importance of the multinationals' own global production network and their reliance on outsourcing to an EMS global production network are seen in the data on international trade—a point to which we will return.

Despite its aggressive search for cost reductions and tax incentives as a competitive parameter, the EMS industry maintains a strong production presence in the United States (table 2.5).[20] Two of the top five EMS companies in 2004 were incorporated in the United States[21] and all of the top five EMS companies had the United States as their number one global sales and asset location. However, consistent with all the data thus far presented on global spending and US multinationals' production, a shift

---

19. *Manufacturing Market Insider* press release, "Annual MMI Top 50 EMS Producer Rankings, 2004," available at www.mfgmkt.com (accessed April 27, 2005).

20. According to the Flextronics International Ltd., 2002 10-K filing (p. 13): "We have structured our operations in a manner designed to maximize income in countries where . . . tax incentives have been extended to encourage foreign investment; or . . . income tax rates are low. We base our tax position upon the anticipated nature and conduct of our business and upon our understanding of the tax laws of the various countries in which we have assets or conduct activities." Available at www.sec.gov (accessed September 30, 2005).

According to the Solectron, Inc., 2002 Annual Report (p. 25): "In general, the effective income tax rate is largely a function of the balance between income from domestic and international operations. Our international operations, taken as a whole, have been taxed at a lower rate than those in the United States, primarily due to tax holidays granted to several of our overseas sites in Malaysia, Singapore, and China."

21. *Manufacturing Market Insider* newsletter, March 2004 and March 2005.

of production locations and assets to Asia from 2000 to 2004 is clearly visible for the top EMS firms as well. Asian sales by the top five EMS companies also rose dramatically, indicating that assets and production follow the markets in this highly competitive industry. Consistent with the other data presented, the growth of EMS facilities in China has been rapid, but this growth has not come solely at the expense of production in the United States. Rather, other developed countries—notably in Western Europe—show declines in EMS production facilities. The US share of sales and assets generally is a little lower for the major EMS companies than for the US IT hardware multinationals covered in the BEA survey data.[22]

What else do EMS firms offer that might underpin their continued strong US presence but also a global location strategy? EMS firms provide both large and smaller US IT companies with accelerated time-to-market and time-to-volume production at their manufacturing facilities. Furthermore, as EMS companies offer more fully integrated product processes, including design, engineering, manufacturing, and postmanufacturing services, adjacency to customers and markets becomes an increasingly important asset, as logistics management and integral production cooperation with name-brand companies form a crucial part of EMS competitiveness. So there is strong incentive for EMS firms to locate in their biggest market, even as they also locate abroad to serve those markets too.

In sum, while outsourcing to contract manufacturers plainly means that parts of the global supply chain will be concentrated in low-cost countries, especially China, it is equally evident that high value-added operations tend to stay in the United States, complementing and facilitating the growth of existing US IT hardware firms. In other words, just because production of IT hardware is outsourced to an EMS company does not automatically mean that is also offshored to China or another low-wage country. When a US IT firm ceases production at a facility in the United States, it may not mean that jobs are lost in lockstep. In some cases, the facility and jobs will change owners and be redeployed, thus contributing to the cost competitiveness of US production overall.

What lessons does the EMS industry offer regarding the nascent globalization of the IT software and services sector? First, even for IT hardware production, where globalized production networks are well developed and have been in place for decades, adjacency and local knowledge matter in choosing a production location, although not necessarily a corporate ownership structure or nationality. Second, assets and production location move with the locus of market demand. Maintaining strong demand in the United States for IT investment throughout the economy is

---

22. The US share generally aligns with the US share of the world IT hardware spending. In 2003, the United States accounted for 32 percent ($119 billion) of world IT hardware spending. See WITSA (2004).

Table 2.5   *Manufacturing Market Insider's* top five electronics manufacturing service companies

Company (country of incorporation)	2004 sales (billions of dollars)	Global locations, owned and leased		Regional sales and asset distribution (percent)	
		2000	2004	2000	2004
Flextronics (Singapore)	14.5 (fiscal year ending March 31, 2004)	Number of locations: United States (21), Sweden (8), China (5), Austria (3), Hungary (3), Scotland (2), Finland (2), Ireland (2), Malaysia (2), Germany (2), Mexico (2), Italy, Brazil, France, Taiwan, Thailand, Switzerland	500,000–2.5mn square feet facilities: Brazil, China, Hungary, Mexico, and Poland 50,000–500,000 square feet facilities: Austria, Brazil, China, Denmark, Finland, France, Germany, Hungary, India, Israel, Italy, Japan, Malaysia, Mexico, Netherlands, Norway, Singapore, Sweden, Switzerland, Taiwan, Thailand, United States	Net sales: Americas (40) Asia (16) Europe (44) Long-lived assets: Americas (34) Asia (28) Europe (39)	Net sales: Americas (14) Asia (45) Europe (41) Long-lived assets: Americas (25) Asia (43) Europe (32)
Sanmina-SCI (United States)	12.2 (fiscal year ending August 31, 2004)	Number of locations: United States (31), Canada (2), Sweden (2), Finland (2), Malaysia (2), China (2), France, Ireland, Mexico	Percent of global square footage: Australia >(1), Brazil (2), Canada (3), China (8), Finland, (3), France (4), Germany (4), Hungary (7), Indonesia >(1), Ireland (1), Israel (2), Japan >(1), Malaysia (2), Mexico (12), Singapore (1), Spain (2), Sweden (2), Thailand (1), UK (7), United States (38)	Net sales: United States (81) International (19) Long-lived assets: United States (86) International (14)	Net sales: United States (27) International (73) Long-lived assets: United States (42) International (58)
Solectron (United States)	11.6 (fiscal year ending October 2, 2004)	Percent of global square footage: Brazil (4), Canada (3), Mexico (9), France (5), Germany (2),	Percent of global square footage: Australia (1), Belgium (1), Brazil (2), Canada (8), China (10), France (3), Germany (1),	Net sales: United States (59) Europe (24) Other (17)	Net sales: United States (28) Other Americas (16) Europe (14)

				Long-lived assets: United States (48), Europe (35), Other (17)	China (16), Other Asia-Pacific (26), Long-lived assets: United States (30), Other Americas (20), Europe (15), Asia-Pacific (35)
		Ireland (1), Romania (2), UK (6), Sweden (2), Australia (2), China (3), India >(1), Japan >(1), Malaysia (8), United States (52)	Hungary (2), Netherlands (2), Romania (4), Sweden (2), Turkey >(1), India >(1), Indonesia (1), Japan (5), Malaysia (9), Singapore (3), Taiwan >(1), Mexico (6), UK (2), United States (37)	Net sales: Americas (61), Europe (28), Asia (11), Long-lived assets: Americas (54), Europe (34), Asia (14)	Net sales 2003: Americas (44), Europe (20), Asia (36), Long-lived assets, 2003: Americas (38), Europe (32), Asia (30)
Celestica (Canada)	8.8 (fiscal year ending December 31, 2004)	Percent of global square footage: Brazil (3), Mexico (6), Canada (17), UK (12), Italy (16), Ireland (4), Czech Republic (3), China (7), Thailand (6), Malaysia (1), United States (26)	Percent of global square footage: Philippines (1), Thailand (5), Japan (5), Singapore (3), Malaysia (8), Indonesia >(1), China (13), Brazil (1), Mexico (9), Spain (6), Czech Republic (3), France (3), Italy (6), Ireland (1), UK, (2), Canada (11), United States (23)		
Foxconn (Taiwan)	8.5 (fiscal year ending December 31, 2004)	Number of locations: United States (5), China (2), Taiwan, Japan, Scotland, Ireland	n.a.	n.a.	n.a.

n.a. = not available

Note: The company operations listed in this table are captured by the aggregate data material used for this book in the following manner: (1) US-located operations are part of the US parent, while foreign operations constitute US majority-owned foreign affiliates. (2) Foreign companies: foreign-located operations are not covered in the aggregate data material, while US-located operations constitute US majority-owned US affiliates of foreign parents. Table is incomplete due to changes in the format of company filings. Due to rounding, percentages may not add up to 100. *Manufacturing Market Insider* 2005 rankings show the same five companies on top ranked Flextronics, Foxconn, Sanmina-SCI, Solectron, and Celestica.

Sources: Company 2000, 2004 10-K filings; Celestica Inc. 2000, 2004 20-F filings; company annual reports; Taiwan Stock Exchange; *Manufacturing Market Insider* March 2004.

an important way of ensuring continued domestic IT production and jobs, and this will be of increasing importance as the demand for IT services and software pervades the US economy.

The Rise of the Global IT and Communications Company

While it is important to focus on IT markets from the perspective of nations, and in particular on differences in trends among countries, so too is it important to examine who the companies are that actually supply these markets and develop much of the new technology. Given the rapid globalization of the IT industry, with many multinational companies located in dozens of different countries, a company-based analysis of the global IT market may yield valuable information about the performance of US multinationals in global IT markets. Such an analysis is an essential addition to the picture of the global marketplace that emerges from using data based on the country as the unit of analysis.

According to the OECD, the world's top 250 technology and communications companies in 2003 made their home in 25 different nations, 18 of which are OECD members.[23] The companies had revenues that year totaling almost $2.5 trillion, and they employed nearly 10 million people. More than half of the 250 firms were American, although this dominance is somewhat less pronounced when looking at revenues and numbers of employees, where US companies account for somewhat less than 40 percent of the total. The EU-25 and Japan account for significantly smaller shares of the number of top technology and communications companies, while both make up approximately a quarter of the top 250 in terms of revenues and employment. Among non-OECD countries, whereas China was the top IT exporter (table 2.1), only three Chinese technology companies are on the top 250 list of IT firms.

An alternative source of information about companies is a composite ranking by *BusinessWeek* magazine based on several different parameters for classification and ranking. (The challenges and risks involved in making such classifications and rankings are discussed in appendix 2B.)

Table 2.6 shows a snapshot ranking of global firms in IT hardware and IT services and software sectors. The table confirms what other data show: US IT hardware companies no longer dominate the global IT hardware market, but they do dominate the software, services, and Internet global market. In corporate rankings of the fastest-growing IT services,

---

23. These figures draw on data from OECD (2004a, annex A). These data incorporate both IT and communications. For the purposes of these data, companies primarily belonging in the following Standard Industrial Classification (SIC) categories are included; 4813, 3663, 3577, 3669, 3661, 8711, 3511, 3651, 3674, 3861, 3571, 3621, 3572, 7373, 5045, 8742, 7374, 7379, 7372, and 4899. See appendix 2B for additional detail.

Table 2.6   Top 25 global IT services/software/Internet and hardware companies, 2004–05

Rank	Firm	Country	Sector	Revenues, 2004–05 (millions of US dollars)	Profits, 2004–05 (millions of US dollars)
IT services/software/Internet companies					
1	IBM	United States	IT services	97,026	8,252
2	Microsoft	United States	Software	38,919	11,224
3	Accenture	US (Bermuda)	IT services	16,145	800
4	CSC	United States	IT services	14,768	519
5	Oracle	United States	Software	10,997	2,852
6	First Data	United States	IT services	10,235	1,762
7	SAP	Germany	Software	9,675	1,682
8	Atos Origin	France	IT services	6,594	13
9	Yahoo!	United States	Internet	3,991	943
10	Google	United States	Internet	3,794	704
11	Fiserv	United States	IT services	3,794	439
12	SunGard Data Systems	United States	IT services	3,662	458
13	Symantec	United States	Software	2,583	536
14	Tata Consulting Services	India	IT services	2,168	503
15	Wipro	India	IT services	1,865	363
16	Adobe Systems	United States	Software	1,716	479
17	Infosys Technologies	India	IT services	1,592	419
18	CACI International	United States	IT services	1,552	83
19	Activision	United States	Software	1,406	138
20	Verisign	United States	Internet	1,338	226
21	Anteon International	United States	IT services	1,330	67
22	Autodesk	United States	Software	1,292	255
23	SRA International	United States	IT services	822	54
24	Satyam Computer Services	India	IT services	794	154
25	Cognizant Technology Solutions	United States	IT services	649	112
Total				238,703	33,036
IT hardware companies					
1	Hewlett-Packard	United States	Computers and peripherals	76,828	2,979
2	Samsung Electronics	Korea	Computers and peripherals	71,585	9,423
3	Dell	United States	Computers and peripherals	51,051	3,246
4	Intel	United States	Semiconductors	35,552	7,964
5	LG Electronics	Korea	Computers and peripherals	33,773	1,405
6	Canon	Japan	Computers and peripherals	33,698	3,376
7	Hon Hai Precision Industries	Taiwan	Computers and peripherals	16,237	892
8	Texas Instruments	United States	Semiconductors	12,616	1,905
9	Apple Computer	United States	Computers and peripherals	11,097	752
10	EMC	United States	Computers and peripherals	8,601	1,001
11	Applied Materials	United States	Semiconductors	8,081	1,489

(table continues next page)

Table 2.6 Top 25 global IT services/software/Internet and hardware companies, 2004–05 *(continued)*

Rank	Firm	Country	Sector	Revenues, 2004–05 (millions of US dollars)	Profits, 2004–05 (millions of US dollars)
12	Taiwan Semiconductor Manufacturing	Taiwan	Semiconductors	7,730	2,748
13	Asutek Computers	Taiwan	Computers and peripherals	7,496	453
14	Compal Electronics	Taiwan	Computers and peripherals	6,889	197
15	Acer	Taiwan	Computers and peripherals	6,746	210
16	Seagate Technology	US (Cayman Islands)	Computers and peripherals	6,710	394
17	Lite-on Technology	Taiwan	Computers and peripherals	6,432	227
18	NCR	United States	Computers and peripherals	6,037	325
19	Nikon	Japan	Semiconductors	5,945	225
20	Tokyo Electron	Japan	Semiconductors	5,919	251
21	BenQ	Taiwan	Computers and peripherals	5,239	228
22	Nidec	Japan	Computers and peripherals	4,524	312
23	TPV Technology	Hong Kong (Bermuda)	Computers and peripherals	3,738	108
24	Chi Mei Opto-electronics	Taiwan	Computers and peripherals	3,535	515
25	Western Digital	United States	Computers and peripherals	3,447	187
Total				439,507	40,813

Notes: Companies selected by *BusinessWeek* must be publicly traded, nonmonopolistic, have a minimum of $300 million in revenues, and not have a stock that has declined more than 75 percent in the last year. They are selected based on return on equity, shareholder return, revenue growth, and revenues. Revenues and profits are for the latest available 12-month period. To ensure continuity over time, the top companies from the 2004 rankings not included in 2005 have been added to each ranking with 2004 data (CSC and Hewlett-Packard).

Sources: Information Technology 100, 2004, *BusinessWeek*, June 21, 2004; Information Technology 100, 2005, *BusinessWeek*, June 20, 2005.

software, and Internet sectors, 19 of the top 25 companies are American (with Accenture classified as a US company), while four are Indian, and only two European. While Indian IT services companies have certainly proven highly competitive in recent years and saw revenue increases of up to 30 percent in 2004–05, table 2.6 indicates that they still have some way to go to become truly global in scale.

In IT hardware, whereas the United States is still well represented among the top 25 (10 companies), the US position is far less dominant compared with the IT services, software, and Internet ranking. The United States is nearly equaled by Taiwan, which places eight companies in the ranking, with the remainder coming from Japan (four), Korea (two), and Hong Kong (one). Notably, not a single European IT hardware company makes the top 25. The data confirm the rise of Taiwanese (not Chinese) companies as subcontractors and producers of IT hardware for other manufacturers.

What with the rise of global producers of IT hardware products, the increase in global supply, even with increased global demand, puts downward pressure on IT hardware prices, as will be quantified in the next chapter. In moving away from this global competition, US firms have focused on the more rapidly expanding marketplace of services and software. But table 2.6 also shows that this is also the more lucrative marketplace: the profit margin of the combined top 25 IT services, software, and Internet companies is significantly above that of IT hardware companies (14 percent versus 9 percent). So it would appear that greater benefits accrue to US firms from dominating the fast-growing IT services, software, and Internet sector, rather than the increasingly commoditized IT hardware sector.[24]

In sum, the global IT marketplace has become broad-based across industrial and developing countries. Growth rates of spending, production, trade, and investment are very rapid around the world. New producers, exporters, and multinationals have emerged. Even as the United States remains the largest market, it is no longer the most important global exporter. The relative importance of the hardware versus the software and services markets appears somewhat different depending on the level of GDP per capita. There is overall a trend toward increased spending on IT software and services, portending the globalization of those markets and products too.

---

24. Rates of return will be particularly volatile in highly cyclical sectors, such as IT hardware. Yet the corresponding numbers from *BusinessWeek's* top 100 ranking of IT firms for 2004 show the same significantly higher profit margin in IT services, software, and Internet sectors, with 11 percent versus only 6 percent for the IT hardware sector.

Appendix 2A
The Shifting Global Market for Semiconductors

The Asia-Pacific region is now the dominant location for immediate demand for semiconductors—one of the fundamental products of the IT and communications industries—but the United States continues to lead in supplying the global marketplace for chips.

As a receiver of shipments, the American market held stable at about one-third of global shipments through 2000, but then dropped precipitously following the dot-com bust to account for about 18 percent of global end use in 2004. Japan's demand continued to decline as that economy remained sluggish. In contrast, the Asia-Pacific share in global demand increased from about 15 percent in 1990 to 20 percent in 1995 and to 42 percent in 2004 (figure 2A.1).

On the other hand, as suppliers of semiconductors, the United States reaches all markets, and is particularly capable in penetrating new markets. American suppliers held their market share through the 1990s, and in 2004 still supplied 60 percent of the American marketplace for chips and about 50 percent of the markets in Europe and the Asia-Pacific region (excluding Japan) (table 2A.1).[25] US exports of semiconductors exceeded imports by an increasing margin through the 1990s, which shows the increasing competitiveness of the highest-technology semiconductors in the global marketplace.

Figure 2A.1   Shares of world semiconductor market, 1982–2004

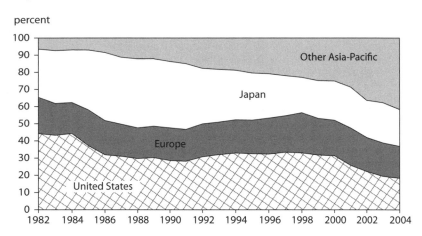

Source: Semiconductor Industry Association, www.sia-online.org/pre_statistics.cfm.

---

25. Semiconductor Industry Association industry statistics on world market shares, available at www.sia-online.org/pre_statistics.cfm (accessed September 30, 2006).

Table 2A.1   World semiconductor market supply and demand, 1982–2004 (percent)

| Supplying region | Demanding region | | | | | Total value (millions of US dollars) |
	Americas	Europe	Japan	Asia-Pacific	Total demand	
1982						
Americas	88.7	54.6	10.1	42.3	56.7	8,030
Japan	10.4	7.1	89.9	25.4	32.5	4,603
Other	0.9	38.3	0.0	32.3	10.8	1,529
1991						
Americas	69.9	45.2	12.5	42.7	39.2	21,193
Japan	19.7	14.7	86.1	33.9	46.4	25,086
Other	10.4	40.2	1.5	23.3	14.4	7,785
1999						
Americas	71.2	57.0	21.1	47.8	51.4	76,781
Japan	11.7	12.2	71.5	27.1	28.5	42,573
Other	17.1	30.8	7.4	25.1	20.1	30,025
2001						
Americas	72.5	54.6	22.8	53.1	51.2	71,149
Japan	11.1	14.3	70.3	18.6	28.1	39,049
Other	16.4	31.1	6.9	28.3	20.7	28,765
2004						
Americas	59.9	49.5	22.8	52.0	46.7	100,123
Japan	12.9	12.5	68.7	17.0	25.6	55,174
Other	27.2	38.0	8.5	31.0	26.8	57,730

Source: Semiconductor Industry Association, www.sia-online.org/pre_statistics.cfm.

Appendix 2B
How to Classify and Rank the Top Technology Companies

The immediate issue when one attempts to compile a meaningful list of the world's top technology companies, as seen in tables 2B.1 and 2.6, is the choice of ranking parameter. At least four such parameters spring to mind, each with separate implications and problems:

- *Current revenues:* Generally the most widely used indicator, this gives an intuitive reflection of the size of the company in the ranking.

- *Market capitalization:* This parameter should (in theory) reflect the present value of future earnings and hence be an indicator of the future of the company rather than its present size. Furthermore, there may be significant distortions imposed on cross-country comparisons arising from the capital market structure of the home country, which may be different from that of the United States. Companies may traditionally be more reliant on bank loans than on issuing equity capital, or frequently may not be listed at all.

- *Profit margin:* This parameter says something about the success of the firm, an issue again of intuitive importance when attempting to identify the top companies. However, this type of data can be both difficult to obtain (and ambiguous to interpret), and may fluctuate highly over time, making robust ranking difficult.

- *Number of employees and plants:* This parameter measures the physical size of the company, which is frequently of political importance when assessing companies. Yet, with the development of automated, advanced production techniques in IT and communications, as well as the adoption of global supply chains, where much of the manufacturing of inputs is done by geographically distant subcontractors, a ranking based on this type of data may not reflect the true size of the company in the marketplace, and could indeed likely be inversely proportional to corporate profitability parameters.

Hence, current revenue is a frequently used parameter, especially when ranking companies within a given industries. Unfortunately, when applied to the IT and communications industries, the current revenue parameter raises several conceptual issues. First, such segmentation of IT companies into subsector categories carries a methodological risk, because many of the world's large technology companies today have business operations in both subsectors of IT.[26]

---

26. For instance, IBM is a large IT services provider, but retains a very substantial IT hardware business as well. Other firms, especially Asian companies of the conglomerate type such as Samsung or LG, manufacture not just IT hardware but also significant amounts of consumer electronics, creating a similar type of issue.

Table 2B.1 Top 50 information technology and communications firms
(millions of current US dollars and number employed)

Rank	Company	Country	Industry	Revenue, 2003	Employees, 2002	R&D, 2002	Market cap, 2003
IT firms							
1	IBM	United States	IT equipment	86,902	315,889	4,750	141,805
2	Siemens	Germany	Electronics	85,894	426,000	5,490	53,873
3	Hewlett-Packard	United States	IT equipment	71,256	141,000	3,312	59,228
4	Hitachi	Japan	Electronics	67,157	306,989	3,307	12,226
5	Sony	Japan	Electronics	63,353	168,000	3,455	33,785
6	Matsushita	Japan	Electronics	62,744	291,232	4,514	21,745
7	Toshiba	Japan	IT equipment	47,944	176,398	2,601	13,679
8	Samsung	Korea	Electronics	47,613	173,000	2,500	40,404
9	NEC	Japan	IT equipment	41,090	141,909	2,661	12,080
10	Fujitsu	Japan	IT equipment	38,480	170,111	2,790	9,226
11	Nokia	Finland	Communications equipment	37,670	57,716	2,879	74,012
12	Dell Computer	United States	IT equipment	35,404	39,100	452	82,350
13	Microsoft	United States	Software	32,187	50,500	4,307	285,413
14	Mitsubishi	Japan	Electronics	30,848	116,192	1,632	n.a.
15	Philips	Netherlands	Electronics	29,947	170,000	2,871	21,471
16	Intel	United States	Electronics	28,527	78,700	4,034	177,332
17	Motorola	United States	Communications equipment	26,293	97,000	3,754	23,947
18	Canon	Japan	Electronics	25,760	97,802	1,864	42,202
19	EDS	United States	Services	21,731	137,000	0	10,608
20	Sanyo Electric	Japan	Electronics	19,856	80,500	853	n.a.
21	Cisco Systems	United States	Communications equipment	18,878	36,000	3,448	133,215
22	Alcatel	France	Communications equipment	18,694	75,940	2,100	13,203
23	LG Electronics	Korea	Electronics	18,080	55,000	551	n.a.
24	3M	United States	Electronics	17,179	68,774	1,066	56,129
25	Emerson	United States	Electronics	17,042	111,500	530	22,757
26	Sharp	Japan	Electronics	16,834	46,518	1,154	11,433
27	Tech Data	United States	Services	15,739	8,000	n.a.	1,900
28	Xerox	United States	Electronics	15,716	67,800	917	7,544
29	Ericsson	Sweden	Communications equipment	14,971	85,198	4,424	23,844
30	Ricoh	Japan	Electronics	14,732	74,600	644	13,997
31	Accenture	Bermuda	Services	13,397	75,000	235	19,691
32	Flextronics	Singapore	Electronics	13,379	95,000	n.a.	6,585
Communications firms							
1	NTT	Japan	Telecom	91,026	213,062	3,118	31,747
2	Verizon	United States	Telecom	67,734	245,000	n.a.	99,159
3	France Telecom	France	Telecom	52,048	211,554	680	24,140
4	Deutsche Telecom	Germany	Telecom	50,528	255,896	849	47,260
5	Vodafone	United Kingdom	Telecom	47,962	67,178	164	122,931
6	SBC	United States	Telecom	42,310	175,980	n.a.	67,703
7	AT&T	United States	Telecom	36,480	71,000	254	18,297

(table continues next page)

Table 2B.1   Top 50 information technology and communications firms
(millions of current US dollars and number employed)   *(continued)*

Rank	Company	Country	Industry	Revenue, 2003	Employees, 2002	R&D, 2002	Market cap, 2003
8	Telecom Italia	Italy	Telecom	32,983	101,713	124	45,812
9	BT	United Kingdom	Telecom	30,460	108,600	540	22,568
10	Telefonica	Spain	Telecom	26,739	161,029	n.a.	47,180
11	Sprint	United States	Telecom	25,604	72,200	n.a.	n.a.
12	KDDI	Japan	Telecom	23,591	9,300	67	13,063
13	BellSouth	United States	Telecom	22,399	77,000	n.a.	41,612
14	China Mobile	China	Telecom	15,527	59,633	n.a.	40,608
15	Qwest	United States	Telecom	15,487	50,788	n.a.	5,984
16	BCE	Canada	Telecom	14,987	66,266	n.a.	17,993
17	Telstra	Australia	Telecom	13,242	44,977	28	31,250
18	Korea Telecom	Korea	Telecom	13,104	48,668	n.a.	n.a.

n.a. = not available

Note: Revenues for 2003 based on financial year reported in 2003 or most recent four quarters.

Source: OECD (2004a, table A.3), compiled from annual reports, Securities and Exchange Commission filings, and market financials.

Moreover, the IT and communications industry is highly diverse. Consider the recent ranking by the Organization for Economic Cooperation and Development of the top 50 global IT and communications companies (OECD 2004a). Twenty-two of the top 50 are IT companies and account for 47 percent of the total revenues included in the rankings. Eighteen of the companies are telecommunications carriers, accounting for 36 percent of revenues, while the remaining 10 are IT services, telecommunications equipment manufacturers, or software companies. Most of the telecommunications carriers are former government monopolies (some remain that), which owe the vast majority of their revenues to a historical legal monopoly and declining marginal costs in their industry. Throwing such old beasts together with software companies—an industry that barely existed 15 years ago, arose from private entrepreneurship, has essentially zero marginal costs at any level of production, and is only now going through a first round of consolidation—will invariably skew the ranking toward telecommunications carriers.

Finally, as with any table based on a single year and in dollar terms, rankings can change.

3

Globalization and IT Prices, Diffusion, and Productivity

Chapter 1 reviewed why the overall impact of networked IT on the US economy warrants deeper analysis, while chapter 2 examined the globalization of the production of and demand for IT and communications products and services and of demand for them. This chapter puts the two pieces together to show the links between globalization of IT, IT prices, and diffusion of investment in IT. It discusses the macroeconomic trends and cycles in IT investment in the United States in response to globalized IT prices and the resulting acceleration of productivity growth at the macro level. Business transformation, particularly with respect to workplace practices, plays a key role in this process.

This chapter also delves deeper into the pattern of IT investment in the United States. It looks at the uneven pace of diffusion of IT into nontechnology sectors in the US economy and the resulting uneven acceleration of productivity growth that underpins the overall macro behavior. This varying pace of IT "uptake" by different sectors of the US economy is of particular interest, and appears to be related to customer and supplier transactional linkages between sectors of the economy, as well as to sector-specific regulations and the size distribution of firms, among other factors.

Finally, the chapter considers the experiences of other countries, given that they too are affected by the globalization of IT, although few of them have exhibited economic performance as it relates to IT similar to the United States. Comparing outcomes cements some of the findings pertinent to US behavior in the face of globalization and IT prices, the resulting investment in networks, and, importantly, changes in business activities and workplace practices.

Globalization of IT and Implications for Prices

What are the implications for the United States of all this globalization of IT production and sales? In short, the globalization of IT hardware production, trade, and sales has made these prices lower than they otherwise would have been. The IT product is a general-purpose investment, and the additionally lower prices further contribute to the diffusion of IT investment throughout the US economy. Globalization of IT increases its power to accelerate change in the US economy.

Forces of globalization are important factors underpinning IT hardware prices, where production and demand have been most globalized. But so far there has been less fragmentation and globalization of production of IT services and software. The globalization forces that affect these prices appear more muted. Going forward, some factors suggest a pattern for IT software and services globalization similar to that for IT hardware, but other factors suggest less of a role for globalization of IT services and software to accelerate change in the US economy.

IT Hardware Prices

This section pulls together the observations on costs in the integrated global network and on new producers and exporters in the global marketplace in order to analyze price trends for two specific categories of IT hardware. In principle, given the lower wage costs inferred from the integrated global production network for IT hardware, globalization of production by US firms should result in lower prices for these IT products. Moreover, increased investment in IT productive capacity around the world, as well as a more diverse set of global exporters, should raise competitive pressures, putting additional downward pressure on prices. Can these effects be quantified?

Research that conclusively links the globalization of IT hardware production to lower prices is elusive, primarily because of difficulties in obtaining adequate and appropriate data. There are problems of matching data on firm operations to data on the prices of products. There is limited information on the geographic location of facilities. And data are neither available for a sufficiently long time frame nor of sufficiently recent vintage for detailed and in-depth analysis across many segments of the IT industry. However, there are two categories of IT hardware for which there is sufficient information to do a structured analysis: dynamic random access memory chips (DRAMs), which are a type of semiconductor chip, and personal computers (PCs). These products offer a paradigm for understanding more generally the forces linking the globalization of IT production and the prices of IT products for US buyers.

Figure 3.1 shows the dramatic declines in the price indices of PCs and DRAMs. The prices of these two IT products are not independent: de-

Figure 3.1   Price indices for PCs and dynamic random access memory chips (DRAMs), December 1992–February 2005

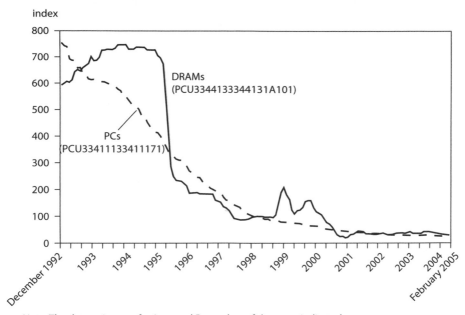

Note: The data points are for June and December of the years indicated.

Source: Bureau of Labor Statistics, producer price index, www.bls.gov/ppi/home.htm.

tailed research on the relationship between the prices of PCs and semiconductors finds that about 40 to 60 percent of the decline in PC prices is due to the decline in price of semiconductors (and about 30 percent of the semiconductors that go into a PC are DRAMs) (Aizcorbe, Flamm, and Khurshid 2002).

What generates the decline in the price of semiconductors (particularly DRAMs), and what additional factors affect PC prices? In particular, what might be the role for the globalization of the IT hardware industry in these price declines?

Technology is the key starting point. Technological change in the production of semiconductors reduces the price, in part by increasing the number of chips on a given-sized wafer, the size of the wafer, and the yield in production (Aizcorbe, Flamm, and Khurshid 2002).

Investment in semiconductor facilities abroad (by US firms and foreign firms, as discussed in appendix 2A in chapter 2) may play a role in technological change in semiconductor production, as these facilities compete with each other to generate the newest advancement in technologies of production and product. For example, innovation in chip speed is critically important as a driver of semiconductor prices (Aizcorbe 2002). As faster chips are introduced, the prices of older chips fall dramatically, which reduces vintage-weighted average prices of semiconductors (such

Figure 3.2   Global capacity and utilization and US prices of dynamic random access memory chips (DRAMs), 1994–2002

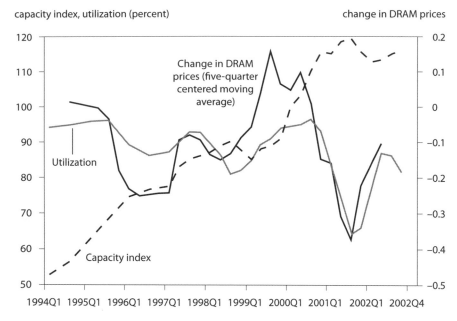

capacity index, utilization (percent)   change in DRAM prices

Sources: Semiconductor Industry Association; Bureau of Economic Analysis, producer price index, www.bea.gov/ppi/home.htm.

as the price index in figure 3.1). Research and development (R&D) is a key factor in innovations involving speed (see chapter 6).

But R&D is not the only factor behind the price declines. Competition also plays a key role. Ana Aizcorbe (2002) focuses on competition in the United States between Intel and AMD (both US companies), but to an increasing degree competition is global both in terms of ownership of the means of production and of geographic location.

Moreover, change in the price-cost margin apparently is an important determinant of semiconductor prices. Research suggests that squeezing margins between production cost and price can account for an average of about 15 percent of the decline in prices; the year-to-year range is huge—from no margin squeeze in some periods (such as the second quarter of 1995 or the third quarter of 2003), to significant margin squeezes of 20 or 30 percent in others (such as the third quarters of 1998 and 2001) (Aizcorbe 2002). Margins can narrow because of the business cycle (demand booms or falls off) or because new production facilities come on line (and supply increases). Increasingly, demand booms and supply increases have global origins—it is not just US demand or supply that matters. Data in figure 3.2 on the global integration of production, opening up of new global markets, and emerging global competitors (all evidenced in the data discussed in chapter 2) show a clear relationship between world-wide capacity and utilization and US DRAM prices.

Regression analysis of the evolution of US DRAM prices as explained by global capacity and global capacity utilization confirms that when a gap opens between capacity and production (that is, capacity utilization falls), the decline in DRAM prices accelerates.[1] Average capacity utilization from 1995 to 2002 was 90 percent, with an average deviation of 2.5 percentage points. Based on the regression analysis, a 2.5 percentage point rise in global capacity utilization (from, say, 85 to 87.5 percent) is associated with a slowing of the pace of decline in DRAM prices from 10 to 2.5 percent (quarterly rate) as producers are able to sell their product into the tighter global demand conditions at a relatively better price. Whereas the bulk of the overall trend decline in DRAM prices is almost surely on account of innovation and technological improvements in chips, the cycling between a greater and lesser pace of price decline is in no small degree due to globalization of chip supply and demand.

As noted, previous research found that the behavior of semiconductor prices explains about half of the decline in personal computer prices. This research finds that global DRAM capacity and capacity utilization play an important role in semiconductor price declines. Are there other global factors that also affect prices of PCs? Figure 3.3 shows the relationship between the net imports of computers, peripherals, and parts (not including semiconductors), which is persistently negative over the time period shown, and the change in prices of the average personal computer and laptop.

Regression analysis of these data indicates that an increase in net imports of computers, peripherals, and parts is associated with accelerating PC (and laptop) price declines. When net imports of personal computers level out (as they did, for example, in the late 1990s), PC prices stop falling so fast.[2] Net imports of PCs averaged $200 million per quarter from 1993 to 2002, with a variation of about $50 million around that average. The regression suggests that if net imports of this category decreased by $50 million (that is, the deficit in PCs and laptops narrowed), then the decline in PC prices would slow by about 10 percent during the quarter due to the decreased net supply of PCs in the US market.

IT Software and Services Prices

If global integration and competition drive reductions in prices of IT hardware, what is happening to prices of IT software and services? For prepackaged software, the price deflators from the national accounts data on software investment reveal an 11 percent smooth decline annually in the

---

1. See Mann (2005) for further regression diagnostics and additional discussion.

2. See Mann (2005) for further regression diagnostics.

Figure 3.3 Personal computer prices and trade, 1993–2002

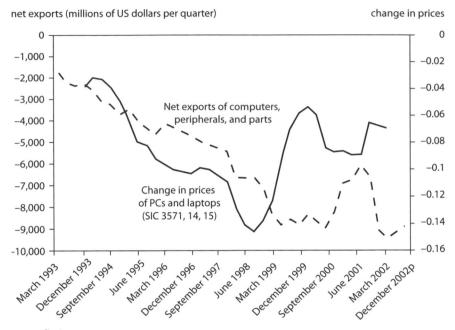

net exports (millions of US dollars per quarter)   change in prices

Net exports of computers,
peripherals, and parts

Change in prices
of PCs and laptops
(SIC 3571, 14, 15)

p = preliminary
SIC = Standard Industrial Classification

Sources: Bureau of Labor Statistics, producer price index, www.bls.gov/ppi/home.htm (accessed September 30, 2005). Bureau of Economic Analysis, international trade statistics, SIC basis, www. bea.gov.

deflator (1990 to 2004; this deflator is adjusted using hedonic methods). On the other hand, for business own-account and custom software, where labor costs play a key role in the construction of the deflator, the index is virtually unchanged from 1990 to 1998, then increases at about 3 to 5 percent per year until 2001, when that rise is abruptly halted and own-account and custom costs once again show no change until 2004.[3]

An alternative source of price indices for software is the Bureau of Labor Statistics (BLS) data based on the North American Industry Classification System (NAICS). The BLS data are designed to measure prices of types of software and services products rather than calculate deflators for types of software investment (figure 3.4). These data reveal that price declines

---

3. See BEA (2000) and BEA table on Software, Investment, and Prices, available at www.bea. gov/bea/dn/soft-invest.xls. See also Grimm, Moulton, and Wasshausen (2002). The price index for prepackaged software is quality-adjusted based on several familiar word processing and spreadsheet programs. Own-account software prices are based on the costs of programmers. Custom programming is an expenditure-weighted average of the two other types. See additional discussion in the next section.

Figure 3.4 Price indices for IT services and software, December 1997–March 2005

index

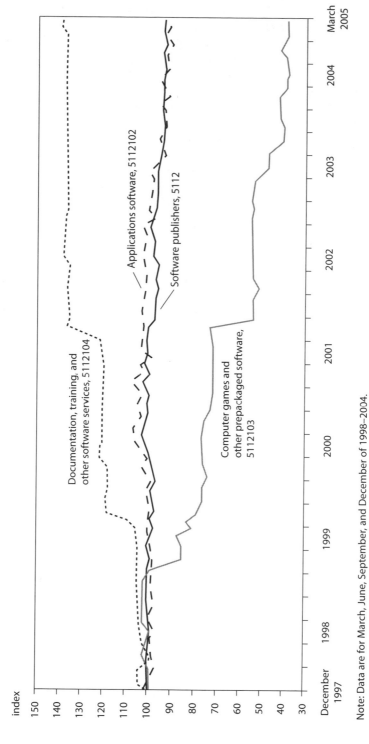

Note: Data are for March, June, September, and December of 1998–2004.

Source: Bureau of Labor Statistics, producer price index, www.bls.gov/ppi/home.htm.

for both "software publishing" (e.g., Microsoft Windows) and "application software" (e.g., customized Oracle database software) have been minimal, much less than for IT hardware. But in the more competitive and global-ized market for computer games and prepackaged software, price declines are significant, although still less than for IT hardware.

Software companies in foreign countries, an increased role for offshore programming in US companies, and competition among the global soft-ware companies may all contribute to the drop in computer game and prepackaged software prices. Data on venture capital funding of software startups reveals a relatively higher share of such funding abroad for these types of software applications. In addition, international trade data show an increase in intrafirm imports of data and information services, which include software among information services (discussed in detail later). The price series and trade data are insufficiently matched to undertake an econometric assessment of the relationship between globalization and IT prices similar to that undertaken for the two types of hardware. But the lower prices of certain kinds of software suggest that the paradigm of globalization of IT hardware and lower IT hardware prices, as detailed above, may be starting to emerge for some types of software as well, par-ticularly software that is less "tailored" or customized for specific clients.

On the other hand, for what are called "documentation and training and other software services," which surely incorporate tailored specifica-tions for the specific needs of sectors and countries, prices continue to rise at about the rate of overall services price inflation. Recall that the IT ser-vices markets are more geographically segmented (perhaps by language, culture, business milieu, and level of sectoral development), with pro-duction and sale of the service mostly in the same market. Data already presented show that wage costs of software and IT services workers at US affiliates abroad tend to be similar to the wages at the US-located parent firm. Finally, segmented markets, ceteris paribus, have lower competition, leading to different prices for different markets.

Overall, some of the factors that have helped to make IT hardware into commodities that can be produced more cheaply abroad appear to be tak-ing hold in some aspects of software and services, but have not extended to the full range of software products or IT services. Even in the longer term, the effect of globalization to reduce prices of all parts of the pro-duction process of services and software may be muted.

The consequence of relatively stable software prices, rising IT services prices, and rapidly declining IT hardware prices is that the share of the overall price of an IT package (which includes IT hardware, services, and software) has become increasingly weighted toward IT services and soft-ware (box 3.1). Reexamining the data on IT expenditure reveals that in 1993, for each $1 spent on IT hardware, firms globally spent $1.25 on IT services and software, whereas in 2003, for each $1 spent on IT hardware, firms spent $1.94 on IT services and software (WITSA 2002, 2004; see also

Box 3.1 Purchasing a computer: Mostly software

Since software and hardware are usually sold as a package, it is difficult for a small business shopping for a computer to figure out which products to buy and what their prices are. However, prices of computers in Dell's catalogue and of software at the retailer Best Buy (visited in July 2005 and April 2006) indicate the high and rising relative importance of embedded software in the computer package.

Suppose two small businesses priced computers in July 2005 and April 2006, respectively. How do the prices and functionality of the computer package change, and how important is the software part of the package in the overall price?

In July 2005, a Dell Dimension 9100 Desk Top at Dell.com cost $1,417 with free shipping. It included a range of hardware and preselected software:

- *Hardware (nonexhaustive list):* Intel® Pentium® 4 processor at 3GHz, 1GB dual channel DDR2 SDRAM at 533MHz, 40GB serial ATA hard drive (7200RPM), 32x CD-RW/DVD-ROM combo drive, and a standard 17-inch CFT monitor.

- *Preselected software:* Windows XP Professional and Microsoft Office Professional.

Given the retail value of the software at Bestbuy.com—Windows XP Professional cost $299 and Microsoft Office Professional cost $499—the above price suggests that more than half of the value of the computer package was embedded software.

Suppose the small business wanted a cheaper package and selected different software options. If it selected Windows XP Home Edition and WordPerfect Office 12 for its Dell machine, rather than the preselected software, the overall price fell to $968, and the share of the package represented by embedded software fell to 30 percent.

Now suppose a similar small business priced computers in April 2006. At Dell.com, a Dell Dimension E310-P4 Desk Top cost $1,093 with free shipping. It included a range of hardware and preselected software:

- *Hardware (nonexhaustive list)*: Intel® Pentium® 4 processor at 3.0GHz, 1GB dual channel DDR2 SDRAM at 533MHz, 80GB serial ATA hard drive (7200RPM),[1] 48x CD-RW/DVD-ROM combo drive,[2] and a standard 17-inch CFT monitor.

- *Preselected software:* Windows XP Professional and Microsoft Office Professional.

Given the retail value of the software at Bestbuy.com—Windows XP Professional cost $299 and Microsoft Office Professional cost $499—the above price

(box continues next page)

Box 3.1   Purchasing a computer: Mostly software   *(continued)*

suggests that almost three-quarters of the value of the computer package was embedded software.

Again, suppose the small business wanted a cheaper package. If it selected Windows XP Home Edition and WordPerfect Office 12 for its Dell machine, the share of the package represented by embedded software fell to about 40 percent.

No doubt software costs of Dell are much lower than those of a software retailer, but embedded software costs are a large and increasing share of the total costs incurred by businesses and consumers when buying a computer.

Over the nine-month period of this example, the overall package price fell by more than did the value of the embedded software. Even over this short period, the relative share of software costs in the computer package rose even when cheaper software was selected for the machine, mostly on account of the falling cost of the hardware component.

Unlike hardware, where globalized production and competition are fierce, software is an area of IT where these forces are just beginning to be felt. Going forward these factors likely will push down further the price of the total IT package, thus putting these productivity-enhancing IT packages within reach of a wider range of businesses throughout the US economy.

---

1. Note that the 80GB hard drive available in April 2006 has twice the capacity of the hard drive available in July 2005.

2. Note that the 48x CD-RW/DVD-ROM combo drive available in April 2006 is 50 percent faster than that available in July 2005.

figure 2.1 in chapter 2). This skew was even greater for US buyers, who spent almost $3 on IT services and software for every $1 on IT hardware in 2003. Faster globalization has reduced the relative importance of IT hardware and increased the relative importance of IT services and software in the expenditure package. It should come as no surprise that users want lower prices for IT services and software, and that US IT firms are trying to meet that demand by fragmenting the production process and moving some activities to lower-cost locations abroad in order to reduce the price of providing the tailored software and services.

Macroeconomic Overview of IT Investment in the US Economy

How have the IT price declines—due to both technological innovation and globalization—been reflected in investment patterns in the United

States? Prices are not the only factor that drives investment demand—so does GDP growth. It is difficult to parse out the relative roles for prices and GDP.

IT Waves in US National Income and Product Accounts Data

IT hardware and communications have been considered investment all along. But software was reclassified from spending to investment as part of the benchmark revision of the national income and product accounts in 1999. Waves of investment spending on IT and communications can be seen in the National Income and Product Accounts (NIPA) data that correspond to the changing emphasis on hardware and software/services already noted in the international marketplace, in the corporate data, and in the data on US multinationals (figure 3.5).[4]

Patterns of importance of IT and communications in the United States can be seen by disaggregating the sector into its main components of communications, IT hardware, and software, and then considering both nominal investment patterns and contribution to real investment growth. Nominal investment in computers and peripherals increased in the 1980s both in absolute terms and as a share of domestic nonresidential investment. Communications equipment is becoming less important in investment. Following the recession pause of 1991–92, investment in equipment and software resumed, but with software investment increasingly being the driving force for growth. In terms of real investment, the contribution of the two components of information equipment and software to real private investment follows a similar pattern, with a hardware wave in the 1980s and then a second wave of both hardware and software in the 1990s, and with the contribution of software investment to real investment becoming more important as the 1990s progressed. Finally, taking these investment patterns and cumulating them to reflect asset stocks yields the same observations, with the software share of total private assets exceeding the hardware share from the late 1990s onward. All told, the NIPA data tell the same story for the United States as do the data based on global expenditure and on multinational production and sales.

Focus on Software

The increasing importance of software investment, combined with the nascent globalization of production and international trade in software,

---

4. Revisions of the historical NIPA data were based on detailed analysis of expenditure and involved construction of new price indices. The consequence of the reclassification to investment affected GDP growth and emphasized the important role for IT investment in the US economy.

Figure 3.5 IT and communications investment, 1970–2005

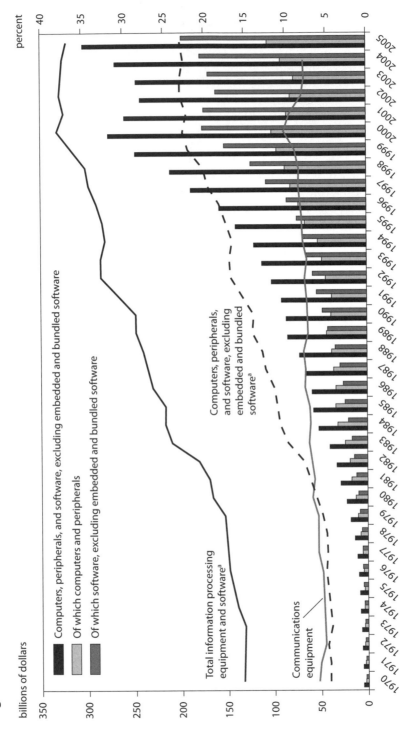

billions of dollars

percent

Computers, peripherals, and software, excluding embedded and bundled software

Of which computers and peripherals

Of which software, excluding embedded and bundled software

Computers, peripherals, and software, excluding embedded and bundled software[a]

Total information processing equipment and software[a]

Communications equipment

a. Share of total nonresidential investment.

Source: Bureau of Economic Analysis, National Income and Product Accounts (NIPA), tables 5.3.5 and 5.5.5, www.bea.gov/bea/dn/nipaweb (accessed April 3, 2006).

make it worthwhile to look more closely at this category of investment. Software investment is classified in three categories: prepackaged, custom, and own-account software. "Prepackaged" software does not imply that it comes in a box—Internet downloadable software, for example, is considered part of this classification—but rather that this software has general applicability without requiring modification. Custom software is tailored to the specifications of a business by third-party consulting firms or individuals. The customization process and expenditures counted as investment in the data may include analysis, design, and new programming, and may also include software that has been customized from pre-existing or standardized modules. Finally, investment in own-account software consists of expenditures including wages, salaries, and related compensation (including indirect costs such as depreciation on the computer equipment) for an enterprise's employees whose job it is to analyze, design, and produce new or significantly enhanced software for the enterprise's own use. Thus, outsourcing of own-account software to third-party consultancies would change the classification of software investment from "own-account" to "custom" software. Offshore outsourcing of this activity would imply a reduction in own-account software investment and a rise in imports in the trade classification of unaffiliated "computer and information services."[5]

Between 1997 and 2003, nominal investment in the three categories of software rose from $128 billion to $191 billion, with the bulk of this investment (about 80 percent) undertaken by business (the remainder is investment by government and by individuals for personal consumption). Investment in own-account software doubled ($42 billion to $80 billion), while investment in prepackaged software rose less quickly (from $40 billion to $55 billion). The middle category—third-party customized software—rose dramatically through 2001 (from $47 billion to $72 billion) and then dropped off in 2003 to $57 billion. Is the drop in customized software related to the technology boom generally, to Y2K specifically, or to offshoring of software services?[6] "Software repair" to avoid Y2K glitches in existing software is explicitly excluded from the software investment data. But new spending for an upgrade or new software would be included as investment, so the Y2K phenomenon would accentuate the technology

---

5. If the new software activity remained "own-account" software but the programmers were located in India, then this offshored but not outsourced activity would appear as an import of affiliated computer and information services, to the extent that such transactions are captured in the data surveys.

6. Y2K is the colloquial term used to address the software issue whereby old software was designed to recognize only the last two digits of the year-date (such as 75 for 1975). There was a real concern that many computer systems that depended on such two-digit dates would fail when the calendar changed from 1999 to 2000. Hence there was substantial upgrading of computer systems to correct this internal glitch. Other businesses saw this as the opportunity to buy new computers and software products.

cycle in the data. Whether the dropoff in the data also suggests offshoring of this customizing activity will be addressed in the sections that follow.

There is a fourth category of software—so-called embedded or bundled software—that is not included in the software investment category, but rather is included in the investment category for computers and peripherals. This software comes preinstalled with the hardware (such as when a personal computer comes with preinstalled Microsoft Windows or even when the software is embedded into the semiconductor chip). The line between hardware, embedded software, and prepackaged software is becoming blurred, further challenging our analysis of the effects of globalization and technological change.

Diffusion of IT Throughout the Economy

Another approach to examining IT trends in the US economy is through input-output tables such as those presented in tables 3.1a and 3.1b. First consider the share of IT hardware and services in total intermediates used in the economy for 1998 and 2004. The share of IT hardware in total intermediates fell from 3.4 to 2.4 percent over that period, but the share of IT services in total intermediates rose from 1.5 to 2 percent. The drop in hardware is consistent with the lower prices, and the two trends together are consistent with the movement away from hardware as well as the growing importance of services in terms of making IT useful to firms as they do business.

Looking at the two-digit sectoral breakdown reveals some changes in the rankings of sectors in their intensity of IT use as an intermediate. For IT hardware, the stability in the rankings is almost complete, in that none of the sectors move more than one place in the rankings. On the other hand, for IT services intensity, there are more changes in rankings. Most notable is the fall in the relative intensity of "health care and social assistance," even though in terms of absolute use of IT services as an intermediate this sector actually increased its use. Other relative decliners include transportation, warehousing and storage, and utilities, all of which actually saw declines in their absolute share of IT services intensity in intermediates used.

These diffusions in terms of IT hardware and services use as an intermediate to production provide important insights into why some sectors lead and some lag in US productivity growth, a topic to which we now turn.

IT Diffusion and US Productivity Growth

US macroeconomic performance in the 1990s was extraordinary (and following the 2001 recession, equally robust). In terms of the standard mea-

Table 3.1a   IT hardware intensity, 1998 and 2004 (percent share
of total intermediate goods used)

NAICS category	Sector	1998 Rank	1998 Intensity	2004 Rank	2004 Intensity	Change in rank, 1998–2004
31–33	Manufacturing	1	6.634	1	4.744	→
51	Information	2	5.227	2	4.411	→
42	Wholesale trade	3	3.978	3	3.201	→
81	Other services, except government	6	2.926	4	2.999	↑
T001	**Total intermediate use**	5	3.396	5	2.440	→
54	Professional scientific and technical services	4	3.605	6	2.160	↓
56	Administrative support and waste management and remediation services	7	1.743	7	1.590	→
62	Health care and social assistance	9	1.093	8	0.973	↑
44	Retail trade	8	1.097	9	0.890	↓
61	Educational services	11	0.964	10	0.863	↑
23	Construction	10	0.986	11	0.852	↓
55	Management of companies and enterprises	12	0.728	12	0.527	→
48	Transportation	14	0.371	13	0.350	↑
52	Finance and insurance	13	0.461	14	0.324	↓
53	Real estate and rental and leasing	15	0.328	15	0.263	→
21	Mining	18	0.151	16	0.193	↑
71	Arts, entertainment, and recreation	16	0.210	17	0.139	↓
22	Utilities	17	0.198	18	0.106	↓
72	Accommodation and food services	20	0.085	19	0.064	↑
49	Warehousing and storage	19	0.097	20	0.055	↓

sures, productivity growth accelerated to rates not seen since the 1960s; GDP growth was sustained at more than 4 percent; inflation was the lowest in a generation; and the unemployment rate fell below where it had been for decades. Research on the underpinnings of this positive economic performance focused on the rising importance of IT, initially in terms of IT production in the US economy and then in terms of investment in and use of IT throughout non-IT sectors of the economy. Now, researchers are examining the role for global engagement and productivity growth through the channels of reductions in the cost of IT, more fragmented production facilitated by globally networked communications, and global competition that enhances forces that promote more effective use of IT by business and in the workplace.

Table 3.1b   IT services intensity, 1998 and 2004 (percent share of total intermediate goods used)

NAICS category	Sector	1998		2004		Change in rank, 1998–2004
		Rank	Intensity	Rank	Intensity	
55	Management of companies and enterprises	1	7.46	1	7.5	→
54	Professional scientific and technical services	2	3.42	2	3.6	→
56	Administrative support and waste management and remediation services	4	2.75	3	3.0	↑
51	Information	5	2.35	4	2.7	↑
48	Transportation	3	2.94	5	2.2	↓
42	Wholesale trade	6	2.21	6	2.2	→
44	Retail trade	7	1.82	7	2.1	→
T001	**Total intermediate use**	8	1.54	8	2.0	→
52	Finance and insurance	9	1.49	9	1.9	→
61	Educational services	11	1.32	10	1.6	↑
21	Mining	15	0.94	11	1.5	↑
81	Other services, except government	12	1.28	12	1.5	→
62	Health care and social assistance	10	1.44	13	1.5	↓
71	Arts, entertainment, and recreation	14	1.13	14	1.3	→
49	Warehousing and storage	13	1.19	15	1.2	↓
72	Accommodation and food services	16	0.78	16	1.0	→
31–33	Manufacturing	19	0.72	17	0.9	↑
53	Real estate and rental and leasing	17	0.77	18	0.8	↓
23	Construction	20	0.39	19	0.4	↑
22	Utilities	18	0.73	20	0.3	↓

Source: Bureau of Economic Analysis, Input/Output Tables, www.bea.gov.

Role of IT in Transforming US Workplaces and Businesses

The most important ingredient to the positive economic outcomes of the 1990s was the sustained increase in productivity growth. Research on US data as well as detailed analysis of data from other economies concludes that investment in and increased use of IT yielded faster GDP growth and higher productivity growth. For the United States, one-quarter to one-

7. See Dedrick, Gurbaxani, and Kraemer (2002, table 2); Oliner and Sichel (2000, 2002); Jorgenson, Ho, and Stiroh (2002).

third of the increase in real GDP growth from 3 to 4 percent (1973–94 versus 1995–2000) came from investing in and using IT.[7] Industry sectors that used IT intensively grew 75 percent faster than other sectors throughout the 1990s (ESA 2002, figure 4.1). Intensive use of IT accounted for 60 to 70 percent of the doubling of labor productivity growth after 1995.[8]

Researchers have investigated four linkages between IT and productivity growth: (1) IT capital deepening and increasing efficiency within the business enterprise; (2) the role of network effects and transactional spillovers between enterprises that both use IT, which raises the productivity of both enterprises; (3) the positive association between increased productivity and changing workplace practices within the firm; and (4) international engagement in IT and productivity growth.

The overwhelming finding is that production and investment in IT capital are not the most important source of economic gain. It is the effective use of IT, a step beyond IT investment, and the transformation of business activities and of the relationships between businesses with networked IT, that most augment productivity growth. To emphasize this key point, it is instructive to put forth a brief historical review of the research on IT, communications networks, and productivity growth.

The earliest research on the relationship between IT and faster US GDP and productivity growth focused only on investment and the use of IT by businesses in the IT-producing sector. This early work suggested that it was extraordinarily high productivity in the IT-producing sector that accelerated US productivity growth. However, as time went on and expansion of the IT-producing sector waned, research turned to the relationship between IT investment and productivity growth throughout an economy rather than the IT sector alone. Using detailed data for the United States and Europe, as well as more aggregated data for a broader set of economies, this research made it clear that investment in and effective use of IT by businesses throughout the economy are what increased productivity and GDP growth.[9] These observations came from comparing productivity and growth for industry sectors (both goods and services) that were more versus less intensive in investment in various kinds of IT capital. IT producers are IT-intensive in terms of purchasing and using IT, but they are neither the whole story nor even the major part of it when it comes to macroeconomic performance.

Making the distinction between fast growth and high productivity in IT-producing firms versus IT-using firms is important for the source and sustainability of robust GDP and productivity growth. First, of course, broad-

---

8. Sixty percent is from van Ark, Inklaar, and McGuckin (2003, appendix table C) and 70 percent from ESA (2002, 36).

9. See van Ark, Inklaar, and McGuckin (2003); Stiroh (2001, 2002); Baily and Kirkegaard (2004); OECD (2003); Wilson (2004); Mun and Nadiri (2002); Atrostic and Nguyen (2005).

based high productivity growth is the foundation for faster GDP growth without generating inflation. If productivity growth is confined to IT producers, then sustaining rising productivity growth overall will require an increasingly large share of IT production in an economy. Moreover, if high productivity comes mostly from producing IT, then an economy without an IT production sector would appear to be doomed to low productivity and slow GDP growth. If, instead, what matters is using IT, then a country can get productivity benefits by importing and using IT products.[10]

One way to measure changes beyond labor productivity that signal the effective use of IT and the transformation of business activities and relationships is with total factor productivity (TFP) growth. TFP measures the additional output obtained by a reorientation of the means of production using the same inputs—in other words, the transformation of business activities, which would include new products, processes, business and customer relationships, and workplace practices. Much of the second wave of research on the role of IT in the economy has focused on how IT changes the internal activities of the firm and the relationships between firms.

This complementarity between IT investment and workers is the second strand for the research on how effective use of IT affects productivity growth. Researchers have focused on the relationship between labor productivity and changing workplace practices in the presence of IT capital.[11] Innovation in four areas where employees interact with the business activities of the firm are considered: (1) the employees' voice, where nonmanagerial staff contribute directly to innovations in business process; (2) work design, where managerial staff can reallocate labor and capital resources to respond more effectively to changing business demands; (3) workforce training, which complements the increased flexibility of labor in the business process; and (4) incentive-based compensation systems, which give nonmanagerial staff an incentive to maximize the financial potential of the business.

Controlling for IT investment (which takes account of the capital deepening component of labor productivity growth), researchers find, both within specific industries and across industries, that application of innovative workplace practices raises productivity further. Perhaps even more important for the understanding of the relationship between IT capital and productivity growth in an enterprise, the researchers find that diffusing computers to the nonmanagerial workers increases productivity, whereas IT capital investment has no effect on overall productivity when computers are diffused only to the managers.

---

10. See Bayoumi and Haacker (2002) regarding this point in the context of developing countries.

11. Black and Lynch (2001, 2003, 2004, and forthcoming); Boning, Ichniowski, and Shaw (2001); Bresnahan, Brynjolffsson, and Hitt (2002); and Ichniowski, Shaw, and Prennushi (1997).

IT and Inflation

Thus far, the gain from lower prices of IT products has been couched in terms of accelerated productivity growth. However, another macroeconomic benefit of lower IT prices is lower inflation.

First, falling prices for computer items reduces measured inflation simply because the falling prices for IT capital are included in the basket of purchases. In parallel to the research on productivity growth, which focused on the IT-producing sector, the price-dampening effect of IT initially was thought to derive mostly from this rapid decline in the quality-adjusted price for computer equipment as it showed up in the producer price index for the US economy. On this basis, some analysts (particularly in Europe) thought that their measured inflation was higher (and therefore their output and productivity growth were lower) simply because they did not quality-adjust their IT producer prices. An examination of this question, however, revealed that quality adjustment had little to do with the inflation (or by extension productivity or growth) dynamics in Europe compared with the United States.[12]

Further analysis finds that, just as for productivity growth, it is the dynamics of the response of prices and costs outside the IT-producing sector that matter most for the overall inflation dynamic. The reduction of inflation on account of IT is more significant for those sectors that have integrated IT into their businesses.[13] The detailed analysis presented here based on US data reveals the systematically lower price inflation of sectors that are IT-intensive. Effective use of IT appears to lower output price inflation. IT intensity could lower price inflation because, within a sector, the more competitive firms integrate IT into their business operations, reduce their prices, and drive less IT-intensive competitors out of business (McKinsey Global Institute 2001, Baily and Kirkegaard 2004). Across sectors, firms with high IT intensity can lower their costs more and reduce prices, which feeds into lower overall price inflation. Translated to the macro level, core inflation might have been 1 percentage point per year higher during the 1990s (3 percent versus 2 percent) had there not been increased use of IT (ESA 2002, 39).

---

12. Triplett (2004); Ahmad et al. (2003); Schreyer (2001); Deutsche Bundesbank (2001); Gust and Marquez (2000); and Landefeld and Grimm (2000). The two main reasons for the limited impact of disparate utilization of hedonic deflators for IT goods across countries is that many of these products are used as intermediate goods, as well as imported from abroad so the "failure" to quality adjust "nets" out.

13. See intermediate costs analysis in Mun and Nadiri (2002).

Globalization, Technology, and Labor Productivity

The forces of global competition and engagement work in conjunction with other factors to affect productivity, including IT intensity, research and development spending, resource reallocation, and trade patterns. There is a long and rich history of research on this broad topic, sometimes specifically addressing IT, sometimes not. Much of the most recent work focuses on the interactions among the various factors, particularly the way global integration and international competition work to strengthen the effect of the other factors.[14] It is worthwhile to briefly summarize key research that links globalization, technology, and productivity growth.

Although the direction of causality is not well specified, the robust research finding is that firms that produce for export markets and face import competition are more productive.[15] What is the additional relevance of technology to the trade-productivity link? The link between productivity and trade is found to be particularly strong both for technologically sophisticated products as well as for firms that use IT (Baygan and Mann 1999; Haskel, Pereira, and Slaughter 2002; Lewis and Richardson 2001). That is, trade in technologically sophisticated products is associated with higher productivity, as compared with overall trade or trade in lower-technology products. But it is also the case that the industries that have invested heavily in IT have a greater propensity to export. This suggests that IT both demands and enhances international competitiveness.

For the United States, there are several transmission channels for these effects. First, research shows that the least productive firms go bankrupt, low productivity firms (likely those least intensive in the use of IT) serve only the domestic market, and the most productive firms export and serve the domestic market (Helpman, Melitz, and Yeaple 2003). Second, multinationals are more robust than domestic-only companies and are more technology-intensive. US-headed multinationals use 31 percent more advanced manufacturing technologies in US plants, yielding 11 percent more labor productivity and a 7 to 15 percent wage premium to blue- and white-collar workers, respectively. Foreign-headed multinational firms in the United States use 27 percent more advanced manufacturing technologies, and have 13 to 19 percent higher wages compared to domestic-only plants (Lewis and Richardson 2001). Thus, global engagement goes hand-in-hand with the use of advanced manufacturing technologies, with benefits accruing to both workers and firms—or at least to those that successfully adjust (an issue we will turn to again in subsequent chapters).

---

14. There are too many works to cite. A short review is found in Navaretti and Tarr (2000). OECD (2003) offers a much longer assessment, along with some original work.

15. See Baily and Gersback (1995); Jensen and Musick (1996); Bernard and Jensen (1997); and Mann (1998). See also the more recent set of papers using plant-level micro data by Bernard, Jensen, and Schott (2002, 2003, and 2005).

Third, import competition can lead to changes in the goods produced and more capital-intensive production technology, both of which promote greater productivity. Competition from imports from low-wage countries, such as China, pushes output and employment toward capital-intensive plants (including those intensive in IT capital), and changes the product mix toward capital- and skill-intensive production methods, both of which tend to increase productivity (Bernard, Jensen, and Schott 2003).

In sum, to an increasing extent the detailed research finds important channels linking global engagement, IT, plant-level productivity, and worker skill intensity. Box 3.2 shows the price reductions and product enhancements that can be facilitated by globalized production for a specific individual product, in this case cell phones.

Evidence and Implications of Uneven Sectoral Diffusion of IT Investment

Whereas the macroeconomic gains from intensive use of IT are clear, large segments of the US economy have not yet integrated IT fully into their business operations. Figure 3.6 shows the relationship between IT intensity and contributions to aggregate productivity growth in the United States by sector, along with the size of the sectors in terms of GDP.[16] The upward slope of the regression line mirrors the relationship as derived from the macroeconomic time series data, as discussed earlier. Considering the economic behavior of different sectors of the economy gives insights as to the source of overall macroeconomic performance, but also presents puzzles about why certain sectors have lagged in their investment and use of IT. Understanding better why some sectors have led in the investment and use of IT while other sectors have lagged may point to the future role for deeper globalization of IT, particularly IT software and services, with implications going forward for the US economy.

A first observation is that many of the larger sectors (in terms of GDP) leading the way in terms of contributions to productivity growth and IT-intensity are services activities, including wholesale trade, securities and commodity brokers, depository institutions, and communications. Retailing is the only notable example of a large services sector that did not use IT particularly intensively across the board but experienced above-average productivity growth.[17] Among manufacturing sectors, electronics

---

16. Analysis by the Economics and Statistics Administration (2002) for the *Digital Economy 2002* report for the US Department of Commerce developed sector-level measures of IT investment, productivity contributions to US growth, inflation, and other important indicators.

17. Although the sector as a whole does not appear to use IT particularly intensively, research shows that much of the productivity gain in retailing comes from more productive establishments replacing less productive ones, and that an important factor underpinning the more productive establishments was IT. See Foster, Haltiwanger, and Krizan (2002).

Box 3.2   Cheaper cell phones for the world through global production

Cell phones today have become the top-selling consumer electronics good in the entire developed world. Of course, the cell phone is actually a bundle of phone and telecommunications carrier (and perhaps other functions as well). Since cell phone prices for wealthy consumers remain heavily subsidized by telecommunications carriers, the average wholesale value of a cell phone was not insubstantial $174 in 2004. And the price is expected to decline only by about 1.5 percent annually until 2009 as phones become packed with more and more new features such as digital cameras, FM/AM radios, and Internet capabilities.[1]

The persistently high wholesale price of cell phones has remained a significant obstacle to large-scale adoption of mobile telephony in developing countries, despite rapidly improving wireless infrastructure and more competitive telecommunications charges. In 2005, while 80 percent of the world's population lived in areas with wireless coverage, only about 25 percent used mobile telephony services.[2]

The spread of wireless services in developing countries represents a huge business opportunity for wireless services providers that face increasingly mature and saturated markets in industrial economies. And a widening body of economic research indicates that rising mobile phone penetration is highly beneficial for economic growth. Leonard Waverman, Meloria Meschi, and Melvyn Fuss (2005) find that a developing country with an average of 10 more mobile phones per 100 inhabitants between 1996 and 2003 would have enjoyed per capita GDP growth that was 0.59 percent higher than an otherwise identical country.

As a result, the GSM Association, Motorola, and a large number of wireless services providers in developing countries launched the "Emerging Market Handset Initiative" in early 2005.[3] The goal was to produce a "no-frills cell phone" by the second quarter of 2005 at a price point below $40 (exfactory) to allow wireless services providers in developing countries to offer consumers phones within their purchasing capacity on a commercially viable basis (i.e., without the mas-

(box continues next page)

is a leader in terms of IT investment and above average contribution to productivity growth (which was why this sector was the focus for the first stage of research on IT and productivity growth), but it is a relatively small sector (in terms of GDP). There are other high-productivity manufacturing sectors, but summed up, "above-average manufacturing" accounts for only about 10 percent of GDP. Instead, the leading services activities account for 31 percent of GDP. In sum, the rapid acceleration of US productivity growth comes more from productivity-enhancing IT use in the services arena rather than from manufacturing.[18]

---

18. Research already cited from Mun and Nadiri (2002) confirms this finding. In addition, researchers from Europe (including van Ark, Inklaar, and McGuckin 2003) have noted that

sive handset subsidies offered to developed-world consumers).[4] In June 2005, Philips Electronics announced a supplementary initiative aimed at a $20 handset (exfactory) with the goal of reaching $15 by 2008.[5]

The operational opportunities for both Motorola and Philips for offering mobile phones within the much lower price range of developing-country consumers comes from both companies' extensive use of low-cost production facilities in developing Asia, in particular. Motorola, for instance, produces all its handsets at facilities located in China, Singapore, Brazil, Malaysia, and South Korea, and relies on electronics manufacturing suppliers (EMS) in Asia for approximately a third of the company's handset production.[6] For its part, Philips Electronics specifically located its low-cost cell phone initiative at its production facility in Shanghai.

The mobile telephony sector illustrates the powerful trend, noted elsewhere in this book, of how technology companies today utilize global low-cost supply not only to offer products at declining prices to consumers in the developed world, but also to offer technology products at affordable prices to consumers in developing countries, thus facilitating the closing of the digital divide.

---

1. Gartner, "Forecast: Mobile Terminals, Worldwide, 2000–2009," July 18, 2005, available at www.gartner.com.
2. GSM Association press release, "GSM Association Announces New Phase for Emerging Markets Initiative," July 4, 2005.
3. Developing countries are defined here as those with GNP below the average of the World Bank's GNP/Capita Index and with a mobile penetration of less than 60 percent.
4. Motorola press release, "Motorola Chosen by GSM Association to Connect the Unconnected," February 14, 2005.
5. Philips Electronics press release, "Philips Launches Global Initiative to Develop Solutions for Ultra Low-cost Mobile Phones," June 29, 2005.
6. Motorola 10-K filing, 2005, available at the SEC EDGAR database at www.sec.gov/edgar (accessed on September 30, 2005).

Three sectors stand out for being large in GDP terms, low in IT intensity, and below average in terms of productivity. All are in services: health, construction, and the highly heterogeneous group of "other services," which among other activities includes engineering, accounting, research, and management services.

Exactly why some sectors have led in the use of IT and others have lagged remains a fertile area for research. There are several nonexclusive hypotheses, including those related to the information content of the activities of the sector; the degree to which firms in the sector were already

---

the disparity in productivity performance between Europe and the United States is due more to productivity performance in services than in manufacturing.

Figure 3.6 IT intensity and contribution to GDP per FTE growth, 1989–2000

annual average contribution to GDP per FTE growth

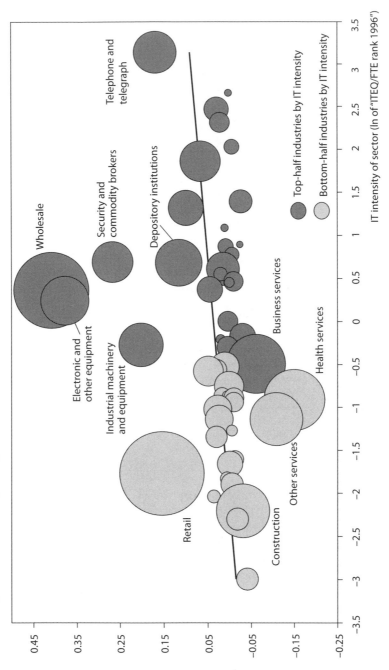

ITEQ/FTE = information technology equipment/full-time equivalent (worker)

Note: Size of bubbles indicates share of GDP by individual sector.

Source: Bureau of Economic Analysis, Digital Economy, 2002, table A4.4.

organized in or around networks; the population of small and medium-sized enterprises in the sector; the extent of sector-specific regulation; and exposure to international market forces (the last hypothesis will be discussed in chapter 4).

With regard to the nature of the sector's activities, research begun by Frank Levy and Richard Murnane (1992) and then continued with a co-author (Autor, Levy, and Murnane 2002) finds that industries intensive in business processes and jobs characterized by routines and explicit rules have invested the most in IT, thus changing the mix of tasks between those done by people and those done by technology. IT-intensive industries then increase their demand for labor with skills such as judgment, problem solving, and communications, and reduce their demand for workers who performed the routine tasks that follow explicit rules. In fact, Daniel Wilson (2004) suggests that these routine tasks increasingly can be done by IT itself using various software programs.

With regard to the second hypothesis on the role of pre-Internet networks, it may be that the sectors that have been the leaders in IT intensity and contribution to GDP growth already exchanged information over telecommunications networks before the advent of the public Internet and IT made this interchange even more integral to the activity of the sectors. For example, in the financial system, interbank payment systems and automated teller machine networks networked financial institutions well before the advent of Internet technology.[19] Similarly, telecommunications firms were well positioned with networks in place to add new services based on IT investments. Finally, lower-cost supply-chain logistics and improved management of supply-chain information have been at the heart of just-in-time inventory management systems and rapid package delivery systems that contribute to improvements in productivity in some manufacturing sectors and wholesale trade (Gereffi 2001, Bair and Gereffi 2001, McKinsey Global Institute 2002).

Research using this same sectoral decomposition finds that the productivity-enhancing effect of IT capital investment is greater among industries with strong transactional linkages (Mun and Nadiri 2002). A related finding is that IT networks appear to be an independent factor in raising the productivity growth of plants. Figure 3.7 shows the reduction in average variable cost in the sector associated with investment in IT by both customers (forward linkages) and suppliers (backward linkages). These IT spillovers show how reductions in costs come from the importance of transactional linkages to other firms' IT. Cost reductions induced by networked IT free up financial resources to be devoted to other activities or investments. Sectors below the 45 degree line are those where IT use by the customer (or forward-linking sectors) are more important in

---

19. This is consistent with the research cited from Atrostic and Nguyen (2005). See also Morisi (1996).

Figure 3.7 Reduction in own costs from IT usage by suppliers and customers

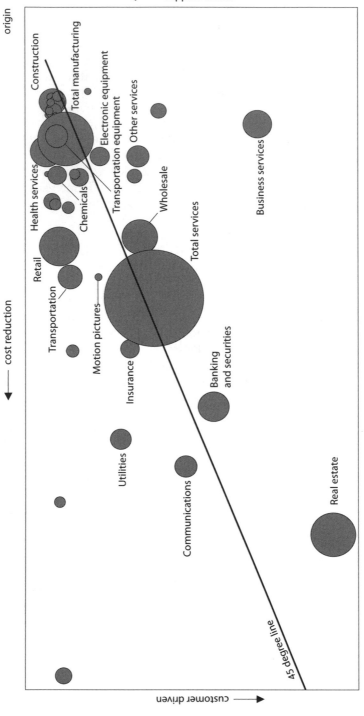

origin

supplier driven

Construction

Total manufacturing

Electronic equipment

Other services

Transportation equipment

Business services

Health services

Chemicals

Wholesale

Retail

Total services

Transportation

Motion pictures

Insurance

Banking
and securities

Utilities

Real estate

Communications

45 degree line

customer driven

— cost reduction

Note: Size of bubbles indicates industry share of GDP.

Source: Mun and Nadiri (2002, table 4).

reducing the sector's own costs. Sectors above the line are those where the IT use by the suppliers (or backward-linking sectors) has the greater impact on the sector's own costs.

Considering the main segments of the economy—manufacturing versus services—this research shows that the benefits of IT spillovers to reduce costs are greater for services sectors (the cost reduction from transactional linkages is greater) than for manufacturing sectors (the services bubble lies to the left of the manufacturing bubble in the figure). In part, these greater spillover benefits come from the greater overall investment in IT by the relatively larger services sector. But it is also the case that services firms have a more diversified set of forward linkages (customers) throughout the economy—in terms of the figure, more of the individual services sectors lie below the 45 degree line. The more diversified the transactional linkage and the more the transaction-linked sector uses IT, the greater the spillover benefits of one's own IT investment to reduce costs.

Just as in the case of overall macroeconomic performance, the diversity in the importance and direction of transactional linkages across sectors in the US economy reveals the source of economic gain from IT investments. Banking, business, and wholesale services have strong forward linkages (i.e., below the 45 degree line) and show significantly reduced costs from these transactional linkages (i.e., well to the left in the figure). Health services, retail, and construction are sectors where, in general, there is little cost reduction coming from IT in transactional linkages (i.e., these bubbles are close to the origin of the figure). This pattern of diversified forward linkages and greater spillover gains is suggestive of the role that competition and tailored customer demands can play in driving IT investment and spillover gains. A key strategy for tailoring IT is through software and services—but these are the relatively more expensive parts of the IT package. Globalization to reduce the costs of IT software and services, just as it has reduced the cost of IT hardware, could play a role in further customization, greater investment, and increased spillover gains for these lagging sectors.

Corroborative research, undertaken using detailed plant-level data, finds an independent role for IT networks (Atrostic and Nguyen 2005). IT networks enhance the productivity of a plant beyond the gain from internal IT investment by the plant. The network impact is stronger in raising the productivity of newer plants. Not only are the newer plants more likely to have made IT investments, but the share of those investments in IT services and software—the necessary tools to link IT hardware together—is likely to be higher, at least judging from the NIPA investments waves presented earlier. Finally, the newer and more networked plants are also likely to have a higher share of skilled workers.[20]

---

20. Specifically, there is a higher share of nonproduction workers, who are often used as a proxy for skilled workers.

Table 3.2   Capital expenditure per employee, by industry sector and size of company, 1998

Sector/size of company	Computers and peripherals (US dollars)	Total equipment (US dollars)	Share of total employment (percent)
Durable manufacturing			
SME: 0–499 employees	942	4,562	38.5
Large: 500+ employees	1,463	20,291	61.5
Construction			
SME: 0–499 employees	112	3,250	89.6
Large: 500+ employees	493	3,731	10.4
Health			
SME: 0–499 employees	231	1,284	43.1
Large: 500+ employees	476	2,760	56.9

SME = small or medium-sized enterprise

Source: Buckley and Montes (2002, table 3).

Why do some sectors seem to lag consistently in IT adoption, cost reductions, spillovers, and productivity growth too? Sectors with a higher population of small and medium-sized businesses appear to lag. The data suggest that these sectors generally have invested less per employee in productivity-enhancing IT. The construction and health services sectors have particularly high populations of small and medium-sized enterprises. Controlling for the same sector, the IT investment per employee has been significantly less than at their large-firm counterparts, and their investment in IT has been drastically less when compared with firms engaged in durable-goods manufacturing (table 3.2).

Culture and regulatory constraints may affect the uptake of IT by the lagging sectors. For example, in health services, privacy and regulatory issues are quite important for software and services design and implementation. Moreover, there are no IT hardware, software, and services packages that are common to the disparate entities that are part of the sector (doctors' offices, pharmacies, hospitals, etc.). Professional licensure, particularly when it varies from state to state, may be important for construction and for engineering services as well. Such fragmentation could increase the costs of producing IT applications appropriate for these sectors and thus reduce IT investment and use by firms in these sectors. Finally, legacy issues of existing training, information management systems, and technology equipment complicate integration and the type of business transformation and networks that are the hallmark of productivity growth in the leading sectors.

In sum, the growing body of research on different aspects of the relationship between IT capital and productivity growth reflects the complementary relationships between IT investments within the plant (hardware, software, and services), communications investments to network the plants, and IT use by increasingly skilled workers. To the extent that globalization of IT reduces the price of investments, and aids or hinders the uptake of IT (including the training needed by workers to use it effectively), productivity growth likely is enhanced or dampened. Going forward, as the software and services component of the IT package increasingly becomes a key part of that package within and between firms (as evidenced by the spending data discussed earlier), there will be a greater and greater premium on reducing the price of these components. As it has for IT hardware, globalization can play a role.

The uneven productivity growth across sectors of the United States raises questions for further research: Why do some sectors lag? Do they face more challenges to using communications networks? Is there greater sensitivity to the cost of IT services and software? Does customization of these parts of the IT package cost more?

Global sourcing of components of software and IT services offer the potential to reduce the module prices on which customized software and tailored services can be built. Econometric estimates show that the demand for software and services is even more responsive to price reduction than is the case for IT hardware. Therefore, as prices fall, demand for services and software is likely to rise more than one-for-one, helping to diffuse IT into the lagging sectors, deepening the use of IT in the leading sectors, and raising productivity growth throughout the US economy (see, for example, Deloitte Research 2003 for finance). Extending the beneficial forces of globalization to the components and activities that matter the most for the lagging sectors of the US economy portend a second wave of productivity growth.

The US Experience Compared with Other Countries

Looking at the US experience by itself is instructive, but there is even more to learn about the role that IT can play in transforming an economy by comparing the US experience with that of other countries. In particular, this cross-country comparison can give some insights into the consequences of the changing share of the United States in global IT production and expenditure. Cross-country analysis will also highlight the role for transformation and networks in the presence of IT as being of particular importance to reap the full benefit of it. Finally, the role for complementary services infrastructure and services (including communications) is highlighted on account of the key role that such infrastructure plays in the development of IT services and software as well as cross-border trade in services more generally.

Production versus Use of IT

Rapid innovation and falling prices for IT products reduce the entry cost to effective use of IT and the benefits that accrue to its use. But many countries still impose tariffs on imported technology capital, sometimes thinking that this will promote development of a domestic industry. Moreover, a number of countries—including Malaysia, the Philippines, Singapore, and Ireland—have expended significant sums of money via direct and indirect subsidies to become globally important producers and exporters of IT products. Are there lessons to be learned from these strategies and their impact on the countries that employ them?

While production and export of IT products obviously should not directly harm an economy,[21] declining prices for IT products mean that the terms of trade (export prices compared to prices of imported products) are moving against these producers. Thus, the gains to the domestic economy that do come from producing IT hardware for export are partly offset by the opportunity cost of not using those increasingly cheaper and more powerful IT products throughout the domestic economy.

One way to document the relative importance to economic well-being of being an IT producer as opposed to IT buyer (or somewhat in between, which is the case for most economies) is to net out the benefits to an economy of being one or the other. "Social savings" is a methodological concept used to assess the benefits of technological change. As prices of a new technology fall, the gains to national income of an economy can be calculated as the difference between what the economy pays for the new technology when it buys and uses it in the domestic economy compared to what it receives when it produces and sells the new product. If spending exceeds production, the economy is a net importer of IT; if production exceeds spending, it is a net exporter. Social savings can be mapped into the more familiar growth accounting framework emphasized in the research discussed earlier on the United States in the 1990s. Broadly speaking, the social savings measure equates to the measure of total factor productivity growth.[22] Figure 3.8 shows scatter plots of Tamim Bayoumi and Markus Haacker's calculations of social savings against net expenditure on IT (net expenditure is the difference between IT as a share of production and as a share of expenditure, averaged for 1996–2000).

---

21. Assuming that the targeting of certain sectors does not lead to corruption or other inefficient activities.

22. See Crafts (2004) for an instructive comparison of the social savings approach to measuring the gains from IT as compared to the growth accounting methodology.

Figure 3.8   Social savings and the difference between IT production and expenditure (percent of GDP)

social savings

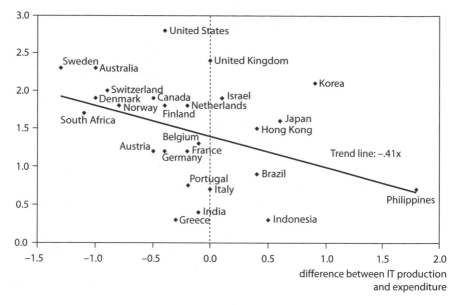

Note: Excluded countries include Singapore, Malaysia, Ireland, Taiwan, and Thailand.

Source: Bayoumi and Haacker (2002).

The figure reveals several points.[23] First, all countries to the right of the zero y-axis are net exporters with the share of IT in production (where falling prices reduce the net gain to social savings and national income) greater than the share of IT in domestic expenditure (where falling prices increases the net gain to social savings and national income). Those to the left of the zero y-axis are net spenders and net importers of IT. Now consider the trend line, which reveals the negative relationship between social savings and the net of IT production and expenditure; when the net gain to social savings and net income is greater, the greater is the gap between expenditure and production. This does not imply that a country needs to be a net importer to gain from IT. The trend line cuts the zero y-axis at a positive net export of 1.4 percent, and many net exporters enjoy

---

23. Five economies with intense concentration in production (Singapore, Malaysia, Ireland, Taiwan, and Thailand) are not included in the figure. For Ireland, Malaysia, and Singapore, net social savings is above 1.5 percent, whereas for Taiwan and Thailand, it is less than 1 percent. However, these economies are such outliers in net production (located at far right of the y-axis) that they mask the relationship relevant for economies with more average characteristics.

positive net income gains from using IT. However, they may well generate even greater gains if they were to use more of their home-produced IT internally.

The trend line shows the "average" social savings for this set of countries; those above the line generate more than average social savings from the IT they do buy, whereas those below the trend line do worse than average. The US experience is notable for being well above average in deriving gains from IT. The experience of several industrial countries (the United States, Australia, and European countries) will be discussed in more depth in the next section, but a preliminary assessment of their experiences can be seen here. The United States, Australia, Canada, United Kingdom, and the Nordic countries stand out as countries that are net purchasers of IT and have used it more effectively than the average country to generate net income and social savings (they are above the trend line and to the left of the zero y-axis). On the other hand, the larger countries of continental Europe represent countries that are net importers of IT, but have not used it as effectively to economic gain (they are below the regression line), suggesting a TFP lower than the average for this set of countries. With respect to net exporters, some are above average in using IT (Japan and Korea) and others below average (Brazil and Indonesia). The social savings concept is a useful strategy for comparing the experiences of the United States against many other countries along the dimensions of production and expenditure.

Contrasting the Experiences of the Industrial Countries

The productivity experience of the United States has not been widely shared. What can be learned from the experiences of other countries about the source of productivity benefits and the relative role for IT, the transformation of activities, or other factors? Research on industrial countries suggests that differences in outcomes are related to differences in patterns of investment and responsiveness of domestic markets to economic signals, as well as to patterns of international trade.

For many European economies, domestic production of technology capital is relatively small. But, unlike the United States (or Australia, as shown in box 3.3), investment in IT has been slower and imports have been unremarkable.[24] On balance, the lower share of technology capital in the capital investment of firms in many other industrial economies to date is an important reason for their relatively lackluster productivity performance from the latter half of the 1990s to 2002. It is difficult to start on the path of transformation if there is not a lot of IT to precipitate the change (Scarpetta et al. 2000, Elmeskov and Scarpetta 2000, OECD 2003).

---

24. OECD (2002b); tables 2.1 and 2.2a in chapter 2.

Box 3.3 The productivity experience of Australia

Australia offers an important example of how the benefits of IT can diffuse throughout an economy that does not have a significant base in IT production. In Australia, the share of IT production in GDP in 2000 was 0.2 percent, whereas it was 1.8 percent in the United States, 5.3 percent in Finland, and 39.2 percent in Singapore. So Australia is not a big producer of IT.

The acceleration in labor productivity growth in Australia was greater even than that experienced in the United States. Labor productivity can increase for several reasons, including increases in the amount of capital that is used, increases in skill levels of workers, and transformation of the activities in the workplace. The contribution of direct investment in IT capital (so-called capital deepening) to acceleration in labor productivity growth was about the same in the United States and Australia during the period examined (line 3). On the other hand, the role of the transformation of activities (total factor productivity, or TFP, growth) in the acceleration in labor productivity was even greater in Australia than it was in the United States (line 5).

TFP measures how an economy uses its existing resources (capital, labor, land, and so on) to produce more output. An increase in TFP reflects the outcome of doing things differently in an economy in order to get more output out of the same or fewer inputs. TFP proxies for the importance of transformation in raising labor productivity. For Australia, the gains from buying IT abroad and effectively using it in the transformation of business activities have also supported the creation of a domestic IT services sector, thus further expanding the gains from IT.

IT and productivity growth: Contributions to labor productivity accelerations in the 1990s (percent)

	United States[a]	Australia[b]
1. Labor productivity growth	0.5	1.0
2. Capital deepening	0.2	−0.1
3. IT/communications capital	0.3	0.4
a. Hardware	0.3	0.4
b. Software	0.1	0.0
4. Other capital	−0.2	−0.5
5. Total factor productivity contribution	0.3	1.1

a. Growth in 1992–2000 less growth in 1986–92.
b. Growth in 1993–94 to 1999–2000 less growth in 1988–89 to 1993–94.

Note: Percent per year and percentage point contributions by IT to labor productivity acceleration in the 1990s cycle.

Source: Parham (2002, table 1 on p. 9); and author's calculations on IT production as a share of economy-wide production.

Table 3.3 Average annual growth of GDP per hour worked in ICT-producing, ICT-using, and non-ICT industries in the European Union and United States, 1979–95 and 1995–2002 (percent)

	1979–95		1995–2002	
	EU-15	United States	EU-15	United States
Total economy[a]	2.3	1.2	1.8	2.5
ICT-producing industries	6.8	7.2	8.6	9.3
ICT-producing manufacturing[b]	11.6	15.1	16.2	23.5
ICT-producing services	4.4	2.4	5.9	2.7
ICT-using industries[c]	2.3	1.6	1.8	4.9
ICT-using manufacturing	2.7	0.8	2.0	2.6
ICT-using services	2.0	1.9	1.7	5.3
Of which:				
Wholesale trade	2.4	3.5	1.5	8.1
Retail trade	1.7	2.4	1.5	7.1
Financial services	1.9	1.5	2.3	5.0
ICT-intensive business services	0.8	−0.9	0.6	0.7
Non-ICT industries	1.9	0.4	1.1	0.2
Non-ICT manufacturing	3.2	2.3	2.1	1.2
Non-ICT services[a]	0.8	−0.3	0.5	0.2
Non-ICT other	3.4	1.4	2.1	0.4

ICT = information and communications technology

a. Excluding real estate.
b. Based on US hedonic price deflators for ICT production (adjusted for national inflation rates) instead of actual national accounts deflators.
c. Excluding ICT-producing.

Notes: Industry groupings into ICT-producing industries are from the OECD; distinction between ICT-using industries and less intensive ICT users is based on share of ICT capital services in total capital services from nonresidential capital; see van Ark, Inklaar, and McGuckin (2003) for exact grouping.

Source: van Ark (2005, table 4).

Detailed calculations of labor productivity for different sectors for selected economies reflect more on the differences across countries in terms of how effectively IT is used (table 3.3). The most notable difference between the United States and the European economies is in the higher level and greater acceleration of labor productivity growth in IT-using industries, particularly IT-using services.

Why have some economies not invested in and effectively used technology capital? If the environment is not supportive of upgrading business capital, changing work activities, or business entry and exit, then there is less incentive for businesses to invest in technology capital (Gust and Marquez 2000, 2002). In the case of Australia, the increased and effective use of IT was accompanied by deregulation and liberalization of the business climate (Gruen 2001). Over a broader set of countries, researchers have found that industrial economies that employ less technology capital also have an environment that is less supportive of the needed resource reallocations across firms and sectors in the economy and needed changes in organizational behavior within firms. Financial markets and perhaps accounting rules may play a role here. For example, by common measures of overall capital, the European countries have a relatively capital-intensive economic structure. So one issue may be that some of this "old" capital needs to be retired and new IT capital purchased instead. Rules and regulations may play an important role in limiting the transformation of activities in IT-using services sectors, such as retailing and securities. Resource reallocations across sectors and within firms interact with organizational change; the OECD has found a positive correlation between technology investments and adoption of new workplace practices. So if IT capital intensity is low, there is less incentive to change workplace practices, leading to a low-level productivity trap.

Does the industrial-country experience deliver lessons for the developing economies? Broad-based research on the link between IT and productivity growth that focuses only on developing economies finds mixed results in terms of the extent to which the experiences of these countries mirror the findings of the studies of industrial economies. Some researchers find little relationship between IT and productivity growth in developing economies and surmise that there is too little IT investment and that supporting communications infrastructure is poor (Pohjola 2001; Dedrick, Gurbaxani, and Kraemer 2002; Kraemer and Dedrick 2000).

In other research, when developing countries are divided into two groups based on the share of IT investment in GDP, the ones above a threshold intensity reveal the link between IT and productivity growth observed in the United States, Australia, and some other industrial economies (Lee and Wan 2001, Haacker and Morsink 2002). Thus, just as for the industrial countries, IT investment is the first step, but not enough to generate the hoped-for productivity gains. Just as for the United States, reaping the full rewards from IT requires not just IT investment but also networks and the transformation of economic activities (Moran 1999, 2001). Thus, one lesson to be discussed in more detail in chapter 4 is the need for liberalization of cross-border services, such as telecommunications, financial systems, and distribution logistics and supply chains, that help create the networked relationships and transactions linkages found to be so important for the US experience.

4

Information Technology, Outsourcing, and the New International Trade in Services

Information technology is both a traded product and a product that enhances the tradability of other goods and services. IT enhances the tradability of itself, as well as other goods and services, by enabling firms to fragment the production process and digitize, organize, and codify information. In the presence of appropriate communications infrastructure, firms can manage the fragmented production networks and related information over distances, including across international borders.

Whereas chapter 2 examined the integrated global production platform for IT hardware, this chapter focuses more explicitly on the cross-border trade in IT hardware and services and software. With respect to hardware, the fragmentation of IT production enables US producers to stay internationally competitive by using cheaper intermediate components and retaining higher value-added production steps. The resulting production for both the domestic market and for exports is globally competitive. But while this fragmentation of production of IT hardware has been in place for some time, such fragmentation and international trade in software and IT services is just beginning. So the impact on two-way trade and global competitiveness is still unfolding.

Moving beyond trade in IT products per se, the digitization, organization, and codification of information and tasks facilitated by IT software applications, and which travel over communications networks, vastly increase the actual and potential tradability of many nontechnology services. Thus, IT and communications networks facilitate international trade in a much broader array of business and professional services. Services overall represent a large share of the US economy and increasingly a larger share of the global economy. Therefore IT and communications together create the potential to expose a significantly greater share of the US economy to the forces of international trade. The accelerated globalization of the US economy is a clear consequence of the rapid pace of technological change embraced by US firms here and abroad.

As outlined in chapter 3 in the context of the US economy, many of the services that are increasingly traded across international borders— including business and professional services, distribution services, financial services, and telecommunications services—play an important role in the domestic economy by increasing the efficiency of domestic production and international trade in goods. Recognizing the increasingly important role for these services, the Uruguay Round of trade negotiations explicitly broached a framework for disciplines on barriers to international trade in services. Negotiations on these disciplines continue in the context of the Doha Development Agenda. In a more narrow context, the role for these services to increase the competitiveness of trade in goods has been taken up in the Doha agenda under the rubric of "trade facilitation." Research on both the broad and narrow assessments shows that liberalization of IT products and telecommunications networks, as well as of other services, is a key factor that enhances economic performance and competitiveness of trade in goods.

For the United States, such multilateral liberalization of services may have the added benefit of reducing the large US trade deficit. Research indicates that the growth elasticity of exports of business and professional services exceeds that of imports, in contrast to what has been estimated for exports and imports of goods.

On the other hand, the notion that fragmentation, digitization, and codification of services will proceed without any stopping point ignores the issues of regulatory jurisdiction and other differences, as well as the importance of local tastes and preferences for face-to-face design, implementation, and delivery. Not all aspects of business and professional services can be globalized.

US Cross-Border Trade in IT Products

Before discussing the new international trade in business and professional services, it is worthwhile to examine international trade flows and the balance of payments in IT products. As discussed in chapter 2, the well-developed global production network in IT hardware and the predominance of local sales for IT software and services mean that US cross-border trade in IT hardware dominates the value of cross-border trade in IT products overall. That said, it is also the case that it is increasingly difficult to disentangle hardware from software in the international trade data (appendix 4A). With these data concerns in mind, this section discusses trends in US cross-border trade in IT products, both hardware as well as services and software.

While some of the discussion that follows was presaged in chapter 2, this section hones in on cross-border trade in IT products. For IT hardware, there is an overall trade deficit, whereas for IT services and software there is a trade surplus. International trade within the multinational enterprise (what is called "intrafirm trade" because it is between a multinational parent and affiliate) behaves differently. Intrafirm trade within US multinational IT hardware firms is falling as a share of IT hardware trade, but it is rising for US IT services firms. Finally, although US multinational IT hardware firms run a trade deficit with their affiliates, these net imports of intermediate components appear to support a higher value in total sales abroad to unaffiliated buyers, so on net, the multinational group runs a trade surplus in sales of IT hardware. It is too early to tell whether a similar pattern of trade is developing for IT services.

Pattern of Trade in IT Hardware

Aggregate trade patterns reveal that real US exports and imports of IT hardware rose dramatically during the 1990s (figure 4.1) hand in hand with the development of global markets and the fragmentation of production, as already discussed. The collapse in 2000 of the technology boom and domestic IT investment then affected both US exports and imports, which declined and remained subdued for several years. Once US domestic IT investment resumed, real imports recovered and by 2004 exceeded their previous peak. Real exports recovered more slowly, but by 2005 were back to technology-boom levels. Despite the continued growth in spending in global markets, as already discussed, IT spending in the industrial-country markets has been much more sluggish. US exports of IT products are concentrated in sales to these more slowly growing markets in part because these richer and more sophisticated users can afford the higher-value US exports.[1]

Intrafirm trade offers another perspective on the implications of the globalization of IT products for the US economy and net exports. Intrafirm trade is an important part of the global activity of IT multinationals, and their pattern of behavior can be observed in the US trade data. The US market is served by US-owned and domiciled firms; foreign-owned but US-domiciled firms (majority-owned US affiliates of foreign parents, or MOUSAs); imports from US-owned firms that are located abroad (majority-owned foreign affiliates, or MOFAs); and imports from unaffiliated parties (also known as " arm's-length" imports). US firms, when they

---

1. See Mann and Plueck (2005) for more in-depth analysis of US trade by broad product category and region.

Figure 4.1   US real IT hardware trade, 1984–2005

billions of US dollars

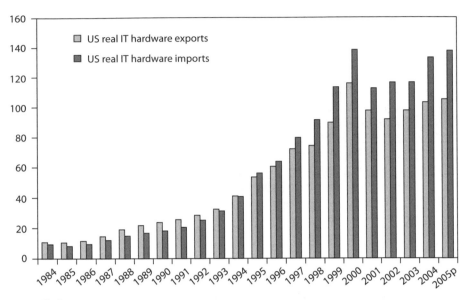

p = preliminary

Sources: Bureau of Economic Analysis, International Transactions Accounts Data, table 2, www.bea. gov; Bureau of Labor Statistics, producer price index, www.bls.gov/ppi/home.htm.

export, can sell to their own affiliates (to their MOFA) or can sell to final buyers (arm's-length exports).

Considering this complex scenario, what can be said about international trade by US IT firms and by foreign players, both intrafirm and at arm's length?[2] Because there is a longer time period of globalization, as well as more data, the initial focus will be on intrafirm trade and overall trade in IT hardware. In sum, it appears that US IT hardware producers are less and less engaged with meeting US demand through imports from affiliate operations abroad. Instead, the US multinational IT firms appear to be relinquishing the lower value-added production to unaffiliated foreign producers while producing and exporting higher value-added IT hardware

---

2. Data on intrafirm trade are generated from mandatory firm-level surveys of US multinationals. However, the international trade classification system differs from the industry classification system used for these surveys, making detailed product-level comparisons of intrafirm trade to arm's-length trade difficult. Moreover, firm-level detail is only available in public aggregates when no individual company can be identified, which frequently poses significant obstacles in the presentation of IT services data. Discussion of intrafirm trade in the IT sector must therefore proceed cautiously (box 4.1).

products to the world. Moreover, the affiliates of US firms abroad are selling more and more to unaffiliated foreign buyers.

Figure 4.1 provides the background for this analysis of the role for US IT multinationals. Overall, trade in IT hardware was in surplus at the start of the technology boom period, but then moved into a deficit, which continues. Net cross-border exports (exports minus imports) in IT hardware posted a surplus of about $3 billion in 1989 but switched into deficit in 1992. Widening steadily, by 1995 the net export deficit was about $22 billion. Since 1995, the US technology and investment cycles appear to be the drivers of the overall IT hardware deficit, widening along with the technology boom up until 2000, narrowing with the bust and recession, and then widening again in 2004 and 2005. Is the behavior of US multinationals a major factor in this pattern?

Against this background of overall trade, data for intrafirm trade within the US IT multinationals reveals a positive correlation between parent sales to foreign affiliates and unaffiliated foreign buyers (a proxy for exports) and sales by the affiliate back to the US parent (a proxy for imports). The data show that net multinational sales are positive when viewed from the perspective of the US IT multinational parent (figure 4.2). Thus, the intrafirm pattern of sales offsets the overall trade deficit in IT hardware. To the extent that the positive net intrafirm sales balance is narrowing somewhat, this offset is becoming less advantageous to the US trade balance.

This positive correlation between intrafirm imports and global sales (in conjunction with the multinational compensation data already discussed) suggests that these intrafirm (or affiliate) imports (sometimes called global "outsourced" production) may well be a source of competitive advantage for US IT exports in the global marketplace. Comparing the total US parent sales outside the United States with the intrafirm sales reveals a consistent $10 billion in additional sales to unaffiliated foreign persons.

As a final note, it appears that foreign multinationals' affiliates operating in the United States have a greater dependence on their foreign parent than being the case for US multinationals' affiliates operating abroad. That is, in 2003, the parent dependence of foreign affiliates in the United States was 80 percent and that of US affiliates abroad was just 37 percent. This asymmetric dependence of foreign affiliates in the United States on trade with their foreign parents is true in general for merchandise trade. However, unlike the average for all merchandise trade, where the share of intrafirm trade has fallen only slowly over time,[3] for IT hardware products the dependence of US affiliates abroad on exports from the US parent fell rapidly from 1989 to 2003. In contrast the (foreign) parent dependence

---

3. From the perspective of the United States as a geographic unit, the share of US total merchandise exports shipped by US multinationals that went to MOFAs was 40 percent in 1989 and 1994, declining slightly to 37 percent in 2003. Meanwhile, US-located MOUSAs relied on the foreign parents for 77 percent of their total merchandise imports in 1989 and 1994,

Figure 4.2   US multinationals' US trade balance in IT hardware, including sales to others, 1989–2003

billions of dollars

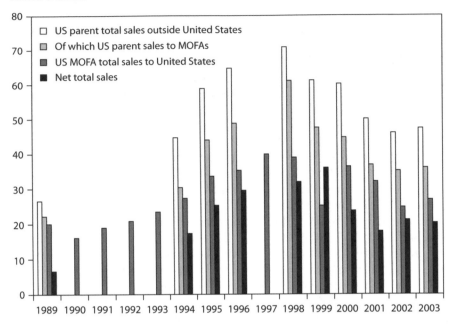

MOFA = majority-owned foreign affiliate

Note: Data for US parent sales outside the United States suppressed by BEA for years 1990–93 and 1997.

Source: Bureau of Economic Analysis, US Direct Investment Abroad: Financial and Operating Data for US Multinational Companies, www.bea.gov (accessed September 30, 2005).

of the affiliate in the United States still stood at 67 percent in 2002. So all in all, US multinationals abroad are becoming less dependent on their US parents and US exports.

The asymmetric parent dependency implies a structural trade imbalance in multinational trade for both US and foreign parent multinationals and their affiliates. As US demand for IT hardware grows, and to the extent that the products are purchased from affiliates of foreign parents in the United States, this will lead to IT hardware imports at a higher rate

---

rising slightly to 79 percent in 2002. Similarly, total merchandise exports by US parents to their MOFAs in 1989 and 1994 accounted for 25 and 27 percent, respectively, of total US merchandise exports, while merchandise imports to US-located MOUSAs from their foreign parents accounted for 26 and 25 percent of total US merchandise imports, respectively. See Mataloni (2005, table 2), Zeile (2005, table 11), and BEA financial and operating data for 1989.

than a similar increase in growth in sales of US affiliates abroad would yield intrafirm sales and IT exports. Taken together, overall trade and intrafirm trade patterns are consistent with a trend that imports from unaffiliated and affiliated foreign producers (the new global entrants) are key for the behavior of the balance of payments deficit in IT hardware. US multinational outsourcing plays a positive but shrinking role in offsetting this trend.

Trade Patterns in IT Services

Turning to overall trade and intrafirm trade in IT services, as seen in figure 4.3, a roughly similar pattern of US trade flows emerges, but the trends of the trade balance and intrafirm trade appear to be reversed from those for IT hardware: The overall trade surplus is rising, but the intrafirm trade is in deficit. In terms of overall trade in IT services, both US exports and imports increased rapidly during the 1990s, albeit from values much lower than for IT hardware. Data that detail both affiliated and unaffiliated trade are available only from 1997. Unaffiliated US exports of IT services rose fivefold from a little over $1 billion to more than $7 billion in 2004, while IT services imports rose from virtually nothing prior to 1989 to a little less than $2 billion by 2004. So by 2004 the US unaffiliated trade surplus in IT services was about $5 billion. If the United States has comparative advantage in IT services, why is this figure so small? Recall the earlier data on growth in the United States and in global markets that revealed a slowdown in growth of IT services spending in Japan and other industrial countries even as IT services and software spending continued to rise in other parts of the world (table 2.1 in chapter 2). Moreover, recall that global *sales* of US IT services firms continued to rise (figure 2.3). One way to square the trade data with the global sales data is to remember that IT services are predominantly delivered in the local market rather than through cross-border trade.

The shorter time series of data including intrafirm trade in IT services reveals potentially important behavior within the multinational enterprises. Surveys of such affiliated (intrafirm) trade from 1997 to 2004 show that imports of affiliated IT services (i.e., what US parents buy from their foreign affiliates and what foreign affiliates in the United States buy from their foreign parents) quadrupled over the period from about $800 million to about $5 billion, with the largest increase between 1998 and 1999. On the other hand, affiliated IT services exports (i.e., what US parents sell to their foreign affiliates and what foreign affiliates in the United States sell to their foreign parents) yielded a somewhat different picture. These affiliated transactions rose only modestly, from about $1.6 billion in 1997 to about $2.3 billion in 2004. In other words, affiliated IT services imports rose much faster than affiliated exports, albeit from a lower base. There-

Figure 4.3 US trade in computer and information (C&I) services, 1986–2004

billions of US dollars

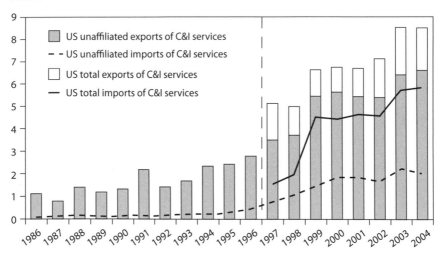

Note: Data prior to 1997 include only unaffiliated imports.

Source: Bureau of Economic Analysis, *Survey of Current Business*, 2005.

fore this pattern of affiliated trade in IT services is negative, in contrast to the overall positive balance of trade for IT services. This negative net balance of trade within IT services multinationals comes from the fact that the share of import trade through affiliates is much larger than the share of export trade through affiliates (64 percent versus 28 percent, respectively).[4] (Note that this US parent dependency on its affiliates abroad is much higher than in the case of IT hardware.) The higher (and increasing) import share through affiliates may be evidence of "offshoring," or the purchase from abroad of, for example, software development services by the US parent.[5] But data are lacking for sales of services to unaffiliated buyers in third markets (which were seen to be an important part of the puzzle of understanding US hardware multinationals). In addition, the low share of affiliate exports could be a consequence of restrictions relating to the establishment of US investment abroad in IT services.

---

4. These figures for cross-border trade in computer-related services do not exactly match the categories for affiliate sales in IT services in previous tables. This is a consequence of different classification schemes for trade and affiliates data.

5. The BEA is proposing a new survey of cross-border trade in services, both unaffiliated and affiliated, which will allow more comprehensive analysis of these trends. But data on sales of services to third-country buyers from foreign affiliates may still elude the statistical net.

IT and International Trade in Business and Professional Services

Just as IT diffusion throughout the US economy has increased productivity growth, IT diffusion into services paves the way for greater exposure of a wide range of these activities to the global forces of technology and competition. Just as our understanding of the role for IT in the domestic economy initially focused on the IT-producing sectors but now has expanded to the role for IT throughout the economy, our analysis of IT and the globalization of services started with IT services but now will be extended to how IT and communications networks facilitate international trade in a broader array of services. This section traces why and how IT globalizes a much wider range of services activities, including business and professional services in finance, advertising, consulting, engineering, legal matters, and other areas. (For analysis and presentation of key data on services, see occasional articles in BEA 2005; see also Borga and Mann 2003, 2004; Nephew et al. 2005)

Globalization of Services: Why Now and How Important?

There has always been a "services" category in the balance of payments and in direct investment accounts. Transportation and communications services bridge the physical distance between a buyer and seller of a good. Tourists travel to experience new cultures, and temporary workers send money home. However, international trade in a wide range of business and professional services is now an increasingly important part of the global economic landscape. Increased use of IT and international communications networks both in the United States and abroad are key factors underpinning the globalization of this broad range of services.

In the past, business and professional services were termed "nontraded" in economic parlance because, as a matter of fact, international transaction costs (measured in time, distance, or otherwise) prevented the close proximity between a buyer and seller deemed necessary for the service activity to take place. Beyond transportation costs, culture, customs, and regulation often required direct contact between a buyer and seller, which limited the extent to which services could be separated from the main activity of a firm or carried out across international borders. For example, financial, legal, and administrative services have required handshakes, physical presence to sign papers, or professional licensing, examination, and oversight that are unique to a jurisdiction and profession (such as for construction, accounting, or law).

In addition to transaction costs, the "production" of many business and professional services has been functionally integral to an organization's business activity or product and therefore could not be done remotely or separately from the main activity of the firm. For example, reading a radiological image has been done on site as part of a patient examination; drafting a blueprint has been integral to an architect designing a building; mortgage applications have been reviewed by the local bank manager before processing. Similarly, the "consumption" of a service, such as responding to a customer service request or fulfilling a maintenance contract, has been delivered in person by someone employed by the parent organization.

Technological change, as well as changes in customer and business attitudes over time, has eroded these attributes of services—transaction costs and functional integration—that heretofore made them "nontradable." These newly tradable activities are sometimes called information technology–enabled services (ITES). This name acknowledges first that the information and communications technologies—both data transmission (the hardware and telecommunications) and data manipulation, classification, and standardization, which involve software—are what enable these services to be fragmented and codified, and therefore undertaken with distance between the core business, the intermediate supplier, and ultimate customer. Second, it acknowledges that the services activities are not just narrowly IT-related (e.g., computer programming or database administration) but more broadly include accounting, financial analysis, call center services, architectural drafting, and health record transcription, among other business and professional services.

At the same time, new businesses have sprung up to specialize in services tasks that have common attributes across many types of businesses—such as human resource management, customer call centers, and standardized financial analysis. These new businesses enjoy the economies of scale in their particular area of expertise, as discussed in the context of electronics manufacturing services (EMS) firms for IT hardware production. Hence, with the availability of technology and with the specialization of some business tasks, firms in many industries are reassessing which of the many services underneath the corporate umbrella truly are integral to their main business function. Those that are not integral have been outsourced to specialized services providers.

International trade in services—sometimes termed offshore sourcing of services—demands not only restructuring by firms in the United States, but also requires that the trading partners have the technology that reduces transaction costs and allows functional fragmentation, and that the foreign workforce has the appropriate skill level for the task. That is, globalization of business and professional services beyond the US border is limited unless both sides of the cross-border transaction have, at least to some degree, embraced technological change. For example, a huge reduction in the telecommunications costs between the United States and India made offshore call centers much more attractively priced; in another example, a sevenfold increase in the penetration of personal computers in the Chinese marketplace networked this production platform into information- and logistics-based businesses.[6] More generally, comparative research, particularly of emerging markets, finds that, controlling for the level of development, adoption of the Internet is related to capital account controls, trade protection (particularly tariffs on personal computers and telecommunications equipment), cost of telecommunications transmissions, and spending on public education (Knight 2003). So some countries, by virtue of their policies and attributes, are more likely to be leaders in international trade in services.

International trade in business services is a reality and much bigger than IT services alone (table 4.1). The United States is the global leader in business services, although not in computer and information services.[7] Does the IT sector (hardware and services, domestic and traded) support the leadership of the United States in international trade in business services? Consider detailed data on US trade in services, focusing on the sectors that use IT intensively and thus might be most prone to rapidly increased two-way trade on account of both the United States and other countries embracing the enabling technology (figure 4.4a). Two important facts are yielded by the US trade data for these services: trade growth is robust, and the US trade balance remains solidly in surplus (figure 4.4b).

For trade in categories such as "finance," "overall business, professional and technical," and "other" categories, aggregate data clearly indicate the United States' competitive position. Recall that these were leaders in investment in IT and in contributing to productivity growth.[8] Moreover, consider that the main markets for US services exports are in Western Europe and Japan, which have been experiencing a synchronized economic slowdown. The stable positive net export balance suggests that the

---

6. Both quantitative examples are based on World Bank data for 1996 compared with data for 2001.

7. A note of caution on the export data for Ireland and India: The Indian data were subsequently revised downward substantially. See appendix A.

8. Two categories of services trade are not shown because their evolution has little to do with either technological change or economic activity: telecommunications and insurance, which together have a deficit of some $22 billion. With regard to the insurance deficit, much of this is due to increasingly higher premiums charged by foreign reinsurance firms to cover past losses and higher rates associated with hurricane and terrorism-related insurance coverage. The accounting framework makes this category highly influenced by geopolitical/terror and weather risks, and conclusions drawn from these data should reflect this, rather than competitiveness per se. With regard to telecommunications, the data show vestiges of an idiosyncratic accounting system, which is being phased out, rather than the underlying state of the international competitiveness of US telecommunications companies.

Cross-border trade in telecommunications is determined by a system of bilaterally negotiated accounting rates for carrying international calls measured in minutes. Calls are billed in the originating country, so a carrier whose outbound calling minutes exceed its inbound calling minutes makes a net payment to its foreign counterpart "delivering the calls." Net settlement payments by US carriers to foreign carriers are subsequently recorded as imports, while net settlement receipts from foreign carriers to US carriers are recorded as exports. The

Table 4.1 World's largest business and computer and information services importers and exporters, 2003
(billions of US dollars)

	Exports (insourcing)		Imports (outsourcing)	
Rank	Business services	Computer and information services	Business services	Computer and information services
1	United States 64.1	Ireland 14.4	United States 44.2	Germany 7.2
2	Britain 44.8	India 12.5	Germany 40.4	Britain 2.9
3	Germany 31.8	Britain 7.0	Italy 24.6	Japan 2.1
4	France 24.1	Germany 6.6	Netherlands 24.6	Spain 1.7
5	Netherlands 22.0	United States 5.4	Japan 23.2	Belgium 1.6
6	Italy 21.0	Israel 3.7	Ireland 22.3	United States 1.5
7	Japan 18.0	Spain 2.9	Britain 20.1	Netherlands 1.5
8	India 17.5	Canada 2.3	Austria 19.1	France 1.2
9	China 17.4	Belgium 2.1	Spain 15.3	Sweden 1.2
10	Austria 15.9	Netherlands 2.1	Belgium 12.3	Brazil 1.1
11	Belgium 14.8	Sweden 2.0	Korea 11.2	Italy 1.1
12	Spain 13.5	France 1.3	Sweden 10.7	China 1.0
13	Denmark 12.4	Luxembourg 1.1	India 10.5	Canada 1.0
14	Singapore 11.4	China 1.1	Canada 10.4	Australia 1.0
15	Canada 11.3	Japan 1.1	China 10.4	Norway .7
16	Sweden 11.1	Australia .7	Denmark 9.6	Finland .5
17	Ireland 6.7	Finland .6	Indonesia 8.8	Russia .5

	Country	Value	Country	Value	Country	Value	Country	Value
18	Korea	6.7	Italy	.5	Singapore	5.1	Ireland	.4
19	Switzerland	6.6	Norway	.4	Russia	5.1	Austria	.4
20	Saudi Arabia	5.3	Singapore	.3	Saudi Arabia	4.8	Luxembourg	.4
21	Norway	4.5	Hungary	.2	Switzerland	4.8	Poland	.4
22	Brazil	4.1	Malaysia	.2	Brazil	4.4	Hungary	.2
23	Thailand	3.9	Austria	.2	Thailand	3.9	Portugal	.2
24	Israel	3.1	Russia	.2	Norway	3.8	Singapore	.2
25	Russia	3.0	Costa Rica	.2	Israel	3.6	Malaysia	.2
26	Luxembourg	2.4	Greece	.1	Malaysia	3.1	Greece	.2
27	Australia	2.3	Poland	.1	Finland	2.9	Czech Republic	.2
28	Finland	2.1	Argentina	.1	Poland	2.5	Korea	.1
29	Egypt	2.1	Portugal	.1	Australia	2.4	Slovak Republic	.1
30	Malaysia	1.9	Romania	.1	Czech Republic	2.3	Syria	.1
Total value of trade (and number of countries reporting data)		427.9 (114)		70.7 (83)		396.1 (117)		31.4^a (85)

a. The very large discrepancy between the total value of reported computer and information services exports and imports is testament to the continued serious statistical problems concerning gathering of these data. See box 2.1.

Notes: Data for China exclude Hong Kong and Macau. Indian business services data from 2002.

Source: IMF's Balance of Payments Statistics, June 2005, www.indiastat.com (accessed March 28, 2006). Data on Indian exports of computer and information services are from the Indian statistical agency, Datanet India, for fiscal year 2003 (April 2003–March 2004).

Figure 4.4a   US trade balance in IT-enabled services, affiliated and unaffiliated, selected categories, 1997–2004

millions of dollars

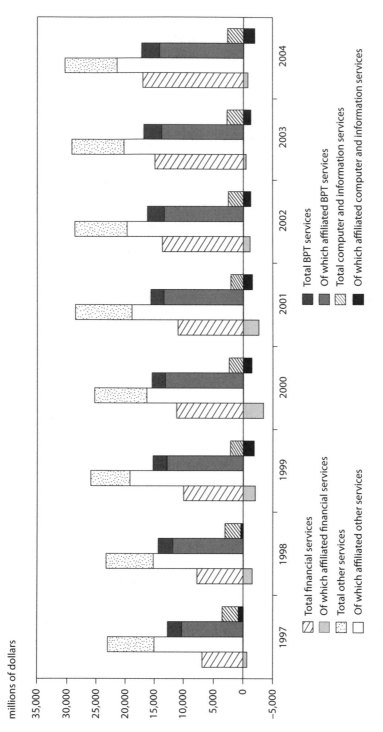

BPT = business, professional, and technical

Note: The "affiliated" and "unaffiliated" trade shown varies between categories. The category "other services" includes any service that is not an education, financial, insurance, telecommunications, business, professional, or technical service.

Source: Bureau of Economic Analysis, Survey of Current Business, *2005.*

Figure 4.4b   US exports and imports of other private services, 1997–2004

billions of US dollars

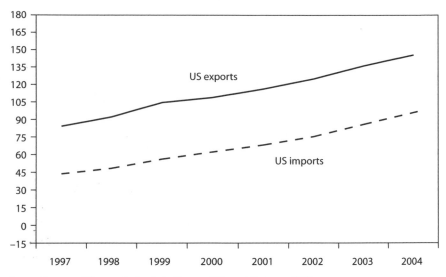

Source: Bureau of Economic Analysis, *Survey of Current Business*, 2005.

competitive US position in IT-enabled services persists, even as more countries engage in cross-border trade in services.[9]

In the narrow category of computer and information services, affiliated trade is in deficit, and the United States is not the global leader in computer services trade (figure 4.4a). However, this negative balance may contribute to the lower costs and international competitiveness of IT-enabled services such as finance and business, professional, and technical services, just as imported IT hardware has contributed to overall cost reductions and productivity growth for the US economy overall.

high level of international calls originating in the United States up until 2002 caused a chronic US telecommunications trade deficit, but the Federal Communications Commission mandated reductions in the accounting rates after 1997 and technological innovations such as Internet protocol telephony have served to improve the US sectoral balance. Since 2002, it has been in modest surplus (less than $1 billion).

9. The United States maintains an "other private services" surplus with all regions of the world, again indicating a strong competitive position. For detailed data, see Bureau of Economic Analysis, international transactions table 11 at www.bea.gov. In addition, Mann (2004) indicates that a slowdown in growth in major export markets has a greater than one-to-one effect on slowing export growth of business and professional services. (Of course, as growth resumes, this has a more than one-to-one effect on raising exports.)

Figure 4.5 Headquarters trade: US intrafirm trade in business, professional, and technical services, 1997–2004

billions of US dollars

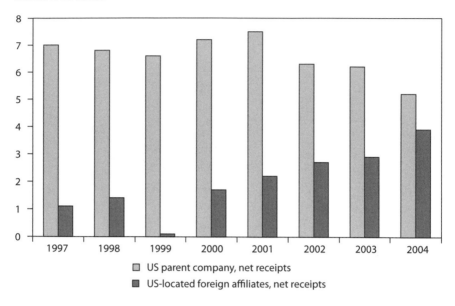

☐ US parent company, net receipts
■ US-located foreign affiliates, net receipts

Source: Bureau of Economic Analysis, *Survey of Current Business,* October 2005, 33 (table E).

The competitive advantage of the US environment in business and professional and technical services is corroborated by data on where multinational corporations conduct their "headquarters" services (figure 4.5). In the figure, "US parent, net receipts" represents the payments made to US-located parent companies from their overseas affiliates, minus payments from US-located parents to their overseas foreign affiliates. An example would be the transactions between IBM in the United States and IBM's subsidiary in India. "US affiliates, net receipts" refers to the payments received by US-located subsidiaries of foreign multinationals from their foreign parent companies, subtracting payments made by the US-located subsidiaries to their foreign parent. Here an example would be transactions between Deutsche Bank in New York and the Deutsche Bank headquarters in Frankfurt. Box 4.1 discusses the decision of whether to keep services under the corporate umbrella or not.

An initial observation is that, although US multinationals are expanding overseas and integrating their operations globally, this has not been associated with a deterioration of the US "headquarters" services trade balance. Even though US multinationals do send some back-office and administrative work overseas to be done by affiliates, on balance, the

Box 4.1   From affiliated services to arm's-length trade: Where General Electric goes, will other companies follow?

For confidentiality reasons, the most recent data for foreign affiliates of US information technology services firms are not disclosed by the US Commerce Department's Bureau of Economic Analysis. However, an examination of recent individual company transactions in the largest provider country of IT services (India) may give insight into possible trends.

In November 2004, General Electric sold its wholly owned Indian affiliate GE Capital Information Services (GECIS) to two US private equity groups (General Atlantic Partners and Oak Hill Capital Partners) for $500 million, while retaining a minority 40 percent stake. GE was one of the pioneers of offshore outsourcing in India, establishing GECIS in 1997 to provide internal business support for GE's other businesses. At the time of the sale, GECIS supported nearly 1,000 business processes across GE's different business units, including finance, accounting, supply-chain management, customer service support, software development, data modeling, and analytical activities. GECIS operated facilities in India, Mexico, Hungary, and China, conducted business in 19 languages, and employed 17,000 people, of whom 12,000 were in India.[1]

In many ways, the growth of GECIS since 1997 into a billion-dollar business has mirrored the rise of the entire Indian IT services industry, which even today remains heavily influenced by US companies. India's National Association of Software and Services Companies (NASSCOM) estimates that in 2004, one-third of the Indian IT services industry was owned by multinational companies, the vast majority US-owned.[2] Does the sale of GECIS portend a trend? Are other US multinationals in the process of selling their captive Indian offshore operations? If so, this would indicate a trend from intrafirm offshoring to arm's-length offshoring— i.e., from sourcing from a majority-owned Indian affiliate of a US company to sourcing from an Indian third party by US multinationals.

A related development is the ongoing consolidation of the Indian IT services industry. In 2004, the top five domestic companies accounted for 44 percent of the entire industry. Should this consolidation continue, it could have significant implications for the presence of US multinationals in the Indian IT services sector, as these US firms might be increasingly likely to sell their facilities to local Indian third-party providers with the sufficient scale to achieve profitability—much like the trend toward consolidation of commodity hardware production in electronics manufacturing services (EMS) companies.

Concerns over access to proprietary company information may color the decision by some multinationals to sell their captive Indian affiliates. For example,

(box continues next page)

Box 4.1   From affiliated services to arm's-length trade: Where General Electric goes, will other companies follow?
(continued)

in April 2005 IBM purchased Daksh e-services for somewhere between $100 million and $150 million, and Citigroup Inc. in August 2004 paid $112 million for e-Serve International Ltd. So even as GE sold its Indian subsidiary, other US multinationals are buying Indian services firms and bringing their activities "in-house."

1. GE press release, "General Electric Partners with Leading Investors to Transform GECIS, Its Global Business Processing Operation, into an Independent Company," November 8, 2004.
2. NASSCOM Indian IT Industry Fact Sheet 2005, available at www.nasscom.org (accessed October 1, 2005).

affiliates import more of these services from the parent. A second observation is that foreign multinationals with subsidiaries in the United States also increasingly do their internal "headquarters" services transactions in the United States. This contrasts with the behavior on the merchandise account and suggests that the United States has maintained a strong competitive position in the services transactions that take place within foreign multinational companies.[10]

To a great degree, the forces promoting tradability and hence the globalization of business and professional services—reduced transaction costs and the functional and physical separation of business functions—are the same forces that underpin the globalization of goods. In what ways is the globalization of business and professional services different from the globalization of goods, and what are the implications for the globalization of America?

First, reducing the cost of network infrastructure in the United States and abroad has quickened the pace of globalization of business and professional services both here and around the world. Global international trade in what are categorized as "other commercial services" (i.e., excluding government services, travel, and transport services) doubled from 1995 to 2004 to $950 billion, and accounts for about 8 percent of global international trade.[11] In the United States, exports of business and

10. Some US firms have moved their headquarters to low-tax jurisdictions, such as Bermuda. When firms do this, what had been recorded as a services export may now be eliminated from the trade balance or be recorded as a services import.

11. World Trade Organization (WTO) online international trade database at www.wto.org (accessed October 1, 2005). All data are for 2004 and include the entire world as reporter and partner. "Trade" is defined as the average of imports and exports. Total global trade is the sum of trade in merchandise and total commercial services trade.

professional services (what are called "other private services" in the US balance of payments accounts) are growing more than three times as fast as exports of goods, and imports of business and professional services are growing about 80 percent faster (1995 to 2004). These services account for about 10 percent of total exports and about 7 percent of total imports.

A second factor that differentiates the globalization of goods from the globalization of services is that the two may differ in how easily firms can change the location of their activities to take advantage of better capabilities in another country. Certainly foreign direct investment (FDI) in services has been growing, with about one-third of the inward and outward stock of US FDI in 2003 attributed to these kinds of activities. Digitized and standardized services require little complementary capital compared with producing goods in a factory (although infrastructure investment in communications, for example, is crucial). Firms that focus on an intermediate segment of the international value chain in services production (and do not serve the domestic market) are likely to be more footloose than factories because their links to the local economy are fewer and physical investment is low.

A third factor is that the globalization of services, in the context of global GDP growth, appears to differentially contribute positively to the US balance of payments. Research shows that the global elasticity of demand for US services exports (particularly BPT) exceeds the US elasticity of demand for services imports (Mann 2004, Marquez 2005). This elasticity "asymmetry" is opposite to that observed for trade in goods. Therefore as global GDP expands, the US balance of payments surplus in services tends to expand as well, offsetting to some degree the balance of payments deficit in goods.

To the extent that both trade and direct investment in services continue to grow both in the United States and around the world, the share of global production exposed to international market forces rises. In industrial countries, where services account for the majority of output and employment, rapid globalization of services means that a large and increasing share of the labor force and the productive economy faces international competition. At the same time, in developing countries, more workers are being drawn into the services sector, due in part to globalization and in part to the developmental transition from agriculture to manufacturing to services. Consequently, an increasing share of the global labor force is engaged in activities that are exposed to technological change and will need to respond to global competition and the resulting international division of labor. In contrast, the shares of agricultural and manufacturing employment have been declining in both industrial and developing countries as technological change increases productivity in these sectors and the share of labor falls.

Prospects for Further Trade in Services

The previous sections have addressed the potential tradability of services. To the extent that the main motivator propelling international trade in services is technology itself, along with lower wages in developing countries and a narrowing education gap, is there no end to the potential fragmentation of services activities, their tradability, and the potential for job changes in the United States? On the other hand, research indicates that the US balance of payments would differentially benefit from faster trade growth and more internationalization of the globally competitive services. So what are the prospects for international trade in services?

Limits to International Trade in Services

There are several limitations on international trade in services. First, not all services are or will be tradable either domestically or internationally—technological change, while powerful, cannot drive transaction costs to zero and divorce all activities from within the firm. Second, substantial variations in customer taste and culture, firm size, management attitude, domestic regulations, and government interventions differentiate markets for the delivery of services and lead to different degrees of functional and physical separation of business functions, depending on locale. Third, there are substantial impediments to international trade in services related to the domestic climate of services provision—such as in the finance and telecommunications sectors, both of which are major IT users and, more importantly, support economywide investment in IT and diffusion of it. In these sectors, as well as other services sectors, domestic and trade liberalization efforts are making only slow progress.

Even as international services trade increases, several factors point as well to a sustained increase in services activities in domestic markets (with attendant job increases). As noted, services as a share of economywide production increases with the level of economic development—the elasticity of the demand for services with respect to GDP is greater than one. Not all services activities can be codified and digitized. Face-to-face interaction is still required at many points in product development, marketing, delivery, and maintenance. Local knowledge is critical, for example, to understand the thicket of healthcare regulations or legal codes. Businesses of a certain size (generally small and medium-sized enterprises) need tailored delivery and demand proximity of the services provider.

More generally, an important constraint to the globalization of services that might otherwise have the potential to be delivered internationally via IT is the interface between the global marketplace and the local jurisdiction of policy and regulation. For example, there are no global rules specifying how cross-border transactions of data should be treated with respect to privacy or intellectual property rules. Consumer and business attitudes toward the balance between market-oriented and government-legislated solutions in these areas are not homogeneous across countries, nor even within a country (Mann 2001, 2002). Professional licensure and regulatory standards vary across jurisdictions. (This is true even in the United States, for example, for lawyers and some engineers.) The best that is likely to be achieved in the long run is mutual recognition agreements, yet in general, these agreements for standards of professional licensure do not yet exist, particularly across country borders. With differing rules across countries, globalization of some business, professional, and technical services will proceed slowly.

Potential for Services Negotiations

A related constraint to greater cross-border international trade in services is that international trade negotiations have made little headway in agreeing on a more liberal trade regime for many of the services that can be done internationally—including those in which the United States has a comparative advantage. By the same token, potential growth around the world, which would tend to augment the demand for products, services, and labor in the United States, is lower than it otherwise would be because services that enable IT to work effectively in an economy—low-cost telecommunications, financial intermediaries that can move money electronically, and delivery logistics that can move products expeditiously—have not been deployed (Mann and Rosen 2001; Mann, Eckert, and Knight 2000).

But does it make sense to focus attention on services trade negotiations when there is so much unfinished business in agriculture and manufacturing liberalization? As it turns out, the various researchers who consider the implications of different multilateral trade negotiation scenarios for global and individual economy GDP find that the gains from services sector liberalization alone could be about one-half of the total gain to global GDP of liberalization of agriculture, manufacturing, and services together (table 4.2) (Brown, Deardorff, and Stern 2001; Dee and Hanslow 2001). Who gains from increased cross-border trade in services? Industrial-country exporters of services, including the United States, gain from liberalized trade in services. For many developing economies, the increased GDP from improvements in domestic services sectors that come from trade liberalization is nearly as large as (and in some cases larger than) the gains to GDP that come from trade liberalization in manufactured and agricultural exports. The reason is because domestic services are an input to all other sectors, whether domestic-focused or export-focused. Poor services are a tax on domestic GDP growth and undermine export competitiveness in all sectors. All told, the welfare gains throughout an economy from improving the performance of the domestic services sector are dra-

Table 4.2 Estimated gains from trade and investment liberalization, selected countries

Country	All sectors[a] Percent of GDP	All sectors[a] Billions of US dollars	Manufacturing only Percent of GDP	Manufacturing only Billions of US dollars	Services only[b] Percent of GDP	Services only[b] Billions of US dollars
World		613.00		211.00		390.00
United States	1.95	177.30	0.34	31.30	1.65	150.00
Japan	1.90	123.70	0.89	57.80	0.95	61.60
EU/EFTA	1.54	168.90	0.58	63.30	0.94	103.40
China	1.50	13.60	0.54	4.90	0.79	7.10
Korea	2.84	14.10	1.40	8.00	0.91	5.20
Malaysia	2.81	3.40	1.99	2.40	0.54	0.60
Chile	2.40	1.90	1.29	1.00	1.17	0.90
Mexico	1.84	6.50	0.32	1.10	1.49	5.20

EU/EFTA = European Union/European Free Trade Association

a. Agriculture, manufacturing, and services.
b. Services coverage includes construction, trade and transport, other private services, and government services. Protection measured by excess operating profits of firms listed on stock markets.

Note: Scenario shows liberalization of implied protection of 33 percent for three sectors (agriculture, manufacturing, and services).

Source: Brown, Deardorff, and Stern (2001, table 2, 25); Dee and Hanslow (2001).

matic. Consequently, liberalizing key services sectors should be a focus of bilateral, General Agreement on Trade in Services (GATS), and Doha negotiations.[12]

Other research and analysis using different econometric models quantifies the potential macroeconomic benefits associated with broad-based trade and investment liberalization, diffusion of networked technologies into business, and domestic policy reforms that ensure that resource reallocations can take place. The approaches are different, but the conclusions are the same: The potential gain to economic well-being is huge from policy reforms that create a favorable environment for IT to take hold. For example, the United Nations Conference on Trade and Development (UNCTAD) considers the long-run effect on GDP of IT, networks, and associated facilitating policies. UNCTAD's simulations with survey data on business costs suggest that the effective use of IT could increase GDP in the industrial world by almost 5 percent (about $1 trillion) in the long run.[13]

---

12. For more on IT issues in multilateral WTO negotiations, see Mann (2000) and Mann and Knight (2000).

13. See Mann and Rosen (2001, 30–35) for a more extensive discussion of the UNCTAD method and adjustments to it.

Table 4.3 Trade and trade facilitation

Variable	Full sample (1)	Developing to industrial country trade (2)	Developing to developing country trade (3)
Tariff rates	−1.555***	−1.512	−1.500***
Port efficiency of importing country	0.307*	0.344	−0.283
Port efficiency of exporting country	0.924***	0.845***	0.949***
Customs environment of importing country	0.472**	1.041	0.202
Regulatory environment of importing country	0.281*	−1.120*	0.816***
Regulatory environment of exporting country	0.620***	2.437***	0.827***
Services sector infrastructure of importing country	0.729***	2.134***	0.866
Services sector infrastructure of exporting country	1.943***	2.124***	3.133***
Adjusted R-squared	0.758	0.702	0.649
Number of observations	7,904	2,188	3,094

Note: The significance levels are denoted as * for 10 percent, ** for 5 percent, and *** for 1 percent.

Source: Wilson, Mann, and Otsuki (2005).

Finally, new research in the area of trade facilitation shows the importance of services for increasing trade flows (Wilson, Mann, and Otsuki 2003, 2005). As tariffs on trade in goods have come down, more interest has focused on the role that services play in fostering international trade. Research indicates that both imports and exports for a country—and for the world—would increase with improvements in trade facilitation as measured by country-specific proxies for port infrastructure (air and maritime), the customs environment, regulatory environments, and services infrastructures (finance, telecoms, logistics). Table 4.3 reports results from this research, while box 4.2 gives a specific example. Increased trade in manufactured goods from trade facilitation improvements in all four areas yields increases in both exports and imports (column 1 in table 4.3). The most important ingredient in achieving these gains is a country's own trade facilitation reform efforts. (To see this, compare the coefficients in the table on the "importing country" versus the "exporting country"). Moreover, among these trade facilitation measures, improved services infrastructure has the greatest impact on trade. Comparing the results for direction of trade (developing countries to the industrial countries, or developing countries to other developing countries) reveals the greater importance of improved infrastructure for services in increasing trade

Box 4.2 The role of services infrastructure in locating a new US multinational plant

Intel Corp. is the premier chipmaker in the world, with its products including chips, boards, and other semiconductor components that are the building blocks integral to computers, servers, and networking and communications products.

As market leader, Intel is always in the process of positioning assets for a global fit for its business strategy. On the one hand, the time from fabrication to assembly and testing and to the finished product for market demand is long. On the other, sufficient capacity must be up and running when demand hits. So Intel is identifying worldwide trends and determining where it will build its next set of facilities even before the next chip exists.

What is Intel looking for (and what will it help to create under the right circumstances)? Common to all types of facilities, Intel first considers the site and infrastructure, the operating environment, and the community. Here the factors that matter include a hub airport, connectivity, and value-chain partners; the quality and quantity of the technical workforce and the nature of intellectual property protection; and whether the overall environment is conducive to a highly educated workforce. Intel works on an ongoing basis with governments to help develop the total package that will be attractive not only to Intel but to other companies as well.

Once through these initial considerations, the site selection process diverges somewhat depending on the nature of the facility. For fabrication facilities, site size, infrastructure, legal issues, and quality and quantity of engineering and technical personnel matter the most. For assembly and testing, the objective is to maintain engineering quality, but at the lowest cost and quickest throughput. So locations with airports and those with tariff- and tax-advantaged privileges are key. For data centers, connectivity, English language proficiency, and amenities are important.

Intel and others are following a pattern of globalization with two key drivers: market access and global production. For the first, heterogeneity matters, with regional headquarters, customer support centers, and research and development located near the target marketplace. For the second, cost sensitivity drives location, with taxes and subsidies playing a role in the selection of a production location where scale economies are important.

particularly from developing to industrial countries (column 2 in table 4.3) and among the developing countries (column 3 in table 4.3).

Collectively, this research makes clear that the developing world has much to gain from broad-based liberalization of trade and investment in the services sectors of finance and banking, telecommunications, and distribution and delivery. This global engagement, in conjunction with a macroeconomic environment of fiscal efficiency and where domestic competition and sufficient education ensure that domestic labor and capital adjust to new opportunities, has great potential to help poorer nations reap the full gains of global engagement and IT.

From the standpoint of the United States, as a net exporter of services and with a positive balance of trade in many services, expanding global opportunities for trade and investment would likely expand the global marketplace for these activities. If, in addition, such globalization of services increases the level of economic development, then the United States stands to gain even more in trade, since consumption of services tends to increase as a share of GDP as per capita GDP increases.

In sum, since domestic services are an input to all other sectors, whether focused domestically or on exports, the liberalization of trade in services can play a role in creating a virtuous circle that would enhance GDP growth and balanced trade in both the United States and the developing world.

Appendix 4A
Challenges of International Trade Data for IT Products

Statisticians face three main hurdles in measuring patterns of international trade in information technology products: distinguishing IT products from other products, determining what crosses international borders, and ascertaining the prices of these traded IT goods and services.

Distinguishing IT products from other products is a challenge because of the rapid pace of innovation in the IT sector. New IT products merge communications (personal digital assistants or PDAs), entertainment (game consoles with Internet access), and "traditional" computer hardware, software, and services. Statistical classification cannot keep up, and, in any case, constant changes in classifications hinder long time series of data. Balancing the desire for up-to-date classification with the desire for time-series consistency implies that statistical classification of the IT sector will lag real-world developments to a greater extent than in other parts of the economy.

The enormous rise in IT services presents another hurdle, as part of the more general challenge, of how best to account for the growing importance of services activities. The reclassification of data from the US Standard Industrial Classification System (SIC) to the North American Industry Classification System (NAICS) in 1997 was partly designed to more validly capture services and new advanced technology sectors. NAICS classifies together economic units according to the processes used to produce goods and services and as such is far better able to capture services in the high-tech sectors.[14]

NAICS created a new sector, "51 Information," which comprises establishments engaged in the following processes: (1) producing and distributing information and cultural products, (2) providing the means to transmit or distribute these products as well as data or communications, and (3) processing data. NAICS's new "computer and electronic product manufacturing category" (NAICS 334) was designed to include only IT manufacturers.[15] So NAICS both captures IT hardware, services, and software, and distinguishes between these categories in trade and production.

The second statistical task is to determine when IT products cross international borders. For IT goods such as semiconductors or laptop personal

---

14. These North American efforts to improve statistical capture of the services sectors have been mirrored internationally since 2002 by the *Manual of Statistics on International Trade in Services*, published jointly by the European Commission, International Monetary Fund, Organization for Economic Cooperation and Development, United Nations Conference on Trade and Development, and the World Trade Organization (UNCTAD 2002).

15. The US Census Bureau definition is from www.census.gov/epcd/ec97/def/51.txt and www.census.gov/epcd/ec97/def/334.txt (accessed March 15, 2006).

computers, this presents no new challenges, as existing administrative systems based on customs collection or export survey for measurement can be used, although the growing fragmentation of production implies a need for increasingly detailed data. For IT services, however, most of which are only recently internationally tradable, experiencing rapid growth, and often intangible, the task of measuring international trade is far more complicated.

IT services are frequently difficult to define and may constitute abstract concepts rather than a physical good, attribute, or function, and very rarely require a physical package (with an inventory description) to cross borders. Hence, contrary to IT goods data, IT services trade data are collected predominantly through surveys of IT businesses, administrative sources, and numerical estimations by statistical agencies. During this collection process, practical considerations of data confidentiality (statistical agencies agree to protect individual corporate data) as well as respondent burden (there are limits to how many surveys businesses can reasonably be expected to fill out) must be weighed against the demand from data users for more detail and validity. Moreover, collecting trade data requires a high degree of "common understanding" of the precise definitions of complicated concepts across different countries' statistical agencies, and also broadly among the players in the IT services industry.

A specific example of such differing interpretations of concepts is revealed by the valuation of US-India trade in "computer and information services." In 2003, the US Commerce Department's Bureau of Economic Analysis (BEA) reported US imports from India as less than a tenth of similar exports to the United States reported by India's National Association of Software and Services Companies (NASSCOM) (Baily and Lawrence 2004). This large discrepancy arose for several reasons. The Indian source included the value of work carried out by company employees on location in the United States, whereas the BEA data, in accordance with the standard balance of payments accounting standards used by the International Monetary Fund, classifies such "wage earnings" not as "trade imports" but as compensation of employees ("worker remittances") in US international transactions tables. Moreover, if the employees in question are in the United States for more than one year, domestic and international accounting standards classify the wages of these employees in the US GDP statistics, not in imports at all. The statistical responsibility for valuating "computer and information services" has since been transferred from NASSCOM to the Reserve Bank of India, and measures of bilateral trade are now comparable.

Many IT services transactions are conducted across international borders but within the same firm as intrafirm trade. Statistical coverage of the scope of transactions within companies is murky—both as to whether a transaction has taken place and at what price—even though US statistical agencies maintain the most comprehensive data collection effort in the world on intrafirm trade. BEA's new surveys of services transactions will significantly improve the coverage of intrafirm trade.

Even when the statistics correctly demarcate the IT products and determine when they cross international borders, the next question is the price at which such international transactions take place. Price declines among IT goods, especially semiconductors and memory chips, have been unprecedented, and rapid innovation means that the product yesterday at price P is not the same product sold today at price p. As the pace of innovation and functionality speeds up, the statistical strategy of "matching models" in the marketplace to link together and create a single price index for a rapidly changing product becomes increasingly challenging.

Pricing of IT products is also complicated by the more pervasive "packaging" of IT hardware, software, and services together. It is becoming more difficult to separate and price the parts of this package, such as for instance the actual value of the "bundled software" preinstalled on personal computers (box 3.1 in chapter 3). At the same time, such "IT packages" are increasingly customized to individual specifications, meaning they contain increasingly disparate amounts of IT hardware, software, and services, adding a further layer of complexity to determining their price.

Finally, many transactions occur within a company itself, making trade pricing vulnerable to transfer pricing by multinational firms. Not unique to the IT sector, it is well documented that multinationals tend to set the level of transfer prices within the company so as to maximize profits in low-tax subsidiaries, rather than at a level that reflects the true value of transacted items (Hines 1996, 1997, and 2000; Desai, Foley, and Hines 2002; Clausing 1998).

The challenges of classification clarity and data integrity are well known to US statistical agencies, which are working with private firms, researchers, and their own staffs to improve the data to better support descriptive insight and policy decision making. Ensuring adequate resources to track this increasingly important sector is critical.

5

Information Technology and Labor Markets

One of the most controversial aspects of globalization is its impact on American workers. However, technology also affects workers, and in much similar ways. A substantial research portfolio focuses on the combined forces of technological change and globalization, although parsing out the specific effects of one versus the other is not possible since globalization and technological change go hand in hand. The successful diffusion of IT throughout the US economy into non-IT-producing sectors, accelerated by the globalization of IT and international competition more generally, means that the US labor market is experiencing significant structural change. This change was already examined in the context of workplace practices that enhance productivity growth; this chapter illuminates the issue in the context of wages and employment.

Even if there were no endogeneity between trade and technology, the pervasive and widespread diffusion of IT across economic sectors would mean that a wider and wider swath of the economy and workforce would face the forces of rapid technological change and the business cycles associated with that investment cycle. Data show that IT investment and IT occupations (at both IT and non-IT firms) go hand in hand. So with widespread diffusion of IT throughout the economy, the technology cycle (such as the boom-bust and slow recovery during 1995–2004) generates a business cycle that affects an increasingly larger segment of the US economy and workforce. Since IT also is an increasingly globalized industry and with communications networks enhancing global links, a greater proportion of activities and workers are exposed to international competition. Therefore, IT and communications do have an explicit role in accelerating structural change and transmitting business cycles to a more globally integrated American economy and workforce.

The transformation of the workplace in the face of networked IT implies rapid changes in the skills that are demanded and, more specifically, rapid depreciation of the skills of incumbent workers in the technology professions. Because more and more labor market functions can be replaced by technology, or fragmented and then carried out from remote locations, the challenge to keep skills current and matched to job demands is greater than ever. The issue of skill depreciation comes on account of IT itself (as technology replaces labor) as well as from communications and network-enabled IT that allows competition to come from labor available abroad.

Finally, a specific interplay between IT, globalization, and the labor markets takes place in America. This is the role that specialized technology immigrant visas play in the US labor market pool of technology professionals.

IT and the US Labor Market

IT and its globalization affect the labor market in a number of ways. First, workers are employed by IT producers—that is, at hardware, software, and services (such as database services) firms. Second, with greater investment and use of IT throughout the economy, another group of workers has emerged, those who have skills to implement and integrate the use of IT in the non-IT-producing sector. These are IT professionals, such as computer network software engineers and database administrators, who work in the non-IT-producing sectors (to be sure, some are also employed in the IT-producing sector). Third, an increasing number of workers use IT products on the job, although IT certainly is not their main or even peripheral job activity (e.g., call center staff or financial analysts). Thus, there are three types of workers affected by IT and its globalization: IT occupations at IT-producing firms, IT occupations at IT-using firms throughout the economy, and IT-related occupations (box 5.1).

Even as IT helped the US economy reach unprecedented rates of macroeconomic growth and low unemployment in the 1990s, it also helped usher in an era of significant restructuring of the labor market that continues today. Indeed, the very transformation and networking of business that has generated the macroeconomic gain has, on the other side of the coin, contributed significantly to the restructuring of labor activities. It is difficult to disentangle the available data to determine exactly how important IT has been, or even more narrowly, how important the globalization of IT has been, to the restructuring of the US labor market. Since, arguably, globalization and technological change cannot be disentangled, it would seem best to look at labor market restructuring overall and make inferences regarding the importance of further globalization as facilitated by IT.

Box 5.1   US labor market statistics

Describing the behavior of categories of workers and tracing the implications of the globalization of IT on each of these worker categories presents a variety of challenges.

A first challenge is the extensive data on the labor market from the Bureau of Labor Statistics (BLS). Most official labor data in the United States come from the bureau's three major survey programs: (1) the Occupational Employment Statistics (OES) survey, which gathers data on wages and employment from approximately 400,000 US establishments annually;[1] (2) Current Employment Statistics (CES), a survey of payroll records that covers more than 300,000 businesses on a monthly basis; and (3) the Current Population Survey (CPS), which gathers information on the labor force status of approximately 60,000 households on a monthly basis.[2] The scope of the official survey data collection is substantially larger and consequently more likely to be reliable than any other source of labor market information in the United States.[3]

There are three principal methodologies for presenting official statistical information on jobs in the United States. One is based on occupations, one on geography, and another on economic sectors (industries). The data can be organized by occupation, by geographic region, by industry, or by more than one criterion, i.e., a particular occupation in a given region of the country or a specific industry. For example, the term "US software publishing employment" would refer to all employees in the industries of the total US economy that produce software,[4] irrespective of occupational category (a CEO or a programmer or janitor) or geographic area. "California computer production employment" would refer to all production-floor employees (not the CEO) in the industries of the economy that produce computers in California.[5] Similarly, the term "US engineering jobs" would refer to the occupational category of "engineer," regardless in which industry or geographic area the job is located.[6]

The Bureau of Labor Statistics administers several other surveys to monitor developments in the US labor market. The Dislocated Worker Survey collects data on what happens to US workers after they have lost their job; the Mass Layoff Statistics reports on mass layoff actions (50+) that resulted in workers being separated from their jobs; several national longitudinal surveys collect information at multiple points in time about the labor market and life experiences of several groups of American men, women, and youth; and the Job Openings and Labor Turnover Survey (JOLTS) collects information and data on job openings, hires, and separations. More recently, the American Time Use Survey (ATUS) has been added to collect information on how Americans spend their time.[7]

(box continues next page)

Job Churn, Business Dynamics, and Structural Change

As a backdrop to any specific analysis of the globalization of IT, it is important to point out that there is a remarkable churning of jobs in the US labor market. That is, there is constant creation and destruction of jobs, with about 7 million to 8 million job increases and decreases occurring every quarter in the United States, accounting for about 6.5 to 7.5 percent of all private jobs. Job churn clearly is related to the overall business cycle, with both increases and decreases in numbers of jobs rising during a business cycle upturn. During such a period, with more creation than destruction, employment rises and unemployment rates generally fall (figure 5.1).

Several researchers have investigated the nature of job churn and job change in recent years (Figura 2003, Schultze 2004, Groshen and Potter 2003, Bradbury 2005). They suggest that structural changes in the distribution of firms and jobs around the economy help to explain labor market behavior of the overall economy since 2000. During previous downturns, people were often laid off but then called back by the same employer during the subsequent recovery to do the same job. But in the recent economic cycle, IT changed the landscape to a greater degree than before—new firms needed new workers with new skills, or old firms changed

Figure 5.1   US job turnover, September 1992–June 2005 (thousands)

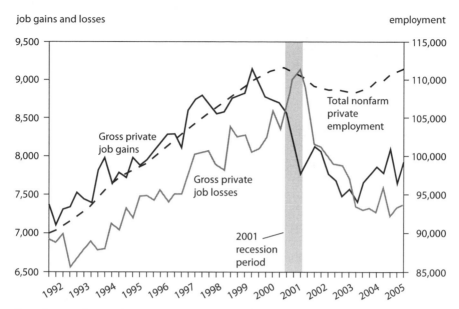

Note: Data are for March, June, September, and December of the years indicated; 1992 includes September and December; 2005 covers March and June.

Source: Bureau of Labor Statistics, Current Employment Statistics and Business Employment Dynamics Statistics.

what they were doing, how they were doing it, and the skills needed in those hired back.

These structural shifts in the demand for labor across different industries result in permanent job losses and delay permanent job gains. That is, when the same types of firms experience a reduction in demand (due, for example, to lower exports or lower consumer demand), they tend to lay off workers who are then recalled when demand picks up again. But if firms think that the downturn in demand is permanent (or the activity can be replicated abroad), then they simply fire workers. It will then take time for firms to believe that an upturn in demand warrants creating permanent positions; if the activity has been permanently moved abroad or replaced by technology, the same positions will never be recreated. Finally, if workers have to move between industry sectors, they have to entertain a similar commitment (for example, to new skills or to a new geographical location) as the firms.

Other research examines these issues through the lens of job tenure. Hypothetically, at one time workers stayed with a single firm for a long time, working their way up the corporate ladder to higher skills, higher wages, and job security (Schultze 1999). Has IT changed this hypothetical?

Tenure by occupational category highlights the difference between the overall trend and the trend in the job categories most affected by technological change. While the overall trend from 1983 to 2002 showed a slight increase in worker tenure, the average tenure for engineers over the same period fell from 6.3 to 5.2 years, and that for math and computer scientists fell from 3.8 to 3.2 years.[1] These data might support the hypothesis that the skills of older technology workers become obsolete. But virtually the entire drop in the average worker tenure for these occupations occurred from 1996 to 2002, a period of very tight US labor markets for these professions. On the other hand, tenure for these two groups lengthened considerably over 2002–04, a period of much looser labor market conditions. By 2004, the average tenure for engineers had lengthened again to 5.8 years, the equivalent of the 1996–98 period, while that of math and computer scientists increased by 1.6 years to 4.8 years, the highest since 1987. There are two interpretations of the behavior of worker tenure in these technology-oriented occupations: voluntary job-hopping was considerable in the IT boom period, then stopped as job opportunities disappeared; and new employees in these occupations entered during the economic boom in the late 1990s but then left after 2000, leaving only those with longer tenure behind. These data do not specifically affirm the notion of a depreciation of skills for technology-intensive occupations.[2]

Against this backdrop of job churn rates and job tenure, is there evidence of any specific role for IT (figure 5.2)? During the boom years when IT was being incorporated widely throughout the economy, job churn increased. After the technology bubble popped, job churn rates (churn/employment) for both job gains and job losses fell for IT employment and less dramatically for all employment. Even as investment in IT started to rebound in 2003, churn rates for IT occupations and for overall employment have stayed low. Sluggish IT investment may temper the diffusion of IT into new sectors and thus slow business transformation, which would tend to reduce the pace of job creation and destruction. A period of strong IT growth may be necessary to boost churn rates again. If this hypothesis holds, the next wave of technological innovation and globalization of IT to deepen its use in the US economy, and in particular to diffuse

---

1. Bureau of Labor Statistics (2002, 2004). Occupational categories here are meta-categories of occupational categories and hence different from those utilized elsewhere in this book.

2. Disaggregating the worker data into different age groups (but all occupation classes) finds some support for the skill depreciation story. Between 1983 and 2002, the job tenure of older men fell substantially, from 7.3 to 5 years for men aged 35–44, from 12.8 to 9.1 years for men aged 45–54, and from 15.3 to 10.2 years for men aged 55–64. However, from 2002 to 2004, men aged 35–44 saw tenure increase slightly again to 5.2 years, while those aged 45–54 saw tenure increase to 9.6 years. Only 45- to 54-year-old men experienced continued shorter average tenure, declining to 9.8 by 2004. Relatively more of these older men whose job tenures shortened were white-collar workers (although through both periods, blue-collar workers were more likely to be displaced). So skill depreciation induced by technological change may be taking its toll on the older workers—or they may be suffering age discrimination more generally.

Figure 5.2 Job churn and IT investment contribution to real GDP growth, 1992–2005 (percent)

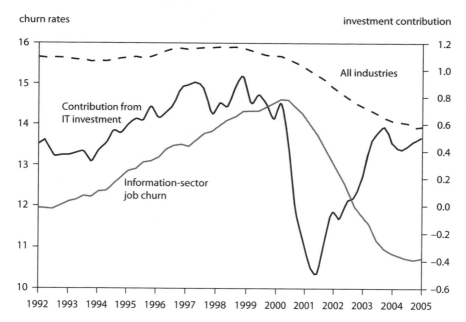

Note: Three-year moving average.

Sources: Bureau of Economic Analysis, National Income and Product Accounts, table 1.5.3, www.bea.gov/bea/dn/nipaweb (accessed October 1, 2005); Bureau of Labor Statistics, Business Employment Dynamics Statistics, www.bls.gov/bdm (accessed October 1, 2005).

it more broadly into the lagging sectors, could propel a new round of business transformation, a rise in job churn (both job losses and job creation), and a second wave of enhanced productivity growth based on that transformation.

IT, Jobs, and the Business Cycle

From an economywide perspective, the higher productivity growth associated with investment and integration of IT translates into higher potential employment and a lower unemployment rate consistent with sustained low inflation. In the mid-1990s, as the US unemployment rate fell below 5.5 percent, pundits and economists thought wage-cost pressures would mount and raise inflation. Federal Reserve Chairman Alan Greenspan interpreted the productivity gains from IT as raising labor productivity and lowering the nonaccelerating inflation rate of unemployment (NAIRU). Thus the Federal Reserve kept interest rates low for a while longer, adding many more jobs to the US economy than would have otherwise been the case.

Figure 5.3 Unemployment rates, total and selected categories of IT-related occupations, 1983–2004

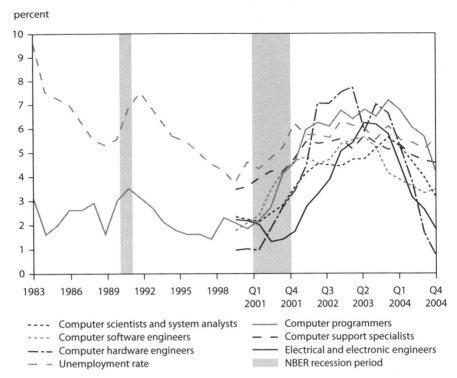

percent

| 1983 | 1986 | 1989 | 1992 | 1995 | 1998 | Q1 2001 | Q4 2001 | Q3 2002 | Q2 2003 | Q1 2004 | Q4 2004 |

- - - - Computer scientists and system analysts
- - - - Computer software engineers
— - — Computer hardware engineers
— — Unemployment rate

———— Computer programmers
— — Computer support specialists
———— Electrical and electronic engineers
░░░ NBER recession period

Notes: Annual data from 1983–99 and four quarter moving averages from 2000–05.

Sources: Economic Policy Institute and Bureau of Labor Statistics.

But IT does not eliminate the business cycle; indeed, the widespread diffusion of IT throughout the US economy appears to have accentuated the impact of the business cycle on workers in the IT profession. As IT becomes more deeply integrated throughout the economy, workers with IT skills will be more exposed to the general business cycle because they are not necessarily working in the IT sector but rather in IT occupations throughout the economy. Data suggest that heretofore, employment of engineers and computer programmers was less cyclical than the economy as a whole, but that now the unemployment rate dynamics for these professions look much more similar to those of the economy as a whole (figure 5.3). In fact, by the end of the 1990s, two-thirds of IT professionals worked outside the IT-producing sector (hardware and services/software).

Not only do those in IT occupations face business-cycle risk, some also face explicit technology risk. Following the completion of Y2K work, as well as the decline of the technology boom and the drop in IT investment, it is not surprising that jobs for IT professionals shrank and unemployment rates for these occupations rose dramatically. But certain occupations (such as computer programmers) face additional risk consistent with an increased "commoditization" of these skills. The fragmentation of the production process of software and the advent of communications links change the skills demanded in the United States and allow some of these skills to be purchased abroad.

IT, Skill Demands, and Dispersion of Earnings in the United States

One of the more notable and intensively studied features of the US labor market during the past 25 years has been the evolution in the dispersion of earnings in the economy.[3] Is there an identifiable role for IT? One hypothesis is that the rising wage dispersion in the United States (compared with other industrial countries) mirrors differential US productivity performance, which, as noted, is driven in part by diffusion of IT. This section takes a look at the labor market side of the story.

Recent research has focused on the particular role for IT in affecting what people do on the job, what skills are demanded, and the wage premium received in the marketplace by those tasks and skills. The link between the globalization, price, and widespread use of IT in the US economy suggests a relationship between globalization and wage dispersion. To the extent that the bulk of the price decline and the power capability of computers and software come from technological innovation, then it is technology, not globalization per se, that is the most important factor affecting wage dispersion in the US economy. From the perspective of a policymaker (as well as the public), the globalization versus the technology effect may engender quite different reactions, even if in the end they have quite similar policy implications.

Much of the original research focused on IT capital investment as driving skill-biased technological change. Individual workers and classes of workers in firms and in industries that use IT tended to also have higher skills, as measured by educational attainment, along with higher earnings (Krueger 1993). Exactly why IT investment raised skill demands, and how that might be related to educational attainment, was not clear and spawned a second stage of research that focused on how workplace practices and product characteristics in a sector interact with IT investment and worker skills to raise the level of skills demanded in the workplace (Bresnahan, Brynjolffsson, and Hitt 2002).

---

3. A large literature on the widening of wage inequality in the United States includes Bound and Johnson (1992); Katz and Murphy (1992); Levy and Murnane (1992); Katz and Autor (1999); Goldin and Katz (2001); Acemoglu (2002); Baily and Kirkegaard (2004); Autor, Katz, and Krueger 1997; and Dunne et al. 2000.

A related question when analyzing the progress of technological diffusion through the economy over time is whether the wage premium received by those skilled enough to use computers was durable or would tend to disappear as computer use became a pervasive requirement of many jobs. Research that disaggregates workers and classifies them by educational attainment shows that the behavior of the wage premium varies by worker education (Valletta and MacDonald 2004). Controlling for various worker characteristics that are known to affect wages (such as age, race, sex, marital status, veteran, union, part-time, and rural/urban), the wage premium to computer use for workers without a bachelor's degree fell from the peak of the wage premium in 1993 (about 22 percent) to about a 15 percent wage premium in 2001. In contrast, for workers otherwise similar except for having a bachelor's degree or higher, the wage premium contracted initially but then widened dramatically—the wage premium to computer use for college-educated workers rose to more than 30 percent by 2001. So, pervasive computer use by workers with lower rates of educational attainment eliminated any wage premium, whereas pervasive computer use by workers with higher rates of educational attainment accentuated their wage premium.

The results suggest that the wage premium that accrues from on-the-job computer use indeed narrowed for most workers as the share of workers using computers as an integral job requirement increased. That the growth in college-educated workers tended to slow over this period also is consistent with the higher wage premium enjoyed by those workers (Card and Lemieux 2000). Did the nature of the jobs change in such a way as to put the workers with lower educational attainment at risk as a result of technological innovation that eliminates their jobs in favor of a computer (e.g., voice and key response technology in answering services) or a foreign worker via low-cost telecommunications networks and codified activities (such as call centers or programmers)?

Key insights on differential returns to computer use come from research on how the availability and price of IT computing capability change tasks (Levy and Murnane 2004; Autor, Levy, and Murnane 2001, 2002). IT complements and enhances some tasks (those that involve problem-solving, judgment, and communications skills) and thus raises the demand for workers in those jobs. IT substitutes for other tasks (those that involve routines that follow explicit rules) and thus reduces the skills demanded by workers in those jobs. This augments the wage premium enjoyed by those using computers for complex tasks on the job and reduces any wage premium heretofore enjoyed by now-routine jobs, even those that may involve use of a computer.[4]

A particularly important result of this research is that the drive to change task content is industry-based. That is, industries that intensively use business processes characterized by routines and explicit rules have invested

---

4. See Wilson (2004) for an example of this substitution for low-skilled workers by software.

the most in IT, thus changing the mix of tasks between those done by people and those done by IT. IT-intensive industries increase their demand for labor with the skills characterized by judgment, problem solving, and communications, and reduce their demand for workers who performed the routine tasks following explicit rules. Within these industries, tasks did not shift away from lower-education workers to higher-educated ones. Rather, the shift in type of task intensive in the occupational mix was found to be pervasive at all educational levels. This research puts the role for IT directly at the heart of wage dispersion in the United States, not so much as it relates to educational attainment across all sectors but as it relates to tasks done within the industry sector.

From a number of different perspectives, factors that have reduced the price of IT and thus facilitated more investment in IT differentially affect US workers with different levels of educational attainment, and who do different tasks in different sectors. Greater investment in IT in some industries yielded higher returns to those workers with educational attainment beyond high school. Industries whose business processes favored investment in IT moved the task mix in favor of workers with higher skills, as often proxied by educational attainment. All told and through several channels, IT appears to play a role in the rising earnings dispersion observed in the data.[5] To the extent that the globalization of IT reduces its price and promotes its diffusion, globalization and IT appear to work together to raise earnings inequality in America.

Globalization of Business Services and White-Collar Jobs

IT and communications networks are not just a US phenomenon. Increasingly, other countries are investing in these technologies, so more cross-border services trade is inevitable. Moreover, because IT and communications networks enable the fragmentation, digitization, and codification of all sorts of services activities, the potential for international trade in services goes well beyond the narrow confines of IT services and software. Chapter 4 discussed how the globalization of IT services and software, in particular, portends a second wave of IT-based productivity growth in the United States. What does the globalization of services to date tell us about the potential impact on different kinds of workers?

Which Workers Are Exposed to Globalization of Services?

Assessing the impact of increased globalization of services on workers first requires identifying which services activities and occupations have

---

5. However, Lawrence Mishel and Jared Bernstein (2003) do not find a relationship between computer use and increased wage dispersion.

the greatest potential exposure to technology-enabled international trade. While it might be desirable to distinguish between occupations at risk for cross-border trade replacement and technology replacement, this is difficult to do, for the very reason that trade and technological change are endogenous.

Nevertheless, one approach, by the Organization for Economic Cooperation and Development (OECD) Working Party on the Information Economy, uses a methodology to identify which occupations may be affected by globalization of services (Vickery and van Welsum 2005).[6] The OECD suggests that workers in occupations with tasks characterized by four criteria are at potential high risk of being affected by technology-enabled international trade: (1) an intensive use of information technologies; (2) out-put that can be traded or transmitted using IT-enabled trade in services; (3) tasks with high explicit information or "codified knowledge"; and (4) little face-to-face contact required.

Examining data from several countries, the OECD classified 68 US occupations at risk from offshore outsourcing. From 1995 to 2002, the share of total employment in the United States in these occupations declined from 19.2 to 18.1 percent. Among the countries examined, only the United States experienced a decline in the share of affected occupations.[7] This may be a direct effect of increased job loss to offshore suppliers of these services, but may also come from more extensive adoption of transformative technology in the United States compared with other countries, which would lead to more American jobs disappearing sooner as they become automated or digitized.

Another data-driven approach to estimating the share of the US workforce potentially at risk from global forces considers the geographic concentration of occupations and industries (Jensen and Kletzer 2005). Geographically concentrated production likely exhibits economies of scale, which is positively related to tradability, whereas geographically dispersed production is less likely to be tradable on account of characteristics such as weight, local regulations, or requirements of face-to-face delivery. Thus, services occupations and industries that are highly geographically concentrated in the US economy may be more likely to be tradable domestically

---

6. Another study with a similar approach is Bardhan and Kroll (2003). The OECD does not take into account three factors mentioned in Bardhan and Kroll: a high wage differential with similar occupations in destination countries, low set-up barriers, and low social networking requirements.

7. The share of total employment made up by occupations at risk of being affected by offshore outsourcing may also decline if this group has lower employment growth than the economy as a whole. Such a scenario may also be caused by offshore outsourcing, as the phenomenon, while not causing an absolute decline in employment, may cause employment growth to rise less than would otherwise have been the case in affected occupations.

and may therefore have greater potential to be traded internationally on account of globalized IT and networks. The research finds that although the services industries are generally less potentially tradable than manufacturing sectors, more workers in services industries may be affected by trade forces because services represent a larger share of employment in the US economy. About 14 percent of employment in US services industries is potentially tradable, as compared to about 12 percent of manufacturing employment. Since what matters for potential exposure to international forces is occupation, not industry, some workers in "nontradable" sectors still can be affected. So over the whole labor force, some one-third of employment could potentially be tradable!

What do we know about these workers? Controlling for worker characteristics and for the sector in which they work, Bradford Jensen and Lori Kletzer (2005) find that workers in tradable services occupations earn about 17 percent more than similar workers in nontradable services occupations. On the other hand, these workers also face a more volatile job environment, with higher rates of job loss. Bringing these characteristics together with others already noted, it can be said that these highest-earning, yet volatile, occupations appear to be in the same sectors that have the highest IT intensity and make the greatest contribution to productivity growth, and where there is comparative advantage in international trade.

A third view on prospects for wages and employment is the projections by the Bureau of Labor Statistics (BLS) for growth (and decline) in occupations, which may shed light on technological replacement of jobs versus technology-enabled global replacement of jobs. A BLS report issued in February 2006 projects that four of the top 10 and six of the top 20 occupations that will grow most rapidly between 2004 and 2014 will be IT-skilled occupations, including network systems and data communications analysts; network, computer systems, and database administrators; and software application and systems software engineers (BLS 2006). For these IT occupations, projected growth of 45 percent is 3.5 times the projected growth of jobs overall in the economy. Because of the higher estimated income elasticity of demand for the products and activities that workers with these skills produce, demand for these workers is projected to expand at well more than the rate of growth of the economy overall. On the other hand, the BLS projects an acceleration in the rate of decline of certain occupations expected to be replaced by technology or characterized by a more routine and codified set of skills, such as data entry, word processing, and typing. For computer programmer occupations, the rate of growth is projected to be well below that for the economy as a whole.[8]

---

8. See the appendix to the BLS report at ftp://ftp.bls.gov (accessed March 15, 2006).

What Do Occupation Data Reveal?

Detailed data highlight several additional perspectives on the US labor market. Since internationally tradable occupations have the potential to cut across industry sectors, employment data should be categorized by occupation (software programmer) rather than sector (information publishing). In addition, it is important to cut through the boom-and-bust period, using the longest time period of consistent data available.[9] What do these data say about trends in US employment in tradable sectors and occupations?

First, the mix of jobs has moved relatively more toward those services occupations thought to be most affected by globalization and technological change (table 5.1). For example, business and financial occupations never declined even through the recession; computer and math occupations (mostly the former) have recovered to the previous technology-boom peak; and architecture and engineering occupations (mostly the latter) have nearly recovered to the previous peak.

Second, over the whole economy, the main decline in jobs has been in the manufacturing sector, but about 20 percent of the job loss in the manufacturing sector is in services occupations within manufacturing industries. This points to the fact that IT, which makes possible the international production of goods, also impacts services workers at manufacturing firms. On the other hand, the services occupations in the manufacturing sector rebounded after the 2001 recession, whereas production occupations did not. Finally, management occupations have been particularly hard hit. Whether this is due to the ability of IT to "flatten" the management hierarchy is an open question.

The occupational categories in table 5.1 are too broad to distinguish skill characteristics that might match the analyses of skill class discussed above. Detailed data on occupations in IT-related fields point to how technological change and globalization together may affect jobs and wages in the US labor market (table 5.2).

Low-wage workers who use IT appear to be particularly hurt by the combined effect of technology and international trade. These occupations, which in general earn about $25,000 annually—telemarketers, switchboard operators, telephone operators, computer operators, data entry keyers, word processors and typists, and office machine operators—experienced very large job losses (almost 712,000) over the entire period of available data (from 1999 to November 2004). The decline represents about 30 percent of all those employed in these categories as of 1999. Over the five-year period, these occupations never experienced a boom and are not likely to return to the United States or indeed anywhere, to the extent that they have been replaced by technology itself.

---

9. See Kirkegaard (2004) for a detailed discussion of alternative BLS data.

Table 5.1 US employment, 1999–2005 (millions)

Sector/occupation	1999	2000	2001	2002	May 2003	May 2004	November 2004	November 2005
Total nonfarm private employment	110.0	111,643	109.3	108.5	108.3	109.8	110.6	112.4
Manufacturing	17.3	17,175	15.7	14.9	14.6	14.3	14.3	14.3
Private services providing	85.4	87,071	86.2	86.3	86.5	87.9	88.6	90.1
Total IT occupations[a]	6.1	6,383	6.1	5.9	5.8	5.8	5.9	n.a.
Of which:								
Nonproduction occupations	5.6	5,875	5.6	5.5	5.5	5.5	5.6	n.a.
Production occupations	0.5	508	0.4	0.4	0.4	0.3	0.3	n.a.
Management occupations[b]	8.1	7,783	7.2	7.1	6.7	6.2	6.1	6.4
Business and financial occupations[b]	4.4	4,619	4.7	4.8	4.9	5.1	5.3	5.1
Computer and mathematical occupations[b]	2.6	2,933	2.8	2.8	2.8	2.9	2.9	2.9
Architecture and engineering occupations[b]	2.5	2,576	2.5	2.4	2.4	2.4	2.4	2.4
Of which engineers	1.1	1,198	1.2	1.2	1.2	1.2	1.3[c]	n.a.

n.a. = not available

a. IT occupations as defined by the US Department of Commerce in *Digital Economy* 2002 and 2003, annual data.

b. The November 2005 number has been generated using the rate of change from November 2004 to November 2005 in the seasonally unadjusted data from the Bureau of Labor Statistics, Current Population Survey, series LNU02032453 (Management), LNU02032454 (Business and Finance), LNU02032455 (Computer and Mathematical) and LNU02032456 (Architecture and Engineering) on the November 2004 data.

c. For time consistency, the current Standard Occupational Classification (SOC) category 17-2199 "Engineers, All Other," existing only in 2004 has been excluded. As such, in November 2004, total engineering employment in the United States was 153,000 higher (at 1.40 million) than the data total indicated in this table.

Source: Bureau of Labor Statistics, Occupational Employment Statistics, www.bls.gov/oes/home.htm (accessed October 1, 2005).

Table 5.2 US technology-related occupations, 1999 to end-2004

Occupation	Number of employees		Total change	Percent change	Annual wage, 2004 (dollars)	Annual real wage change 1999–2004 (percent)
	1999	End-2004				
Call center–type occupations						
Telemarketers	485,650	407,650	–78,000	–16.1	23,520	–0.3
Telephone operators	50,820	36,760	–14,060	–27.7	29,980	–0.3
Low-wage technology workers						
Switchboard operators, including answering service	248,570	202,980	–45,590	–18.3	22,750	0.3
Computer operators	198,500	133,230	–65,270	–32.9	33,140	0.8
Data entry keyers	520,220	307,400	–212,820	–40.9	24,560	0.6
Word processors and typists	271,310	161,730	–109,580	–40.4	29,800	1.6
Desktop publishers	37,040	30,340	–6,700	–18.1	34,210	–0.7
Electrical and electronic equipment assemblers	387,430	207,050	–180,380	–46.6	27,960	2.5
Semiconductor processors	42,110	43,420	1,310	3.1	32,080	0.6
Total call center and low-wage technology workers	**2,241,650**	**1,530,560**	**–711,090**	**–31.7**	**26,539**	**0.7**
Comparable production workers in the manufacturing sector				–19.0		
Total mid-level IT workers						
Computer support specialists	462,840	491,680	28,840	6.2	43,660	–0.5

High-wage technology workers

Computer and information scientists, research	26,280	26,950	670	2.5	90,860	3.7
Computer programmers	528,600	396,100	−132,500	−25.1	66,480	1.3
Computer software engineers, applications	287,600	439,720	152,120	52.9	78,570	1.1
Computer software engineers, systems software	209,030	321,120	112,090	53.6	83,460	2.2
Computer systems analysts	428,210	497,100	68,890	16.1	69,470	1.2
Database administrators	101,460	100,420	−1,040	−1.0	64,380	1.6
Network and computer systems administrators	204,680	262,930	58,250	28.5	62,300	1.9
Network systems and data communications analysts	98,330	176,840	78,510	79.8	64,080	0.3
Computer hardware engineers	60,420	79,670	19,250	31.9	85,540	2.5
Electrical engineers	149,210	147,120	−2,090	−1.4	75,540	1.6
Electronics engineers, except computer	106,830	133,410	26,580	24.9	78,620	1.8
Total high-wage technology workers	**2,200,650**	**2,581,380**	**380,730**	**17.3**	**71,680**	**1.7**
Comparable total CES employment				3.0		

Sources: Bureau of Labor Statistics, Current Employment Statistics (CES) data, 1999, 2000, 2001, 2002, May 2003, November 2003, and May 2004 national occupational employment and wage estimates, www.bls.gov/ces/home.htm (accessed on October 1, 2005).

On the other hand, jobs held by high-skilled, judgment-oriented, and problem-solving IT workers—applications and systems software engineers, database administrators, and network systems engineers and administrators, earning on average $72,000 annually—increased by about 380,000 from 1999 to November 2004. This represents a 17 percent increase in employment in these high-wage IT professional occupations for the period against a 3 percent increase in employment for the economy as a whole.

However, the data also show the rising skill "bar" against which domestic and foreign workers compete in the global marketplace.[10] Between 1999 and November 2004, the number of "programming" jobs earning on average $65,000 fell by 132,000, or 25 percent of the number of these jobs held as of 1999. Whether US programmers were replaced by workers abroad or whether US programmers upgraded their skills to become systems software and network engineers cannot be determined from the data. Clearly the consequences for both individuals and the US economy differ based on the outcome, with spillover gains to the US economy (and individuals) enhanced by skill upgrading but job destructive for those unable to raise their skills.[11]

In sum, BLS data on IT-related occupations suggest that as US firms have integrated technology into the workplace, there has been a reduction of commoditized jobs and a rise in jobs with "integrating" skills—skills that design, customize, and integrate IT applications and services. These workers, although they are in the occupational category of "IT occupations," work throughout the US economy and have a wealth of sector-specific knowledge that is absolutely crucial to their work. Although some technology skills can be replicated remotely, the knowledge specific to a customer need is unique to the location where the worker resides.

International Trade in Skilled Labor: Cross-Border Movement of IT Professionals

The increased globalization of services has another new element—the cross-border movement of skilled workers. That is, rather than firms fragmenting the production of IT-related services and doing some part of the activity abroad, they import skilled workers to do the job in the United States. During the technology boom period, domestic skilled labor was augmented by US companies' use of temporary foreign labor, predominantly through so-called "intrafirm transfers" of L-1 visa holders—employees

10. Samuelson (2004) argues that "catch-up" by foreign countries leads to pressures on higher-skilled workers.

11. Jensen and Kletzer (2005) examine the dislocated worker survey in the broader context of understanding the consequences of potential trade in services employment. A more detailed examination of labor market data, and continuing to collect these data, are necessary to appropriately design labor market policies.

hired outside the country and then transferred to work at company facilities in the United States—as well as the use of "foreign specialist workers" (H-1B visa holders).[12] After the IT bubble burst, there was an extended period of minimal net job gains, and in particular, an unexpectedly high unemployment rate of IT professionals. The impact of the bust in IT investment and skill depreciation on incumbent US workers has already been discussed. But were the foreign workers a further drag on the wages and employment prospects of incumbent US workers with IT skills?[13] Moreover, looking forward, what do the data suggest with regard to this new international trade in professional labor services for businesses and workers in the US IT services sector?

Characteristics of Visa Holders

How many visa holders are in the United States, where do they come from, and what do they do?[14] It is actually rather difficult to answer these questions, although box 5.2 does provide some of the information available. The longest time series available is on annual admissions, which is the number of times a visa holder enters the United States. Of course, any given visa holder might enter the country more than once a year (figure 5.4). The number of admissions of L-1 and H-1B visa holders rose substantially from 1990–2004. But the statistics clearly reflect the technology and business cycle, with a peak in admissions in 2001 and a decline of about 10 percent from 2001 to 2003, before a modest rebound in 2004.

What do we know about the nationality and occupation of these visa holders? The L-1 visa is for an intrafirm transfer within a multinational enterprise; it is issued for three years, and renewable for either two or two times two more years (a maximum of five or seven), depending on the position within the company. Countries with close economic relations in terms of direct investments in and cross-ownership of companies, such as the United Kingdom, Japan, and Germany, consistently top the list of countries whose citizens are admitted on L-1 visas (Kirkegaard 2005). However, the admissions of L-1 visa holders from India rose tenfold from about 2,000 in 1996 to some 22,000 in 2003. The Indian IT sector developed very rapidly in that decade and about a quarter of the Indian IT sector is fully owned by US-parent multinationals.[15] Both factors would tend to ac-

---

12. H-1B holders must hold a minimum of the equivalent of a US bachelor's degree to be eligible for this visa category, as well as adhere to a list of other requirements. See link to "Temporary Workers" at www.uscis.gov (accessed March 15, 2006).

13. See Tim Gray, "Brain Drain in the Tech World?" ZDNEWS, July 15, 2005; Adam Geller, "Outsourcing Themselves," Associated Press, June 21, 2005; and Richard Ernsberger Jr., "The Big Squeeze," *Newsweek International,* May 30, 2005.

14. This section draws extensively on Kirkegaard (2005).

15. National Association of Software and Services Companies (NASSCOM) IT Industry Fact Sheet 2005, available at www.nasscom.org (accessed March 15, 2006).

Box 5.2   US visas for "highly skilled" workers

First, what data are available to measure "imported" highly educated workers? US immigration authorities register information regarding L-1 and H-1B visa holders in three main ways: the number of times a visa holder has been admitted to the United States, the number of visa petitions granted, and the number of visas actually issued to foreign citizens.[1] Official statistics on admission numbers by visa category are the only data available for the entire period of the 1990s. But clearly the number of times in a year a given group of visa holders is admitted to the United States (i.e., crosses the border) is likely to exceed the annual number of visa petitions granted and issued, particularly since both L-1 and H-1B visas are multiyear visas and may be extended.

Next, detailed statistics on the number of visa petitions granted are available only for the H-1B category and only from 1999 to fiscal year 2003. Some detail on actual issuances at US overseas consular offices of other types of visa—including the L visa—is available from 1996 to 2003.[2]

Finally, the number of actual visas issued is significantly lower than the number of visa petitions granted, as multiple employers (frequently different entities within the same organization) often petition for the same individual worker. On the other hand, an actual H-1B visa issued may last for up to six years, so an individual foreign citizen may be issued only one visa but require two successful three-year H-1B petitions during his or her time in the United States.

All told, the precise number of L-1 or H-1B visa holders working in the United States at any given time cannot be precisely determined, only approximated, from available official data. Nevertheless, bringing together all the data does bring some focus to the issues broached above.

---

1. In all cases the data are collected by fiscal years, rather than calendar years.
2. US Department of State, *Annual Report of the Visa Office,* 2002, 2003, and 2004. The 2003 data are from OECD (2004b).

celerate recent L-1 visa usage by Indian nationality worers. Without more comprehensive data that classifies L-1 visa holders by occupation and distinguishes between stock and flow of workers in the United States (rather than simply by the number of admissions), it is not possible to assess the impact of L-1 visa holders on employment and wages of the US industry as a whole, or within specific occupations, such as computer programmers. Given the importance and widespread use of these visas, additional information on the holders, at least as comprehensive as the H-1B discussion that follows, is warranted.

Turning to H-1B visas, the American Competitiveness and Workforce Improvement Act (ACWIA) of 1998 requires US immigration authorities to collect and present to the US Congress information on the countries of

Figure 5.4 H-1B and L-1 visa holders admitted into the United States, by fiscal year, 1990–2004

number of visa holders

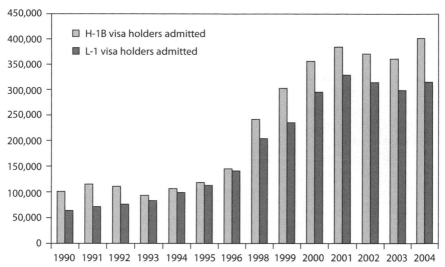

Note: No data available for 1997.

Source: USCIS (2004b).

origin, occupations, educational attainment, and compensation paid to foreign citizens who obtain H-1B status.[16] In addition, the US State Department collects nationality data for H-1B visas issued at overseas US consular offices. Even so, for a number of reasons, these data do not reveal the precise number of H-1B visa holders inside the United States at a given point in time, nor whether a "new" H-1B visa represents a "new" foreign worker.[17]

H-1B visas are issued for three years and can be extended for another three years. Key challenges to interpreting the details of the H-1B data are,

16. Public Law 105-777, Division C, American Competitiveness and Workforce Improvement Act, Section 416(c)(2).

17. Moreover, these data are almost entirely unrelated to the frequently quoted number of "available H-1B visas under the Congressional cap." This cap was 65,000 from 1992 to 1998, before being raised to 195,000 until the end of fiscal year 2003, when it reverted to 65,000. Under the H-1B Visa Reform Act of 2004, an additional 20,000 H-1B visas were added to the 65,000 exclusively for foreign citizens with a master's degree or higher from a US institution of higher education (US Citizenship and Immigration Services press release, May 4, 2005). Finally, many H-1B visas "do not count" toward this cap—in particular, H-1B visa extensions (for a second three-year period), "visas issued to educational organizations," and those issued to "nonprofit institutions." (The latter two categories are not likely to be particularly relevant when considering the impact of H-1B visas on the US IT services sector.)

first, that H-1B visas can be issued to foreign citizens already in the United States on another visa, and second, that they can be extended. Thus, there is a stock-flow issue when interpreting visa data. As the trends regarding visas issued and extended are similar, table 5.3 focuses on "new" H-1B visas granted for initial employment in the United States.[18]

The pattern of H-1B visas has several features related to the technology cycle, but also to the post-9/11 environment for granting visas and to policy responsiveness to labor market concerns. First, the number of H-1B visas granted (both new and extensions) rose from 2000 to 2001 before dropping significantly in 2002 and rebounding modestly in 2003 (row 2 in table 5.3).[19] This pattern is similar to overall technology employment discussed earlier. Second, the share of new H-1B visas granted among the total peaked at 61 percent in 2001, after which both the number and share of new H-1Bs granted dropped (row 3). Finally, the share of new H-1B visas granted to foreign citizens outside the United States dropped significantly in 2002 and 2003, from well above 50 percent of new visas granted to foreign citizens outside the United States (1999 to 2001) to 60 percent or more granted to foreign citizens inside the United States (2002 and 2003) (rows 4 and 5).

Who are the potential H-1B recipients already inside the United States? The foreign citizen could be inside the United States and already part of the US labor force at the time an employer files for the H-1B visa, as the foreign citizen may be transferring from another US visa category.[20] Comparing the peak of the technology boom to the post-boom and 9/11 period, US-located companies did "import" about 270,000 highly skilled workers from abroad from 1999 to 2001, and this group constituted the majority of H-1B visas granted for initial employment to foreign citizens. However, in 2002 and 2003, US-located firms hired many more foreign graduates from US educational institutions and reduced imports of foreign high-skilled labor from abroad. This difference between foreign citizens inside and outside the United States at the time of the H-1B application is further

---

18. For both extended and new visas, see Kirkegaard (2005).

19. This is further supported by data from a General Accounting Office (2000) report, which shows that from 1992–98, the number of "new H-1B non-immigrants approved" was between 50,000 and the annual cap of 65,000. This is substantially lower than the approximate 100,000 entries of H-1B visa holders seen in figure 5.4. However, the data from the GAO publication refer only to those H-1B visas granted, which count toward the annual Congressional cap.

20. For example, a transfer of visa status could occur if an alien transfers from an academic F-1 visa, which gives the alien an option of one year of work (called optional practical training, or OPT) in the United States after graduation from an accredited US educational institution with a bachelor's degree or higher academic degree. An H-1B visa granted to such a student would not result in an addition to the US labor force if the visa were granted to a student at a time when he or she was already working in the United States during his or her OPT.

Table 5.3　US Citizenship and Immigration Services statistics on successful H-1B petitions, fiscal 1999–2003

	1999[a] (1)	2000 (2)	2001 (3)	2002 (4)	2003 (5)
Petitions for initial employment					
1　Number of times an H-1B visa holder was admitted into the United States	302,326	355,605	384,191	370,490	360,498
2　Total number of H-1B petitions granted (percent of admittances)	n.a.	257,640 (72)	331,206 (86)	197,537 (53)	217,340 (60)
3　Of which: Number of H-1B petitions granted for initial employment (percent of total petitions granted)	134,400 (n.a.)	136,787 (53)	201,787 (61)	103,584 (52)	105,314 (48)
4　Of which: Alien was outside the United States at the time of employer petition (percent of total initial employment petitions granted)	81,100 (60)	75,785 (55)	115,759 (57)	36,494 (35)	41,895 (40)
5　Of which: Alien was in the United States at the time of employer petition (percent of total initial employment petitions granted)	53,300 (40)	61,002 (45)	85,320 (43)	67,090 (65)	63,419 (60)
6　Of which: Number 1 country of origin (percent of total)	India 63,900 (48)	India 60,757 (44)	India 90,668 (45)	India 21,066 (20)	India 29,269 (29)
7　Of which: Number 2 country of origin (percent of total)	China 12,400 (9)	China 12,333 (9)	China 16,847 (8)	China 11,832 (11)	China 11,144 (11)
8　Of which: Number 3 country of origin (percent of total)	United Kingdom 4,400 (3)	Canada 5,465 (4)	Canada 9,184 (5)	Canada 7,893 (8)	Canada 6,201 (6)
9　Of which: Number 1 occupational group (percent of total) and median earnings		Computer-related occupations 74,551 (55) $50,000	Computer-related occupations 110,713 (55) $51,600	Computer-related occupations 25,637 (25) $55,000	Computer-related occupations 28,879 (27) $50,500

(table continues next page)

Table 5.3 US Citizenship and Immigration Services statistics on successful H-1B petitions, fiscal 1999–2003 *(continued)*

		1999[a] (1)	2000 (2)	2001 (3)	2002 (4)	2003 (5)
10	Of which: Number 2 occupational group (percent of total) and median earnings	n.a.	Occupations in architecture, engineering, and surveying 17,086 (12) $51,480	Occupations in architecture, engineering, and surveying 25,365 (13) $56,485	Occupations in architecture, engineering, and surveying 14,467 (14) $52,000	Occupations in education 15,008 (14) $36,000
11	Of which: Number 3 occupational group (percent of total) and median earnings		Occupations in administrative specializations 11,468 (8) $38,000	Occupations in administrative specializations 15,573 (8) $40,000	Occupations in education 13,996 (14) $35,000	Occupations in administrative specializations 13,892 (13) $38,900
12	Of which: Number employed in IT services industry (percent of total)[b]	n.a.	n.a.	88,613 (44)	17,803 (17)	19,347 (19)
13	Of which: Number employed in IT hardware industry (percent of total)[c]	n.a.	n.a.	4,824 (2)	2,210 (2)	1,554 (1)
14	Addendum: Number of H-1B visas issued by the US State Department (percent of total H-1B petitions granted)[d]	116,513 (n.a.)	133,290 (52)	161,643 (49)	118,352 (60)	107,196 (49)
15	Addendum: Number of H-1B visas issued by the US State Department to Indian nationals (percent of total H-1B petitions granted to Indians)	55,062 (n.a.)	61,530 (49)	74,078 (46)	44,012 (68)	42,245 (53)
16	Addendum: Number of H-1B visas issued by the US State Department to Chinese nationals (percent of total H-1B petitions granted to Chinese)	5,775 (n.a.)	7,489 (33)	9,076 (33)	7,576 (40)	5,608 (28)

(table continues next page)

17 Addendum: Number of H-1B visas issued by the US State Department to British nationals	6,664	7,304	8,462	6,842	6,095

Petitions for continuing employment

1 Number of times an H-1B visa holder was admitted into the United States	302,326	355,605	384,191	370,490	360,498
2 Total number of H-1B petitions granted	n.a.	257,640	331,206	197,537	217,340
3 Of which: Number of H-1B petitions granted for continuing employment (percent of total)	n.a.	120,853 (47)	130,127 (39)	93,953 (48)	112,026 (52)
6 Of which: Number 1 country of origin (percent of total)	n.a.	India 63,940 (53)	India 70,893 (54)	India 43,914 (47)	India 49,897 (45)
7 Of which: Number 2 country of origin (percent of total)	n.a.	China 10,237 (8)	China 10,483 (8)	China 7,009 (7)	China 8,919 (8)
8 Of which: Number 3 country of origin (percent of total)	n.a.	Canada 2,900 (2)	Canada 3,542 (3)	Canada 3,867 (4)	Canada 4,959 (4)
9 Of which: Number 1 occupational group (percent of total) and median earnings		Computer-related occupations 73,875 (61) $65,000	Computer-related occupations 80,684 (62) $69,000	Computer-related occupations 49,477 (53) $64,739	Computer-related occupations 54,235 (48) $63,000
10 Of which: Number 2 occupational group (percent of total) and median earnings	n.a.	Occupations in architecture, engineering, and surveying 14,298 (12) $65,000	Occupations in architecture, engineering, and surveying 15,023 (12) $68,000	Occupations in architecture, engineering, and surveying 10,730 (11) $63,600	Occupations in architecture, engineering, and surveying 14,292 (13) $64,756

Table 5.3   US Citizenship and Immigration Services statistics on successful H-1B petitions, fiscal 1999–2003 *(continued)*

	1999[a] (1)	2000 (2)	2001 (3)	2002 (4)	2003 (5)
11 Of which: Number 3 occupational group (percent of total) and median earnings		Occupations in administrative specializations 6,951 (6) $50,000	Occupations in administrative specializations 8,221 (6) $54,429	Occupations in education 7,250 (8) $39,000	Occupations in administrative specializations 9,180 (8) $50,000
12 Of which: Number employed in IT services industry (percent of total)	n.a.	n.a.	60,071 (46)	35,814 (38)	39,323 (35)
13 Of which: Number employed in IT hardware industry (percent of total)	n.a.	n.a.	4,347 (3)	2,293 (2)	3,774 (3)

n.a. = not available

a. Period from May 1998 to July 1999.

b. Defined as North American Industry Classification System (NAICS) categories (3341) Computers and Peripheral Equipment and (3344) Semiconductor and Other Electronic Component Manufacturing.

c. Defined as NAICS categories (5415) Computer Systems Design and Related Services, (5141) Information Services, (5142) Data Processing Services, and (5112) Software Publishers. Data not available for all categories each year.

d. Actual issuance by the US State Department of H-1B visas in 1996, 1997, and 1998 amounted to 58,327, 80,547, and 91,360, respectively. India, China, and Britain ranked one, two, and three, respectively, in terms of visa issuance for 2000–2003, followed by Japan, the Philippines, and Germany. Individual country data provided by the US Office of Public and Diplomatic Liaison, Visa Services.

Note: Shaded areas denote H-1B petitions that are exempt from the congressional cap on H-1B visas.

Sources: US Immigration and Naturalization Service (INS 2000a, 2002a, 2002b); US Citizenship and Immigration Services (USCIS 2003, 2004a); US Department of State, *Report of the Visa Office 2000, 2001, 2002*; and OECD (2004b). It must be emphasized that the USCIS qualifies its annual reports to Congress on H-1B visas by stating that "very little editing has been done to the data," and that, consequently, there may be some errors in the data. Whether these are systematic cannot be discerned.

illustrated by the significantly lower number of H-1B visas actually issued to foreigners at overseas US consular offices—107,200 in FY2003 compared with the 161,643 granted overseas in FY2001 and to the total number of H-1B petitions granted in FY2003 (217,340). Indeed, only about half the H-1B petitions granted result in an actual H-1B visa being issued to a foreigner overseas (row 14).[21]

In terms of country and occupational detail, Indian citizens accounted for about half of all H-1B visa petitions granted in 1999–2001, followed distantly by China, Canada, and Britain. "Computer-related occupations" is by far the biggest occupational category of H-1B recipients, and about half of all H-1B recipients were employed in the US IT services and hardware industry. This suggests that "imported" Indian labor was widespread during the technology boom years. The rapid rise in imported IT workers by US-located firms during the 1990s is evidenced by the fact that, in 1992, only about 6,000 H-1B visas (of approximately 50,000 granted that year) were issued to IT-related occupations (rows 6–8, 9–11, and 12–13).[22]

On the other hand, Indians account for about 70 percent of the total decline in numbers of H-1B visa petitions granted for initial employment from 2001 to 2002 (70,000 of a total decline of 98,000). This decline corresponds closely to the decline in the number of petitions granted in computer-related occupations and the number of petitions granted and employed in the US IT services and hardware sectors.[23] Individual petitions cannot be "cross-tabbed" across petitions, but the similar size of the decline in all three categories suggests that there was a very large decline from 2001 to 2002 in the number of H-1B visas granted for initial employment to Indians in computer-related occupations employed in the US IT services and hardware sectors, and that the level in all of the categories remained low in 2003.[24]

---

21. Row 14 differs from row 4 (49 percent versus 40 percent) because of the timing of the data collection. Row 4 is a snapshot measured at the time of the USCIS granting (or rather receipt of application) of the H-1B petition (regardless of whether the beneficiary was inside or outside the United States), whereas row 14 measures over the entire year how many visas were actually issued and relates them to the number of petitions granted.

22. Fiscal year 1992 was the first year that the H-1B visa could be granted to aliens under the Immigration Act of 1990, and hence most visas granted that year would count against the 65,000 annual cap, especially as no extensions could logically be granted. Earlier, H-1B visas were referred to as "specialty occupation visas" and had no upper limit (GAO 2000, 8).

23. A similar trend is observed for recipients of extensions of H-1B visas, where the number of Indian recipients, computer-related occupations, and IT services and hardware employees all declined by about 30,000 from 2001 to 2002.

24. These data are in part confirmed by other sources. For example, NASSCOM, the Indian IT industry association, estimates that the number of Indian IT professionals traveling to the United States on H-1B visas dropped from 77,000 in 2001 to 33,000 in 2002. NASSCOM expected the number in 2003 to be about 30,000, according to Wipro Ltd.'s 2004 20-F filing with the Securities and Exchange Commission, available at www.sec.gov/edgar (accessed on August 3, 2005).

How large are these numbers in comparison with overall IT employment? In 2002 and 2003, there were nearly 30,000 H-1B visa petitions granted for initial employment in "computer-related occupations" in each year. Occupational detail for L-1 visas is not known. And BLS occupation categories cannot be mapped directly into the visa occupation category. However, the number of jobs in the medium- and high-wage IT occupation categories (as in table 5.2) fell from 2,892,000 to 2,847,000 and then rose to 3,073,000 (2001, 2002, 2004 respectively). There were declines in the number of jobs only in the "programmer" category (which at about 500,000 employed in 1999 was the largest subcategory). Comparing wage rates, foreign workers' average wages—$50,500 in 2003 for new H-1B visa holders in computer-related occupations and $63,000 for H-1B holders continuing their employment, probably with three years of work experience—lies between the average wage for the medium- and high-wage IT occupations (table 5.2). Over 2001–04, average wages for high-wage IT workers rose substantially, about twice the rate for the mid-level IT occupations. Would employment and wages of incumbent workers have been different over the period if there had been no H-1B or L-1 visas? More detailed information on numbers, occupations, and wages is needed for this research question.

Taking the 1990s as a whole, the H-1B program reflects the US technology and business cycles as well as homeland security issues. US companies imported foreign high-skilled labor in periods of rapid economic growth (such as 1999–2001), while in periods of slower US economic growth (2002–03) US companies hired highly skilled foreign graduates coming out of US universities and other high-skilled foreign citizens already in the United States. Additional research is needed to gauge the impact of these imported workers on the incumbent workforce, including the existing stock of visa holders.

Corporate Use of Visas and Wages Paid

Which US companies hire H-1B or L-1 visa holders? Detailed data reveal only which US-located companies *apply* for permits to employ H-1B visa-holding foreign citizens.[25] But these data cannot be used to infer anything about the number of H-1B visa holders that a US company might employ in the United States. This is because an application for an H-1B visa entails two separate filings: a filing of a labor condition application (LCA) request at the Department of Labor Office of Foreign Labor Certification (DOL-FLC) and a filing for an H-1B visa with the US Citizenship and Im-

---

25. In 2000, the INS published a list of the leading US employers of H-1B visa holders in the first part of FY2000 (INS 2000b). The US Department of Labor maintains an online database of all the US companies that file the required LCA petitions for employing H-1B visa holders. See www.flcdatacenter. com/CaseData.aspx (accessed March 15, 2006).

migration Services (USCIS), with the former required for the latter petition to be granted. The filing by an employer of an LCA does not mean that an H-1B visa will automatically be issued—indeed, the Department of Labor explicitly states that no one-to-one relationship exists. In fact, there typically are three times as many LCA requests as the number of H-1B visa petitions granted.[26] With such large discrepancies at the aggregate level, the FLC database cannot be used to infer anything valid about the numbers of H-1B visa holders that individual companies employ.

An alternative approach examines selected large US-located employers of H-1B visa holders in 1999–2000 using special data for actual H-1B visa petitions granted directly from the US Immigration and Naturalization Service (INS 2000b) and cross-tabbed with information from filings with the Securities and Exchange Commission (SEC) (table 5.4). Most of the corporate users of H-1B workers from late 1999 to early 2000 were household names in the US IT industry, including Motorola, Oracle, Cisco, Intel, and Microsoft. But the US finance industry and major educational institutions also were well represented. Only seven of the top 100 US-located employers were Indian IT services companies. On the other hand, several companies, both US and Indian, relied heavily on foreign H-1B (and L-1) visa holders in their US workforce in 2003.[27] This could be taken as an indication that some companies have as their primary US business model to bring in foreign (in all likelihood mostly Indian) IT workers to work in the United States.

Even if H-1B and L-1 visas are crucial to the business model of some firms, does this extend to paying wages below the prevailing wage of the incumbent workforce? The DOL-FLC database of employer-filed LCAs contains data for both the wage to be offered the individual H-1B recipient should an H-1B visa be granted by the USCIS, as well as the regional prevailing wage for the occupation in question. By taking all the individual FLC petitions for each of the Indian companies and similar American companies listed in table 5.4, one can see whether, for petitions for FY2004, these companies systematically underpaid their foreign workers and thus directly put downward pressure on US wages in IT occupations. Looking at all incidences of filings, a scatter plot of the prevailing wage against FLC

---

26. See www.flcdatacenter.com/CaseData.aspx (accessed March 15, 2006).

27. Many of the companies in table 5.4 do not make H-1B or L-1 data available. The companies for which data are available generally provide these data in SEC filings as part of their general description of their business model and risk associated with it. Hence, companies are likely to provide information about the number of H-1B/L-1 visa holders in their US workforce if the number is so big that it is important to their business model. For public companies that do not report such data, it is likely that the share of H-1B/L-1 visa holders is low and not crucial to the business model. The same cannot be said for privately held Indian companies, which do not provide filings to the SEC or other similar entities. For the private Indian companies that are in direct competition with public Indian companies, the average number of H-1B/L-1 visa holders is likely to be of the magnitude found in those in Indian companies and US competitors for which data are available.

Table 5.4   Leading US employers of H-1B visa holders

Rank	Company	Number of H-1B visas approved[a]	Country of parent company	Share of US workforce on H-1B or L-1 visas, 2003–04 (percent)
1	Motorola Inc.	618	United States	n.a.
2	Oracle Corporation	455	United States	n.a.
3	Cisco Systems	398	United States	n.a.
4	Mastech (iGate)	389	United States	13 (H-1B only)
5	Intel Corporation	367	United States	n.a.
6	Microsoft Corporation	362	United States	n.a.
7	Rapidigm	357	United States	n.a.
8	Syntel Inc.	337	United States	59 (486 H-1B, 268 L-1)
9	Wipro Ltd.	327	India	>50 (1,130 H-1B, 1,491 L1)
10	Tata Consulting Services	320	India	n.a.
11	PWC LLP	272	United States	n.a.
12	PeopleCom Consultancies	261	Unknown	n.a.
13	Lucent Technologies	255	United States	n.a.
14	Infosys Technologies Ltd.	239	India	>50 (3,200 H-1B, 700 L-1)
15	Nortel Networks, Inc.	234	Canada	n.a.
16	Tekedge Corporation	219	United States	n.a.
17	Data Conversion	195	United States	n.a.
18	Tata Infotech	185	India	n.a.
19	Cotilligent USA, Inc.	183	United States	n.a.
20	Sun Microsystems, Inc.	182	United States	n.a.
26	Hewlett-Packard Co.	149	United States	n.a.
33	Birlasoft	128	India	n.a.
35	IBM	124	United States	n.a.
39	Satyam Computer Services	123	India	Close to 100 (687 H-1B, 635 L-1, March 2002)
42	University of Washington	113	United States	n.a.
52	University of Pennsylvania	97	United States	n.a.
58	Merrill Lynch	87	United States	n.a.
65	General Electric	80	United States	n.a.
71	Goldman Sachs	75	United States	n.a.
75	Stanford University	73	United States	n.a.
79	Morgan Stanley	71	United States	n.a.
82	Harvard University	70	United States	n.a.
94	Ramco Systems	63	India	n.a.
99	Yale University	61	United States	n.a.

n.a. = not available

a. Data are for October 1999 to February 2000.

Sources: US Immigration and Naturalization Service (INS 2000b); company 10-K or 20-F filings with the Securities and Exchange Commission; and company Web sites.

petitions shows that, at least for H-1B petitions in FY2004, none of these companies systematically underpaid their foreign workers (figure 5.5).[28] Indeed, the average offered wage was 111 percent of the prevailing wage. None of the individual H-1B requests offered less than 95 percent of the prevailing wage.[29] (However, see box 5.3 and Kirkegaard 2005 for more discussion of "prevailing wage"; moreover, these data are only for H-1B visas, with no comparable information available for L-1 visas.)

Since the employer applies for the H-1B visa on behalf of the foreign recipient, the opportunities for the foreigner to seek employment elsewhere in the United States are conditional upon finding another employer to sponsor him or her. Hence the opportunities for "job-hopping" in search of better wages for H-1B visa holders are limited, which offers employers some scope for downward wage pressure, despite what the FLC filing may state. As such, the official filing data from the FLC database should not be viewed as a definitively valid official data source. Rather, it is simply the best data source available.

Large US IT companies show a similar pattern, with no filings below 95 percent of the prevailing wage and an average offered wage of 116 percent of this prevailing wage (figure 5.5). But US firms show a much wider dispersion of wages offered compared with the Indian firms as well as a higher average wage. This suggests that US firms consider a wider diversity of candidates in terms of skills and specialized knowledge. In contrast, the Indian firms appear to be filing petitions for a more standardized type of worker and at a lower average wage offered. Incumbent US workers in that occupational and skill class could experience a more concentrated exposure to the H-1B candidates being considered by the Indian firms. By the same token, how technology impacts the mix of narrowly defined skills has changed, and this too will affect the prospects for employment and wages, regardless of whether the worker is incumbent or "imported." Both trade and technology point to potential policy initiatives with regard to skill upgrading and job matching for incumbent workers to move away from more exposed occupations. More data and research on the occupations of visa holders and incumbent workers are needed.

---

28. The figures are constructed such that if a dot is above the diagonal line, it indicates that the H-1B visa recipients are offered a wage above the prevailing wage, while if it is below the diagonal, the wage offered is below the prevailing wage. It is important to emphasize that each dot represents a single LCA filing, which may be on behalf of more than one H-1B recipient. The number of dots in the figure is therefore only vaguely indicative of the actual number of individuals on whose behalf a company is applying for H-1B visas. Fiscal 2004 is the only time period for which data for all petitions—whether filed electronically or by fax—are available.

29. Average prevailing wages and offered wages can be calculated and compared for all petitions by the companies in question. However, such "average prevailing and offered wages" are only indicative of the average wages actually offered and paid to H-1B recipients, since it is not known which of the individual cases in the FLC database ultimately received H-1B visas from the USCIS.

Figure 5.5   Labor condition application requests, FY2004 (US dollars)

Tata Consulting Services, Tata Infotech, Wipro, Infosys, Satyam, Birlasoft, and Ramco

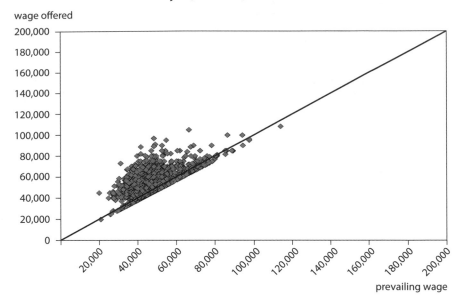

Dell, HP, IBM, Intel, and Microsoft

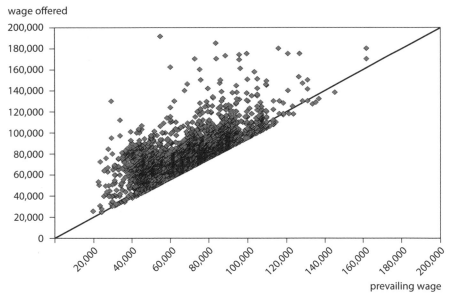

Note: For presentational reasons, five labor condition application filings offering wages above $200,000 were excluded.

Source: Department of Labor, foreign labor certification datacenter, www.flcdatacenter.com.

Box 5.3   H-1B visa holders and the "prevailing wage"

Because wage rates vary so substantially across countries, US law has very specific rules about what H-1B visa holders have to be paid. They must be paid either the actual wage or the prevailing wage. The actual wage is the rate paid by the employer to all other individuals with similar experience, qualifications, education, job responsibilities and functions, specialized knowledge, and other legitimate business factors for the specific employment in question. However, in the absence of similar existing US workers at the workplace, the H-1B recipient must be paid the prevailing wage for the occupational classification in the area of intended employment.

How is the prevailing wage determined for a given H-1B visa petition? A request for a prevailing wage determination may be filed with a local State Employment Security Agency (SESA). Other sources of consultation can be the Bureau of Labor Statistics Occupational Employment Statistics (OES) survey (www.bls.gov),[1] the federal government online wage determination (www.wdol.gov), or other independent authoritative sources, including private compensation surveys by such companies as Watson Wyatt (www.watsonwyatt.com), the Economic Research Institute (www.erieri.com), and the American Society of Employers (www.aseonline.org).

It is the responsibility of the employer that files the H-1B petition to guarantee the truthfulness of the information. Since there are numerous potential sources of information on prevailing wages, can employers choose the lowest estimate? The US Department of Labor must determine whether a source is acceptable as authoritative, and the foreign labor certification will be denied if the prevailing wage information provided is deemed nonauthoritative. Third parties may launch a complaint with the Labor Department alleging inaccuracy of prevailing wage information provided in individual petitions.

US employers are required to post the wage offered to H-1B visa holders at a public location at the workplace. If the majority of H-1B petitions use official prevailing wage data,[2] it seems unlikely that employers can systematically depress wages by providing inaccurate data. On the other hand, federal law CFR 665.731 (d)(4) explicitly states that "[n]o prevailing wage violation will be found if the employer paid a wage that is equal to, or more than 95 percent of, the prevailing wage . . ." (www.dol.gov). Therefore it is essentially legal for US employers to pay H-1B recipients 5 percent less than the prevailing wage—yet that is not the case for the fiscal year 2004 data reported above. However, if US employers are found by the Labor Department to pay their H-1B workforce less than 95 percent of the

(box continues next page)

Box 5.3   H-1B visa holders and the "prevailing wage"   *(continued)*

prevailing wage, they will be required to pay them the full 100 percent. Therefore, companies face no significant financial penalty for not paying their workforce the prevailing wage.[3] While challenges to systematic underpayment of the workforce cannot be dismissed, no data are available from the Labor Department with regard to such investigations.

1. Web sites cited in this box were accessed on March 15, 2006.
2. See appendix A for more on this point as well as details for selected employers in the IT sector.
3. See Kirkegaard (2005) for other, nonfinancial sanctions.

6

Globalization of Innovation

Since the Nobel Prize–winning work of Robert Solow (1957), innovation has been viewed as the cornerstone of economic growth. How is research and development (R&D) related to innovation, and does the type or source of R&D affect the innovative process and thereby growth? The foundations of innovation are research dollars, research scientists, and a policy-supported research system of industry, people, and academic institutions. But the composition of the mix (and of the policies) is not fully known and certainly is not static. Moreover, the lesson from examining IT is that innovations applied to market needs outside the narrow confines of the innovating sector matter a lot for overall productivity and growth; that is, the "D" in R&D—the practical application of research findings to market needs—is crucial and complex. Finally, linking innovation to growth requires having educated customers (consumers and businesses) to demand the output of R&D, a financial sector that is willing to take risks on new ideas, a business climate and managers desirous of using new methods, and workers able to complement the innovations in the workplace. Given the complexity of these linkages, it is not surprising that academic analysis of the relationship between R&D, innovation, and growth is voluminous and mixed in its findings.

An important lens of focus is to gauge and balance the gains to the United States from cheaper innovations obtained through foreign sourcing of science and engineering talent that may lead to even more US productivity growth (through the channels already discussed) against the potential threat of losing the technological edge that could come from innovating only at home. Being the technology leader confers economic gains to the extent that technology is protected by intellectual property law and so yields first-mover revenue gains. But, more generally, failing to retain research talent and development facilities may imply a loss of innovation tailored to domestic needs and local demand. This can have long-term consequences to the extent that innovation responsive to domestic needs is a particularly catalytic source of productivity growth.

This chapter reviews several aspects of the data and academic analysis on the potential implications of a more globalized R&D function, with particular reference to R&D activities in the IT sector. With the globalization process of R&D having just begun, implications must remain speculative.

R&D, Innovation, and Growth

Looking at R&D in the context of the domestic National Income and Product Accounts (NIPA) is one approach to evaluating the importance of R&D in general and the IT sector in particular. In the standard presentation of NIPA, R&D is expensed rather than capitalized as an investment. If it were instead treated akin to software, as investment, then R&D appears to play an important role in productivity performance and US economic growth—perhaps accounting for between 5 and 9 percent of growth in GDP over 1996–2000 and between 3 and 10 percent of GDP over 1961–2000. The upper range of importance is derived from the importance of R&D spillover effects; that is, R&D appears to have a particularly high rate of return, indicative of its ancillary effects beyond the sector in which it is invested.[1]

In the academic analysis, the relationship between trend productivity growth and innovation as measured by domestic R&D variables such as patents, expenditures, and researchers has a long history. Despite the logical relationship whereby R&D spending should increase measures of innovation (patents and citations) and thereby increase productivity, finding these positive correlations has been challenging. This has been disappointing to policymakers who see research funding as a sure-fire way to enhance growth.

The more recent research that links globalization, R&D, and growth points to a possible answer as to why the logical relationship is not necessarily evidenced in the data. Dollars spent on research tend to spur productivity growth only when the environment is open and competition is strong. For example, R&D expenditures in sectors that are protected from global competition do not translate into higher labor productivity in those sectors, whereas R&D expenditures in sectors facing global competition do enhance productivity both for high- and low-technology types of products (Baygan and Mann 1999).

Other research points to ways a country can obtain growth-enhancing technological innovations beyond its own research undertakings. Two ways

---

1. See Fraumeni and Okubo (2005) for a detailed discussion of the accounting methodology and a possible R&D "satellite" account for the NIPA.

that globalization enhances the relationship between R&D and growth are trade in imported intermediate products that embody innovation and direct investment that may fund and transmit innovation (Coe and Helpman 1995; Bayoumi, Coe, and Helpman 1996; Eaton and Kortum 1996; Keller 2001a and 2001b; Lee and Wan 2001). Analysis shows that countries with greater exposure to trade, particularly imports of capital goods, intermediates, and R&D-intensive products, enjoy greater technology spillovers. The results are particularly strong for smaller countries and those farther away from the technological frontier.

The United States is big and at the technology frontier, so do the benefits of foreign R&D, foreign investment in the US economy, and imports of technology-intensive products hold for the United States? The answer is yes. Inward foreign direct investment (FDI) (as measured by the detailed activity of workers in the affiliates of foreign multinationals in the United States) is a quantitatively important source of US productivity growth. Research finds that US productivity growth is about 30 percent higher in industry sectors where there is inward FDI and high R&D intensity, suggesting positive spillovers between global and domestic technological innovation. Perhaps 14 percent of the increase in productivity growth in the manufacturing sectors between 1987 and 1996 came from inward FDI (Keller and Yeaple 2002).

International spillovers have their greatest impact on domestic productivity when domestic competition works to ensure that innovations are taken up by firms. Research on innovation usually focuses on stimulating innovation and protecting it via property-rights laws. Yet, much of the benefit of international spillovers depends on the ability to generate similar kinds of products on one's own (i.e., to "imitate") (Haskel, Pereira, and Slaughter 2002; Griffith, Redding, and Van Reenan 2000). Robust product-market competition, entry and exit of firms, and responsive labor markets are key to allowing domestic firms to both innovate and imitate other countries' and firms' innovations.

Can IT itself (abstracting from the globalization of IT) affect these linkages and R&D spillovers? IT increases the tradability of ideas and cross-border transfer of innovations, both through communications networks and because IT increases the ability of firms to engage in global production. Moreover, IT increases the tradability of many services that are part of the overall package of IT innovations. Hence, IT is an enabling technology that has its preponderant impact via the new and cheaper ways it allows existing occupations, products, and activities to be organized, produced, and delivered. So globalized IT most likely does enhance R&D spillovers, both into the United States and abroad.

Despite this broad evidence of the importance of global two-way spillovers associated with trade in technologically advanced products, there is a nagging concern that the United States is falling behind international competitors in research intensity or output. Moreover, some question whether the spillover benefits of globalization extend to the research function itself. Instead, globalized R&D may hamper US innovation or hand technological leadership to countries where US firms engage in R&D. One difficulty in assessing the issue is measurement of innovation inputs and outputs.

Information Technology R&D: Who, How Much, and Where?

As was discussed earlier in the context of IT hardware and communications, technological innovation in IT products has been perhaps the most important source of economic gain in the United States over the past decade. Globalization plays an important supporting role, but technological change is key to the price reductions that are so important in driving the growth and diffusion of IT investment and the concomitant acceleration in productivity growth. Thus there is some concern about anecdotes that imply that US IT firms are not just globalizing production and sales but increasingly are globalizing their innovative (R&D) activities. Will the innovation gains accrue to the country in which the innovating actually takes place? And, therefore, will US innovation slacken if R&D is fragmented abroad like so many other activities? Data on R&D workers and funding do confirm that IT is a research-intensive activity, as compared with other sectors of the US economy. The available intrafirm data do not confirm anecdotes that R&D is being fragmented, but some other indicators, available on a more timely basis, do confirm such fragmentation, although implications of this fragmentation are unclear.

Measuring Research Intensity

What are the characteristics of R&D for US industry overall, in the IT sector in particular, and for US-located firms versus affiliates abroad of US-owned firms? If the research intensity of US firms is declining, or if US parent firms are doing more research abroad in their affiliates rather than at home, this trend should manifest itself in declining research intensity of firms in the US economy.

Research intensity can be measured in a number of ways, such as scientists and engineers as a share of total employees, research spending per research employee, or research spending as a share of sales. Several features of the data are worth considering: the change in research intensity over time, the difference in research intensity across different industry sectors, and differences in research intensity of different parts of a multinational enterprise. By almost all of these metrics, the data suggest a rising research intensity for the US economy overall, a much higher and ris-

Figure 6.1   R&D intensity: R&D workers, 1997–2001

R&D workers per 1,000 employees

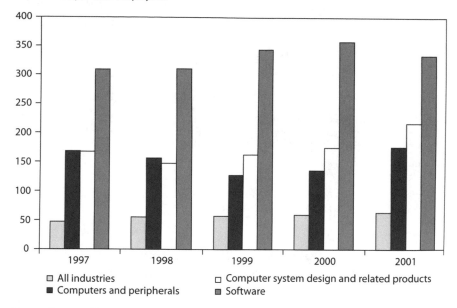

□ All industries
■ Computers and peripherals
□ Computer system design and related products
▨ Software

Sources: Bureau of Economic Analysis, US Direct Investment Abroad: Financial and Operating Data for US Multinational Companies, www.bea.gov (accessed September 30, 2005), and Foreign Direct Investment in the US: Financial and Operating Data for US Affiliates of Foreign Multinational Companies, www.bea.gov (accessed September 30, 2005).

ing research intensity in the IT sectors, and a dramatically lower research intensity at US affiliates abroad compared with their parents in the United States. But most of these data are badly out of date, ending in 2001 or 2003, for such a dynamic activity and for the IT sector characterized by globalization and technological change. Both more timely data and more research to match and analyze the data are needed. Nevertheless, these data are useful to review.

First, consider the level and change in research intensity over time across the whole of the US economy and selected IT sectors (figure 6.1). Research intensity measured by scientists and engineers (research employees) as a share of total employment at the firm addresses how research worker–intensive technologically advanced sectors might be. R&D employment as a share of total employment has risen modestly for the whole economy. One reason for this economy-wide increase is the rising share of IT, which has a much higher research worker intensity. The computer and electronics products sector has 2.8 times more research workers than the economy overall, while software has 5.3 times more.

Table 6.1   R&D spending per full-time equivalent R&D scientist or engineer, 1999–2001

Industry	1999	2000	2001
All industries	179,990	192,322	189,918
Computer and electronic products[a]	172,294	207,637	187,265
Computers and peripheral equipment[b]	(D)	232,125	(D)
Software	153,635	158,554	159,568
Computer system design and related products	(D)	124,254	167,606

(D) = Data suppressed by the BEA for confidentiality reasons.

a. Imputation of more than 50 percent.
b. No imputation.

Source: National Science Foundation Research and Development in Industry statistics, table A39, table A34, and table A38 for 1999, 2000, 2001, respectively.

In the IT sector, research worker intensity is shifting from IT hardware to IT software and services, consistent with the pattern of production and demand already observed. In the software sector, the modest drop in 2001 in research worker intensity is consistent with the bust of the technology bubble, although the offshoring of some software research jobs is also a possibility. The occupation data presented in chapter 5 revealed job losses in only one category of technology professional—programmers—whereas other research-oriented job categories saw job gains.

A second metric addresses how financially intensive the innovation process might be (table 6.1). The very short time series of data reveals mostly that firms producing IT hardware spend more research dollars per worker than firms in software and computer system design, which are more research worker intensive. This matches the relatively more capital-intensive nature of production of manufactured products. Because research spending per worker intensity is about the same for IT firms as for all industries, it appears that the number of R&D workers is the key driver of the higher research intensity of the IT sector. So as IT producers (particularly of services and software) expand as a share of the US economy, the much higher research worker intensity of these sectors should raise the economy-wide average. These data imply that research workers, and their education and skills, are critical to the IT innovative process, particularly as firms move into services and software.

Analysis more specifically focused on the role of globalization in research is revealed in the data for IT multinationals (table 6.2). The difference in research intensity across the form of incorporation of the firm gives important insight into the question of the globalization of R&D. First, as with the other metrics of research intensity, the IT sector's research intensity is much

Table 6.2 Research intensity in multinational firms, 1999 and 2003 (R&D cents per dollar of sales)

| | | | Multinational affiliates | | | | |
| | US parent | | Affiliate in United States with foreign parent | | US affiliate abroad with US parent | | US affiliate abroad: R&D funded by affiliate 1999[a] |
Industry	1999	2003	1999	2003	1999	2003	
All industries (2001)	2.11	2.12	1.34	1.38	0.82	0.77	1.24
Computer and electronic products	8.91	10.79	4.81	5.57	1.70	1.44	1.03
Information and data processing services	(D)	2.68	(D)	(D)	0.27	0.26	(D)
Computer systems design and related services	8.39	10.86	5.58	3.06	0.78	0.96	2.13

(D) = Data suppressed by the BEA for confidentiality reasons.

a. Measured as R&D dollars performed at affiliates/R&D funded by affiliate.

Sources: Bureau of Economic Analysis, US Direct Investment Abroad: Financial and Operating Data for US Multinational Companies, www.bea.gov (accessed September 30, 2005), and Foreign Direct Investment in the US: Financial and Operating Data for US Affiliates of Foreign Multinational Companies, www.bea.gov (accessed September 30, 2005).

higher than that for all industries, and has increased over the short time period of the sample. In terms of research spending as a share of sales, research intensity is very similar comparing IT hardware and IT services (although data processing services has a much lower research spending intensity). This suggests that firms are willing to spend the same amount on new product development for IT hardware as for IT services.

With respect to research by globalized affiliates of a multinational firm, the US parent is vastly more research spending–intensive than its own foreign subsidiaries. For example, in 2003 the "computer and electronic products" parent spent about 11 cents on R&D for each $1 of sales but only spent about 1½ cents or even less on R&D at its foreign affiliates. These data also reveal that the research spending intensity of US-located affiliates of foreign parents is about half that of the US IT parent. Together, these data show that research spending intensity is much higher in the United States and suggest that very little of the R&D dollar is being spent abroad. However, the data lag the most recent innovations in cross-border communications and fragmentation and digitization of services. More current data would improve the analysis of where research spending is being undertaken.

Finally, the 1999 benchmark data show how much of the research being undertaken at the affiliate is funded by and spent at that affiliate. Overall in the industry, the R&D spending at the affiliate is funded by that affiliate with some additional contribution from the parent (1.24). Within the IT sector, in IT hardware, the affiliates' R&D activities are self-funded (1.03), whereas for software and services, it appears that the affiliate gets substantial funds (about double its own funding) from the parent to perform R&D (2.13). Whether the parent would have funded more of its own research at home is unclear. It may be that the parent was funding research at the affiliate that ultimately was destined for the parent's market, not the affiliate's market; or, particularly for IT services, the opposite could well be the case given the high share of affiliate sales that are destined for the local market.

Finally, mandatory business surveys of all US multinationals imply that R&D spending by the IT sector continues to be concentrated in the United States (figure 6.2). Among US-owned IT firms, about 95 percent of global R&D expenditure was spent in the United States in 2002, amounting to about $30 billion (hardware and services).[2] Foreign-owned IT hardware firms located in the United States (as discussed in chapter 2) are three times more R&D intensive than are US firms located abroad; these firms added about $2 billion to US-located R&D activities in the IT sector in 2002. Expenditure data are corroborated by benchmark data from 1999 on the share of US-located employment in the R&D activity, at 92 percent.

---

2. Table 6.2 suggests that the parent funds R&D that is performed by the affiliate, particularly IT services. Discussions with industry confirm this activity. Hence the data in figure 6.2 may overstate the spending by multinationals in the United States.

Figure 6.2   Global R&D expenditure by US IT hardware and services firms, by industry of parent, selected years

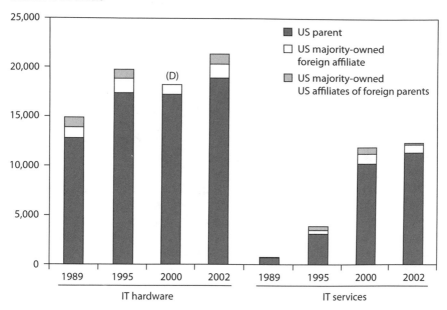

millions of US dollars

(D) = Data suppressed by the BEA for confidentiality reasons.

Sources: Bureau of Economic Analysis, US Direct Investment Abroad: Financial and Operating Data for US Multinational Companies, www.bea.gov (accessed September 30, 2005), and Foreign Direct Investment in the US: Financial and Operating Data for US Affiliates of Foreign Multinational Companies, www.bea.gov (accessed September 30, 2005).

Consistent with the trend from IT hardware to services, the share that US IT firms spent on R&D for IT services increased from 5 percent of R&D expenditure in 1989 to 37 percent in 2002. The next detailed benchmark data for 2004 (to be released in 2007) for US and foreign multinationals will be key for tracking the role that it and communications infrastructure play in fragmenting and globalizing R&D.

Another approach to gaining information regarding firms' global R&D strategies is through surveys of companies. A narrow survey of California-based IT manufacturing firms reveals that R&D activities are outsourced— but more often to other domestic locations, rather than offshore. In addition, most of the outsourced R&D is within a corporate entity, consistent with most models where intellectual property is best protected within the corporate ownership structure. Finally, the survey responses reveal that the more innovative and cutting-edge the research, the more likely it is to remain within the core firm (Bardhan and Jaffee 2005).

Patents and R&D

Corporate data confirm that IT is a research-intensive activity led by the US private sector. Available data for individual firms in the global marketplace show that 32 of the top 50 global IT and communications companies that focused on the IT subsector (that is, excluding telecommunications carriers) spent a combined $73 billion on R&D expenditure in 2002. This is more than triple the R&D expenditures by the US government ($24 billion) that year and surpasses the combined expenditure of the Organization for Economic Cooperation and Development (OECD) countries ($65 billion).[3] Within the United States, R&D expenditure by US IT hardware firms accounted for about 38 percent of R&D by the manufacturing sector in 2000, up from about 32 percent in 1990 (OECD 2002b, 27; OECD 2004c).

Some measures of innovation present a more mixed picture of US innovation and potential. One measure of R&D output is patents registered by the US Patent and Trademark Office (PTO). Patents rose during the last two decades, with a particularly dramatic increase since 1998 (figures 6.3a and 6.3b) due in large part to a particular kind of IT patent—the so-called business method patent—that is somewhat controversial (Mann 2001). The US share of US PTO patents to US-located first-named inventors has remained relatively stable, although with a bit of a decline in recent years.

A look at the corporate identities of the patenting organizations implies that despite the change in the average US position, individual US firms continue to lead patenting and that IT firms are increasingly represented in the top ranks of patenting firms. First, US-headquartered corporations represent 23 of the top 50 and 45 of the top 100 organizations ranked by number of patents filed between 1995 and 2004. The next nationality represented is Japan, with 17 and 33 companies represented in the top 50 and top 100, respectively. No other country comes close, nor even does Europe as a group (figure 6.4).[4]

On the other hand, consider how the patent-weighted share of the United States changes over time (figure 6.4). Prior to 1995, the US patent lead was extreme, with more than 55 percent of patents granted to US firms. In comparison, the 1995–2001 period shows a drop in the share of patents granted to US firms and a rise in those to Japanese firms. However, during 1995–2004, the US lead stabilized. From 1995 to 2001, the US share of all patents was 43 percent, whereas it was 40 percent for Japan. From 2002 to 2004, the US share rose just slightly to 44 percent, but the

---

3. US and OECD government R&D data are from the OECD (2004c), as noted in "#52 Government Intramural Expenditure on R&D." Government expenditures in the OECD database are calculated in current purchasing power parity (PPP) dollars. Adjusting the current dollar expenditure for the OECD from PPP terms to current exchange rates yields $65 billion in current US dollars.

4. Examining patent data from the standpoint of the European Patent and Trademark Office may yield a somewhat less skewed picture.

Figure 6.3a   Patents granted by US Patent and Trademark Office, by residence of first-named inventor and ownership category, 1998–2004

number of patents

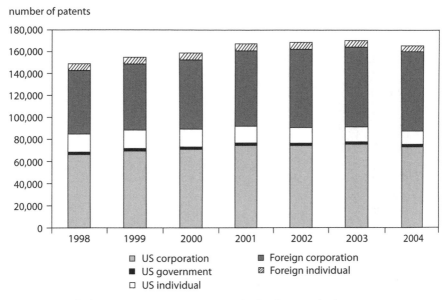

Note: The data for foreign governments are too small to be shown in the figure.

Figure 6.3b   Patents granted by US Patent and Trademark Office, by residence of first-named inventor, 1981–2001

number of patents

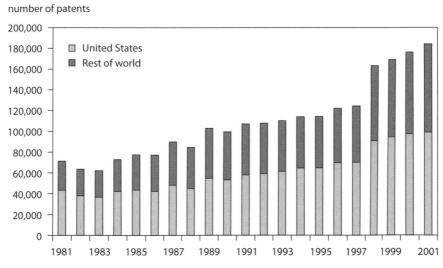

Source: US Patent and Trademark Office.

Figure 6.4   Share of patents granted to top 100 companies, selected periods

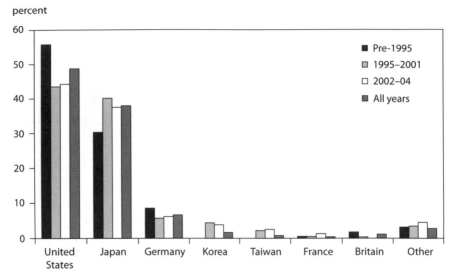

percent

Note: The top 100 are drawn from the total number of companies that have ever been granted more than 1,000 patents by the US Patent and Trademark Office.

Source: US Patent and Trademark Office.

Japanese share fell to 37 percent. Thus, from 1960 to 2004, the US dominance in patenting fell. But in recent years, the US share has ticked upward again. Other countries do not play a big role, although the share of patents granted to "other countries" has risen to 5 percent for the last two years of the sample, from about 3 percent in previous time periods.

A perusal of the corporate identities over time shows that the leading patenting corporations are all multinational household names, and increasingly they are IT names (although only four are US IT names). The top 10 firms granted patents for 2004 were IBM, Matsushita, Canon, Hewlett-Packard, Micron, Samsung, Intel, Hitachi, Sony, and Toshiba. A look at the lifetime of patents awarded suggests a fair degree of stasis more than a change in the ranks. The top 10 lifetime patenting firms are IBM, Canon, Hitachi, General Electric, Toshiba, NEC, Matsushita, Mitsubishi, Sony, and Motorola.

Examining the details of the corporate identity data over time, however, reveals that US IT firms have been moving up the ranks in numbers of patents granted (tables 6.3). For example, Micron Technologies was ranked 248th in total patents granted prior to 1991. But its rank was 130th in 1991 and 166th in 1995, and then it vaulted to seventh in 2000 and fifth in 2004. Intel was ranked 271st by total patents granted prior to 1991, then steadily moved up the ranks to 57th in 1991, 34th in 1995, 18th in 2000,

Table 6.3 Rank of company by number of patents granted by year, selected years

Company	Total pre-1991	1991	1995	2000	2004
IBM	3	8	1	1	1
Hewlett-Packard	77	32	19	15	4
Micron Technologies	248	130	166	7	5
Intel	217	57	34	18	7
Microsoft	261	259	188	43	26

Note: Companies ranked must have been granted at least 1,000 patents to be included in the list.

Source: US Patent and Trademark Office.

and seventh in 2005. Microsoft was ranked 261st by total patents granted prior to 1991, then steadily moved up the ranks to 26th by 2004. IBM leads for most of the 1990s, and recovered from the challenges of its restructuring (discussed in box 2.2) to regain the top spot.

The patenting data reveal the companies that were granted the patents, but not where the research was undertaken. Publicly available data from six large US-based IT firms suggest a more globalized picture of R&D activity, with research facilities located around the world (table 6.4). How important these R&D facilities in foreign countries are for innovation in the industry is not clear. IT firms may engage in R&D abroad for a number of active and passive reasons. A passive reason is to purchase a foreign firm that has significant R&D activity and technologies pertinent to the firm's US and global business strategy (box 6.1). An example of a more active strategy is that of Intel. Since 1990, Intel Capital has invested in more than 1,000 IT companies in some 30 countries, with its 2003 investments ($700 million) in 120 companies, of which 40 percent were located outside the United States (Intel Corporation 2004, 8). Yet a third rationale for global R&D is that bringing together scientists with different academic training raises overall creativity, and speeds a product to market, as box 6.2 shows in the case of the iPod. There may be more R&D activity being undertaken abroad than is suggested by the research worker and R&D expenditure data, but there is no clear implication of the effect of that activity on US innovation or technological leadership.

All told, specific examples indicate that research is now more global, and the specific examples and survey results suggest that there are gains to this globalization. At the same time, the data do not point to a reduction in the R&D intensity of US IT firms, and surveys confirm that innovation within the firm remains key, although parent firms do spend R&D dollars at their affiliates. US IT companies are patenting at an increasing rate, and are amply represented in the top ranks of firms that patent. These data suggest a lively environment of innovation is being maintained in the United States and by US IT firms in their global operations.

Table 6.4   R&D facility locations abroad for US companies ranked among the top 50 global IT and communications firms[a]

Company	Location	Number of employees
IBM	Haifa, Israel	490
	Zurich, Switzerland	250
	Tokyo, Japan	188
	Beijing, China	150
	Delhi, India	110
Hewlett-Packard	Bristol, United Kingdom	n.a.
	Haifa, Israel	16
	Tokyo, Japan	20
	Bangalore, India	14
Intel	China	n.a.
	India	n.a.
	Israel	n.a.
	Malaysia	n.a.
	Philippines	n.a.
	Russia	n.a.
Motorola	Shanghai, China	n.a.
	Tianjin, China	n.a.
	India	n.a.
	Paris, France	n.a.
	Basingstoke, United Kingdom	n.a.
	Wiesbaden, Germany	n.a.
EMC	Belgium	n.a.
	India	n.a.
	Cork, Ireland	n.a.
Dell	China (design)	n.a.
	Taiwan (design)	n.a.
Microsoft	Beijing, China	n.a.
	Dublin, Ireland	n.a.
	Vedbaek, Denmark	n.a.
	Hyderabad, India	n.a.
	Haifa, Israel	n.a.
	Cambridge, United Kingdom	n.a.
Xerox	France	n.a.
	United Kingdom	n.a.
	Canada	n.a.
3M	None	
Cisco	None	
Emerson	n.a.	

n.a. = not available

a. Excluding telecommunications services.

Sources: Company Web sites and 2003 and 2004 10-K filings.

Box 6.1   See it, like it, buy it: Purchasing foreign innovations

The US information technology industry has created some of the most innovative institutions in the world in the Hewlett-Packard (HP) Palo Alto or IBM Thomas J. Watson research labs. Yet not all innovations that firms might desire come from "blue sky" laboratories. US IT companies increasingly seek access to cutting-edge technology via strategic partnerships through outright purchases of R&D-intensive start-ups located both inside and, increasingly, outside the United States. When the parent company possesses sophisticated global marketing and distribution networks, its acquired new technology ramps up quickly into higher value-added product categories, and the value of intellectual property is leveraged via sales to all the major global markets.

For example, in September 2001, HP purchased the Dutch industrial printing company Indigo N.V. The transaction was aimed at promoting HP's image and printing businesses by obtaining Indigo's state-of-the-art Digital Offset Color™ technology. The purchase followed a three-year alliance between the two companies, during which time HP had injected a $100 million equity investment into Indigo and had become the global original equipment manufacturer (OEM) distributor of particular Indigo products.

At the time of acquisition, Indigo N.V. was among the technological leaders in its field, with more than 20 percent of its workforce and 12 percent of total revenues dedicated to R&D. In addition, Indigo received about 3 percent of its total revenues in R&D grants from the Israeli government, which hosted many of the company's facilities. However, Indigo was critically dependent on the continued success of its principal printing technology and had never had a profitable full fiscal year. It continued to finance itself through outside capital injections and short-term bank loans. The company increasingly was forced to rely on strategic marketing and distribution relationships with third parties to continue to grow its business, which was already dispersed, with offices in eight countries and customers in more than 40 countries.

HP's purchase was advantageous for both companies: HP got access to a high value-added new technology—partially developed through the support of a foreign government—that it could now sell globally. Indigo was relieved of its problems of financing continued growth, distribution problems, and its mono-technological risk. The globalizing business environment in the IT industry provides for increased competition as well as new opportunities, regardless of company size.

As will be discussed in the next section, however, the future pipeline of researchers may be stressed, and, recalling the data from table 6.1, the work of these researchers is crucial to R&D in IT.

Concerns remain over the globalization of R&D because it is the foundation for innovation, and therefore an important ingredient in productivity

Most people will have seen it—the sleek-looking gadget with the white plug earphones. The phenomenal success of the Apple iPod portable music player neatly illustrates several aspects of globalization of the IT industry.

First, the iPod conveys novel benefits that are next to impossible to include in statistical GDP estimates. You can take it on a jog without fearing that shaking it will scratch your favorite music (i.e., compact disc); it holds thousands of songs, so you no longer need to bring with you scores of cassette tapes for the Walkman; you can tailor-make your own prolonged play list and do not have to purchase entire albums to get a particular song you like; and, of course, the iPod interface is ergonomically and intuitively designed. Such benefits that consumers derive from new technological innovations are almost never included in GDP estimates. This is just a small example of how the gains from particularly innovative products or transactions, such as IT, frequently are underestimated by standards statistics.

Equally important, though, is that the iPod illustrates just how globalization of the IT industry brings these benefits to consumers rapidly and at an attractive price. The iPod, despite being sold by Apple, is not 100 percent "American as apple pie": whereas the iPod is an example of the California-based firm's core strengths of innovative "cool" design and user-friendly high-tech interfaces, its components come from companies all over the world.

Look inside the iPod. There is a hard drive from the Japanese company Hitachi, a battery from Sony (also Japanese), a controller semiconductor chip from California-based PortalPlayer Inc., a stereo digital-to-analog converter from Wolfson Microelectronics in Edinburgh, UK, a flash memory chip from Sharp Electronics (Japan), an interface controller from US-based Texas Instruments, and a power management and battery charger from Linear Technologies in California. More recent iPod generations also include power management chips from Dutch Royal Philips Electronics, Korean DRAM from Samsung Electronics, USB interface chips from Cypress Semiconductors in San Jose, California, switching

(box continues next page)

growth. If R&D is globalized, does that lessen its potency in raising productivity growth in the United States? Or does purchased foreign R&D or the immigration of research scientists enable the United States to maintain overall innovative superiority? The previous chapter concluded decisively that innovation that interacts with the marketplace of workers and firms is critically important to generating the greatest value to society that innovation

Box 6.2 *(continued)*

regulator controls from National Semiconductor Corp. in Santa Clara, California, and control support from International Rectifier in El Segundo, California, and Synaptics, Inc. in San Jose.[1]

The globalization of the iPod does not stop with the big companies or with the tangible inside pieces. It is also a result of globalized R&D. That established global giants in the IT industry such as Hitachi, Sony, Sharp, Texas Instruments, Philips, or Samsung have a global presence is not a surprise. But much smaller companies involved in the iPod also deserve the label "global company." For instance, Cypress Semiconductors from San Jose, in addition to nine US-located design centers, has R&D facilities in Moscow, Bangalore (India), Hyderabad (India), Cork (Ireland), Istanbul, and Mechelen (Belgium), while maintaining three US production facilities and one in the Philippines.[2] Similarly, National Semiconductor Corp. from Santa Clara has 15 US design centers, as well as in the Netherlands (2), Germany, Scotland, Finland (2), India, China (2), Taiwan, South Korea, and Japan, while maintaining production facilities in the United States (2), Scotland, Malaysia, Singapore, and China.[3] Smaller non-US IT companies, such as the UK's Wolfson Microelectronics, also have a distinctly global profile, with production outsourced to South Korea, China, and Singapore, while carrying out product testing in Malaysia and the UK.[4]

So while it is conceivable that the iPod may have been invented in a nonglobalized world, it certainly would not have come to market in 2001 for only a few hundred dollars.

---

1. All information is from "Inside the Apple iPod Design Triumph," *Electronic Design Chain* magazine, summer 2002, and John H. Day, "Inside iPod," Electronic Design Online, January 20, 2005, http://elecdesign.com (accessed June 15, 2005).
2. See the company's Web site at www.cypress.com (accessed June 15, 2005).
3. See the company's Web site at www.national.com (accessed June 15, 2005).
4. See Wolfson Microelectronics Annual Report 2004, www.wolfsonmicro.com (accessed June 15, 2005).

can offer. Hence, almost without regard to the location of the R&D, the key to continued US productivity growth is to maintain the environment that is conducive to developing as well as using those innovations and allowing the transformation of business to take advantage of them, even when generated abroad. A key ingredient to this success is the people who are part of innovation and transformation, and here the challenges appear more daunting.

R&D in the US Balance of Payments

One area where the nationality of R&D does matter is in the macroeconomic measures of the US trade balance. Research and development outputs, once they receive a patent, copyright, or other forms of intellectual property protection, generate a stream of license or royalty fees from the user. These streams are reflected in the US balance of payments as receipts (inflows of fees from users of US intellectual property outside the United States) and payments (outflows of fees from users located in the United States to foreign owners of intellectual property). US technological leadership and ownership of intellectual property yielded a net positive stream of royalties and license fees of some $32 billion in 2004, against the projected negative current account figure of about $635 billion for that year.

Much of this international trade in intellectual property, such as royalties, is intrafirm trade, with about 80 percent of intellectual property imports and 70 percent of exports between affiliated parties. On the export side, virtually all of the flows are receipts to the US parent for use of intellectual property by majority-owned foreign affiliates abroad. On the import side, virtually all of the flows are payments to the foreign parent from US-located, majority-owned US affiliates of foreign parents.

The intellectual property trade surplus has continued to rise. US receipts for intellectual property rose eightfold from about $4 billion in 1982 to $33.3 billion in 2004 (manufacturing and services). In contrast, payments for intellectual property were essentially zero until the mid-1990s, and crept up to about $2.8 billion in 2004. The bulk of the increase in intellectual property receipts comes from rising net intellectual property in services, whereas net intellectual property receipts for manufacturing has only recently started to grow after stagnating at the turn of the century (figure 6.5).

Is the slower growth of intellectual property in manufacturing due to a movement abroad of manufacturing R&D to the affiliated operation (with the associated return flow of licensing payments)? The data on research intensity for "all industries" and "computer and electronic products" (e.g., IT hardware) presented in table 6.2 show that research expenditure per sales dollar rose at home and fell at the affiliate location. The research intensity of the US affiliate of the foreign multinational also rose, and intellectual property payments back to the parent raised imports. But, it does not appear from these data that manufacturing intellectual property moved abroad with the manufacturing facilities. The data in figure 6.5 essentially are another manifestation of the trend away from manufacturing toward services.

To the extent that more R&D is done abroad and the rights to the intellectual property asset are held in the location where the research is done, the magnitude of the receipt and payment flows may be affected. Intellectual property might become "just another company asset" that multinational companies move around the world as they try to optimize the tax situation of their operations. A change in the national location of the in-

Figure 6.5   US parent firms' receipts and payments of royalties and license fees, by sector, 1982–2004

billions of US dollars

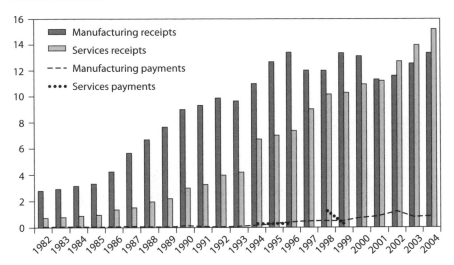

Note: Detailed payments data in services have only been collected since 1994 and are so small that the data are frequently suppressed by the Bureau of Economic Analysis.

Source: Bureau of Economic Analysis. US Direct Investment Abroad: Balance of Payments and Direct Investment Position data, www.bea.gov (accessed October 1, 2005).

tellectual property asset—say, from being held on the books of a US taxable entity to the books of a foreign entity—would affect the direction of trade flows and perhaps give a mistaken impression of where the innovative activity in fact was taking place.[5]

Another set of data on R&D is cross-border international trade in what is called "research and development and testing services" (available only from 2001 to 2004) (figure 6.6). Overall, exports have increased to $10 billion, against imports of about $5 billion. Almost 90 percent of R&D and testing services exports is intrafirm trade; receipts by US affiliates from their foreign parents represent the majority of that export activity. This direction of trade indicates that R&D and testing services done in the United States by foreign-owned firms contributes in an important and positive way to the

---

5. Do firms report intellectual property receipts and payments by where the property is actually generated, so that receipts and payments truly reflect cross-border exchange from the location where intellectual property is generated to the location where it is used? The Bureau of Economic Analysis survey is clear in asking that the R&D expenditures be accounted for by location where the research activity is undertaken. But firms pay substantial attention to potential opportunities for tax arbitrage in the booking of intellectual property activities, just as multinational firms are attuned to tax arbitrage throughout their operations. See Desai and Hines (2002) and Blonigen (2005).

Figure 6.6 US intrafirm trade in R&D and testing services, 2001–04

billions of US dollars

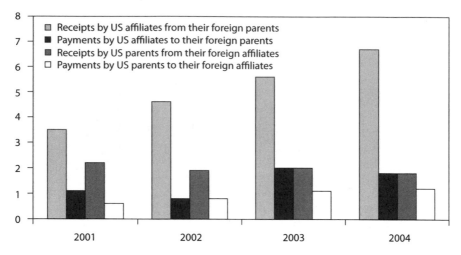

Source: Bureau of Economic Analysis, *Survey of Current Business,* October 2005, 33 (table E).

exports of this type of international R&D trade. On the import side, the share of trade between affiliated parties has been stable at about 70 percent. Since there has been little change in the value of cross-border trade between the US parent and its affiliate abroad, this suggests that imports of R&D services increasingly come from non-US firms located abroad.

Human Capital and Innovation

The picture of the US workforce—which needs to be able to work with and buy innovative products—is not salutary and is particularly striking when considered against the historical position of the United States. When the generation of soon-to-retire scientists and workers was young, they stood out among the industrial countries for their level of educational achievement. The current generation of US workers, on the other hand, is of middling quality compared with other industrial countries, and the younger-generation pipeline of potential science and technology workers (currently in grades K to 12) appears to be falling behind. So one important perspective on US capability in innovation today is to compare the relative achievement levels of those who are currently old, as well as those who are currently young, to their global competition. (The metric of measuring human capital potential by the sheer numbers of science and technology graduates is not appropriate, as discussed in box 6.3.) In any event, the picture is sobering.

Box 6.3 How many engineers are really out there?

The concerns are well known: Millions of new engineers from China and India, working at a fraction of US wages, have already started and will in the coming years continue to undermine US engineering employment. US bachelor's degrees earned in engineering in 2000 stood at just below 60,000, down by a quarter in 15 years.[1] In comparison, India in 2004 graduated 185,000 engineers[2] and China in 2003 a staggering 645,000.[3] So at first glance it would seem that many US positions might be under serious threat. (Although note that engineering graduates were in high demand in 2006 topping the lists of both offers and salaries.)

However, as pointed out by the McKinsey Global Institute (2005) in a report on the global labor supply, there are many reasons why an Indian or Chinese engineering graduate may not be truly comparable, and thus in direct competition, with US engineering graduates. Hence the headline numbers for graduates should be approached with caution. The report was based on interviews with locally posted human resource managers from multinational companies, who were asked whether Indian and Chinese graduates, among others, could successfully work at their companies. The response prompted MGI to note the significant obstacles to a successful career for Indian or Chinese graduates at a multinational company, including lack of language skills; low quality of significant portions of the educational system; limited practical skills; lack of cultural fit and interpersonal skills; attitudes about teamwork and flexible working hours; and geographical availability (proximity to international airport).

Indeed, only 10 percent of Chinese engineering graduates were deemed suitable for a career at a multinational company, and 25 percent of Indian graduates. The share of US engineering graduates that would be suitable for a similar career was not directly covered by the MGI report, but the total suitable pool of engineering talent for multinational companies was estimated to have been almost twice as large in the United States in 2003 as in China and India combined. Therefore, it should not come as a complete surprise that total US engineering employment—with many of those engineers working for multinational companies—actually increased between the peak of the boom in 1999–2000 and 2004.

On the other hand, the rapid rise in the sheer number of engineers in China and India will continue to make it more attractive for US and other multinational IT and software companies to conduct research in those countries. It also will make such a research presence in these two countries a competitive necessity for many companies. It should also be kept in mind that an expansion in the hiring

(box continues next page)

of engineers in China and India can be complementary to, rather than a substitute for, the US engineering workforce, so long as there is demand for local design and implementation for products germane to US needs along with the skilled engineers to do those tasks.

---

1. In 1985, 77,572 bachelor's degrees were earned, according to science and engineering indicators from the National Science Foundation's Science Resource Statistics WebCASTER database, http://caspar.nsf.gov (accessed March 15, 2006).
2. This figure is from the National Association of Software and Services Companies of India (NASSCOM), www.nasscom.org (accessed March 15, 2006), and India's Ministry of Human Resource Development.
3. National Bureau of Statistics of China, *China Statistical Yearbook 2004,* table 21.11, www.stats.gov.cn (accessed March 15, 2006).

Technological Change, Global Competition, and Education Profiles

Synergies between the skill profiles demanded by globalized services, policy changes in key countries to reduce communications costs, and relative wage differentials around the world are likely to speed the fragmentation and globalization of services. The educational demands for internationally traded services range from low (e.g., call center and transcription services) to high (engineering design and computer programming). But underlying both is a generalized set of skills that is not industry- or firm-specific (Autor, Levy, and Murnane 2001).

Technology unleashed by policy reforms in developing countries augments the global pool of labor with appropriate skills. Thus, the share of the US labor force with the level of educational attainment pitted against workers in developing countries may well *increase* over the next 15 years. At the same time, wage differentials between the industrial and developing worlds remain large. Together, the narrowed education advantage to US workers and the large wage differential favoring some foreign workers, along with rapid deployment of IT and communications, enhance the potential for international trade in services and for job and skill competition and volatility in the United States.

As IT has diffused throughout the US economy, the types of labor potentially affected by technology-enhanced globalization of services are both broader in terms of the sectors affected and higher in terms of the thresholds for educational attainment. Both the absolute and, importantly, the relative position of US educational attainment and the associated return to US workers' skills in the global marketplace therefore are key.

With a rising skill bar and enhanced global skill competition, how does the United States fare in comparisons of educational attainment and functional skills?

Examining educational attainment by age cohort across countries reveals some of the characteristics of the US workforce and the global competition (figure 6.7). The heart of the current US workforce (ages 45–64) is still the best-educated workforce among the OECD countries. In terms of both secondary and tertiary educational attainment, US prime-aged workers are better educated than similarly aged cohorts in other OECD countries. This cohort of US workers has enjoyed the prosperity of a US economy increasingly technology-driven and integrated with a world that has been, on balance, less educated.

The younger workforce in the United States is not so well positioned, and, with faster technological change and deeper global integration, the stakes are higher. The generation of Americans entering the workforce today (25- to 34-year-olds) barely makes the top 10 ranking and, nearly uniquely among OECD countries' 25- to 34-year-olds, they have on average a lower level of educational attainment than their parents' generation. This younger group faces significantly higher skill demands than did their parents when they entered the workforce. Because technology enables a wider range of jobs to be done remotely, US job seekers face a much more competitive, and available, foreign workforce. And the younger worker today, particularly with less than a tertiary education, is paired with a global workforce that has narrowed the gap of educational attainment. For those educated at the tertiary level, 25- to 34-year-olds in the United States fare substantially better against the global standards,[6] although they are not the best educated, and many other countries are catching up rapidly.

This concern regarding educational attainment is deepened when viewed against survey evidence on the functional skills of the US workforce. The OECD, in its 2003 Adult Literacy and Life Skills Survey (ALL), evaluated three types of functional skills:

- *Prose literacy:* the knowledge and skills needed to understand and use information from texts, including editorials, news stories, brochures, and instruction manuals.

- *Document literacy:* the knowledge and skills required to locate and use information contained in various formats, including job applications, payroll forms, transportation schedules, maps, tables, and charts.

- *Numeracy:* the knowledge and skills required to effectively manage the mathematical demands of diverse situations.

---

6. Other OECD countries have even bigger problems; their shares of tertiary educational attainment have declined.

Figure 6.7 Percentage of population that has attained at least tertiary education, by age group, 2003

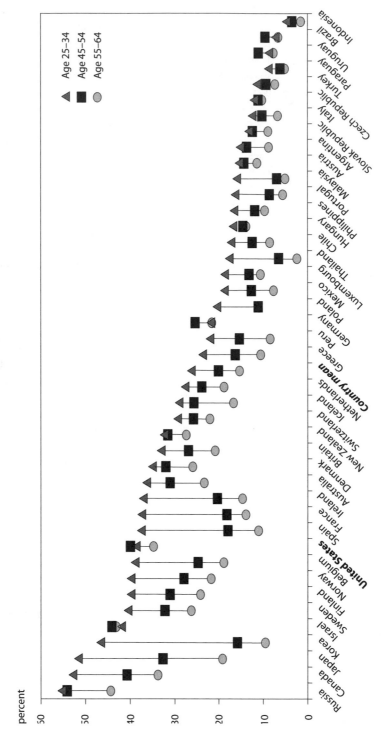

Note: The definition of "tertiary education" varies between countries but does require an educational content equivalent to a bachelor's degree.

Source: OECD (2005a).

Figure 6.8   Document literacy by age group, 2003 (percent)

share of total in attained level

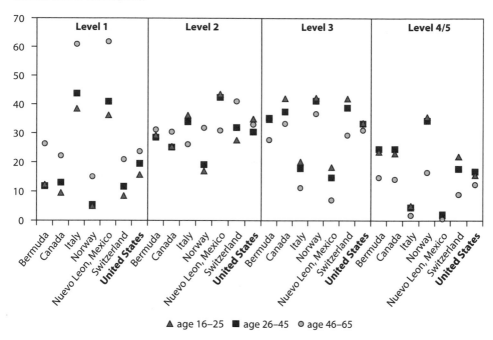

▲ age 16–25   ■ age 26–45   ○ age 46–65

Source: OECD, International Adult Literacy and Life Skills Survey, 2003.

On a scale of 1 to 5, the middle range (level 3) is the level considered by experts as a suitable minimum for coping with the increasing demands of the emerging knowledge society and information economy. In 2003, 60 percent of US adults surveyed did not reach this level of proficiency in numeracy, and more than 50 percent did not reach this level of proficiency in document and prose literacy. Only about one-third of US adults achieved the middle range of the scale for these three types of literacy. And it is not that older adults who lower the average: 50 percent of young adults aged 16–25 scored below the minimum proficiency in document literacy (figure 6.8).

An even greater concern is that, compared with 1994 (for which comparisons only for prose and document literacy are available),[7] the share of US adults in the lowest two quintiles increased, the share of adults in the middle range increased just 1 percentage point, and the share of adults in the top two quintiles of literacy fell. Based on these surveys of functionality, the US performance has not improved over the decade, even as glob-

7. The 1994/1998 OECD International Adult Literacy Survey (IALS) uses a similar methodology as does the 2003 ALL Survey. See OECD (2000, 2005b).

alized technology demands and the US workplace have rewarded higher skills.

Examining other surveys of educational attainment, such as the Trends in International Mathematics and Science Study (TIMSS) and the Program for International Student Assessment (PISA),[8] reveals similar conclusions. Other countries are catching up to or exceeding US levels of educational attainment, even as some US students are doing better on these examinations compared to previous years.

Importantly, these studies also reveal that lower socioeconomic status is correlated with a lower level of educational attainment. A widening disparity of earnings in the United States has already been observed (see chapter 5), so this correlation between socioeconomic status and educational attainment suggests a dynamic that could further widen the existing disparity of earnings and education in the future. Globalized networked technology increases the power of the negative dynamic by adding the wage premium to analytical and judgmental IT-related skills at the top end of the educational distribution, and by heightening global competition at the middle and lower rungs of educational attainment.

In sum, with US educational attainment and functional skill levels on average stagnating, possibly declining and showing a widening dispersion at a time when technology is becoming more sophisticated and other countries are improving rapidly, there is a clear risk that Americans in the future may lose some of the many benefits they have so far enjoyed from globalization. The response must be to improve the incentives to educate people to meet the technological challenges of a globalized economy.

Science and Technology Researchers in the United States

A second concern for the future innovative capacity of the United States is the human capital foundation—people schooled in the sciences and technology. The overall picture of educational attainment is already rather bleak. This does not improve when considering the pipeline of science and technology talent in the United States. Further, the fast pace of technological change also undermines the "stock" of science and technology talent, in that rapid technological change depreciates human skills, just as it depreciates the productivity of physical capital. Rapid skill depreciation suggests that a new approach is needed for ongoing training and "reskilling" so as to keep the US stock of human capital fit for the innovative frontier.

---

8. TIMSS is a comparison of mathematics and science achievement that has been carried out three times since 1995 by the International Association for the Evaluation of Educational Achievement (IEA), an international organization of national research institutions and governmental research agencies. The PISA is a system of international assessments that measures 15-year-olds' capabilities in reading literacy, mathematics literacy, and science literacy every three years. It is administered by the OECD. See www.pisa.oecd.org (accessed March 15, 2006).

About 40 percent of all graduate students and all science and engineering PhDs awarded at US universities (rising to more than half in mathematics/computer sciences and engineering) go to non-US citizens and nonpermanent residents. By itself, this may not be an issue, since in the past these students have tended to stay in the United States and contribute to US innovation here. To the extent that the brightest students from around the world come to the United States for science and technology training, this implies that frontier innovation still inhabits the US university and laboratory setting.

However, the most recent information suggests that two factors may be affecting the inflow and retention of foreign talent. First, with rapidly improving career and business opportunities in the home countries of many foreign students (notably India and China), an increasing proportion of these students appear to be returning home. Not only does this reduce the US return on its investment for having funded a US education for these students, but it also reduces the stock of highly educated workers in the US university and research setting (and increases that stock abroad).

Given these science and technology demographics, and in conjunction with the locus of demand for technology products shifting to rapidly growing economies abroad, it is not surprising that R&D facilities are being opened in foreign countries. A further impetus to this global shift of R&D is the sheer numbers of science and technology graduates in some countries. Against the US graduation numbers of 60,000 engineers in 2004, India graduated about 185,000 in 2004 and China some 645,000 in 2003 (see box 6.3). Many of these graduates are not researchers, and their local environment will not spawn or support innovation, but the fact is that the global pool of science and technology graduates increasingly is not located in the United States. This trend comes at a time in the 21st century when literacy, numeracy, and analysis—skills developed in a program of study in science, engineering, and technology—are needed pervasively throughout the process of research, design, production, marketing, and sales of goods and services both at home and abroad.

Globalization of Venture Finance

How are globalization, venture capital, and innovation linked? On the one hand, the globalization of venture finance, whereby finance raised in the United States is extended to foreign firms to engage in innovative activities, could dilute the US economic dynamic, putting future US prosperity at risk. On the other, this globalization of venture finance could spawn the development of more ideas, and at less cost, which in turn can be taken to the marketplace, thereby bolstering US productivity and growth. The possible scenarios start with the question of whether US venture finance has globalized. A second set of questions considers the type of activities being undertaken abroad and their potential impact on US performance.

Figure 6.9 Total venture capital invested, by source and destination, 1980–2005

billions of US dollars

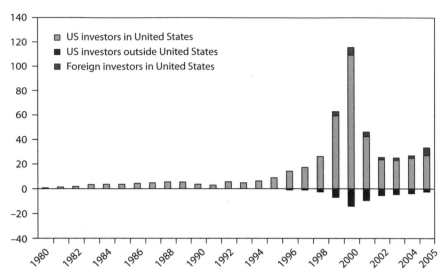

Source: Thomson Financial VentureXpert database.

According to the Thomson Financial VentureXpert database, venture finance has been globalized for some time. In the 1990s, 5 to 10 percent of US-raised venture finance was spent on firms in foreign countries and about 5 percent of foreign-raised venture capital funded US firms.[9] In the first couple of years after the Internet and stock market crash in the United States (2001–02), foreign firms received almost 20 percent of US-raised venture finance; but that share has since fallen back to under 15 percent. The number of foreign countries receiving venture finance has increased, particularly in the last 15 years, with firms in more than 50 countries currently receiving funds. China has been among the top five recipient countries in seven of the last 12 years, whereas India has appeared only once among the top five. Of course, these shares of total funding mask the dramatic boom and crash in venture finance, which is the overwhelming hallmark of the period (figure 6.9).

Waves of financing of IT-related activities appear in these data, with IT investments receiving from one- to three-quarters of all venture finance. Three successive waves can be identified. In the 1980s, venture finance supported computer hardware; in the 1990s, the Internet wave dominated the data; and following the Internet crash, financing associated with software and computer services increased. Other technologies, such as those

9. See http://banker.thomsonib.com/ta/ (accessed October 1, 2005).

Figure 6.10   US venture capital investments in the United States, by industry, 1980–2005

percent of total

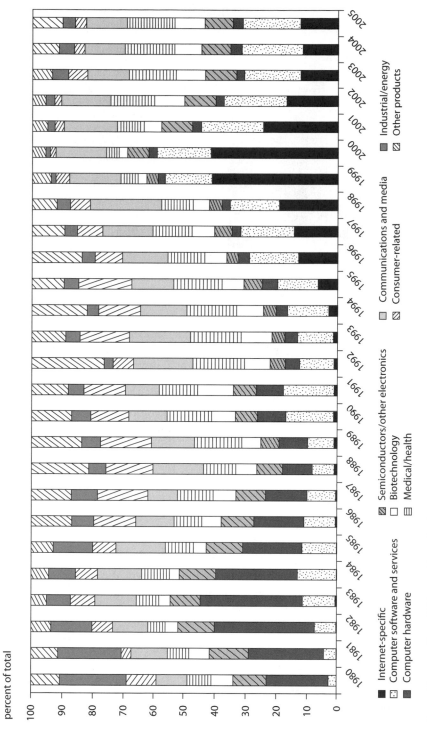

Source: Thomson Financial VentureXpert database.

Figure 6.11　US venture capital flows to the rest of the world, 1999–2005

millions of US dollars

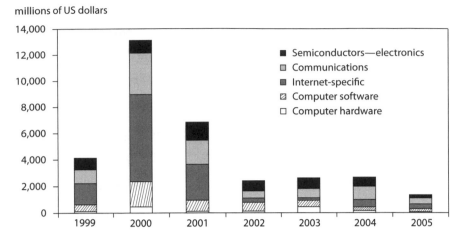

Source: Thomson Financial VentureXpert database.

associated with biotechology and medical/health account for between 15 and 30 percent of financing, generally receiving a higher percentage when IT's fortunes wane. Communications and media firms increased their share in 2005, whereas the share for consumer-related products has fallen since the mid-1990s (figure 6.10).

A clear trend emerges with respect to the stage of financing supported by venture finance. It is common to disaggregate venture finance into five categories: seed or start-up, early stage, expansion, later stage, and buyout or acquisition. The share of venture finance going to seed or start-up ventures in the United States has fallen throughout the period covered by the Thomson database, with the declining share accelerating since 1995. On the other hand, against a backdrop of much smaller dollar values and shares, the share of start-up and early-stage funding to foreign companies does not exhibit this declining trend.

The focus on later-stage investment in the United States may imply that venture finance goes more to firms that are beyond the concept and vision stage and, rather, are expanding in a more mature market. If so, then the globalization of venture finance may point to enhanced productivity growth in the United States coming more through ideas being implemented and brought to market, rather than through "next-big-thing" innovation. On the other hand, funding of start-ups abroad may indicate a greater willingness of US venture firms to take small dollar-value risks abroad that they are not taking at home.

Figure 6.11 focuses attention on just the IT sector and on US venture funding that goes abroad. The technology cycle is obvious, but so too is

Figure 6.12 Top countries and regions receiving US venture finance, 1999 and 2005, share of total (percent)

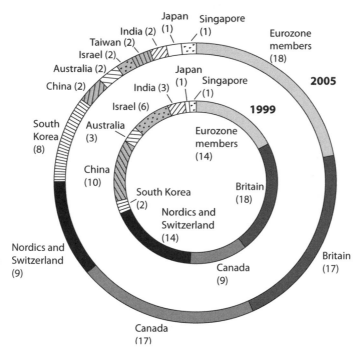

Note: Other countries excluded amount to approximately 20 percent in 1999 and 2005.

Source: Thomson Financial VentureXpert database.

the balance between the various subsectors of the IT industry. In these data, the shift toward spending on services and software, rather than hardware, is less apparent. That is, there is about equal spending on ventures in hardware and software. This is consistent with the spending data discussed in chapter 2—that is, spending on IT hardware in developing countries was relatively larger than for IT software and services but expected to become more balanced over time.

Figure 6.12 shows the top countries and regions receiving US venture finance and the distribution in 1999 and 2005. The EU countries, United Kingdom, and Canada are the largest recipients of funds. Considering the geographic pattern in 2005 versus 1999, it is clear that while the industrial countries continue to dominate venture investment, there is rising interest in funding portfolio companies both in the developing world and in countries with key skills such as Israel.

A Look Forward
with a Policy Agenda

Increased productivity growth supports the "trifecta" of faster GDP growth, lower inflation, and higher-wage employment. Networked information technology fuels this productivity growth in two ways. First, innovations by IT firms in hardware, software, and services spearhead an acceleration of productivity growth. Second, IT products increasingly are purchased, networked via communications, and used by non-IT firms throughout the economy, thereby transforming business activities and workplace practices. Changes outside the IT-producing sectors are even more important than IT itself in generating sustained, widespread, and accelerated productivity. The globalization of IT and communications networks reduces the cost of investing in IT and raises the return to using it, thus playing a key role in the diffusion of IT throughout the economy.

Limiting or otherwise slowing technological change and its globalization forgoes real and large gains—productivity growth, job creation, and innovation. The economic pie is smaller without innovation and globalization of IT and, more importantly, the change they elicit. On the other hand, failure to address adjustment costs that can be a consequence of such globalized technological change also limits economic potential. If labor and capital are not well matched to changing economic needs, maximum economic potential will not be achieved because available resources will not be fully utilized. Labor and capital mismatches result in macroeconomic sluggishness as well as personal anxiety, both of which shrink the economic pie inside its potential frontier. Therefore, policy must both promote innovation and technological change and facilitate adjustment to change—not limit or avoid change or ignore redistribution—to ensure that all resources of the economy are used efficiently and effectively.

The fastest-growing international players, including India and China, change the landscape for innovation and globalized production in ways both positive and threatening to continued US productivity growth. As markets, US firms are attracted to the growth potential of these and other countries and see product differentiation to meet those market needs as new opportunities. As production platforms for the sale of products to the United States or to third markets, they are attractive for their geographical location and labor resources and skills. More generally, industrial policy, tax strategies, policy reforms, and economic openness have enhanced economic vibrancy in many key new markets and competitor countries.

Investment in and use of information technology in the US economy have had important effects that have been magnified by the globalization of the sector and the competitive pressures on the entire economy that come from global engagement. The transformations that yield these gains may also have yielded more rapid job churn in the economy, which some see as beneficial and others see as worrisome. Moreover, at the same time that these benefits have accrued to the American economy overall, IT investments have increased and changed the educational and skill requirements to perfect job matching and mobility, which may have increased the overall wage disparity in the United States. Since the pace and economy-wide scope of technological change and globalization are quickening and broadening, urgent attention to appropriate policies to improve job matching and mobility is crucial to maintain productivity growth and forestall widening income disparity so as to ensure that gains are widely shared.

There are, as well, policy imperatives outside the United States. In some countries, the domestic environment dampens the potential benefits of transformative technology. Some buyers do not benefit from falling global prices of IT products because of taxes and tariffs. Some companies cannot transform their business activities to reap the benefits of IT because of labor and product market rules and regulations. Some workers do not have the skills to use the equipment or services. Some sectors are not allowed to receive the technological benefits that come with foreign investments. Overall, to reap these benefits, to promote IT development tailored to local needs, and to encourage skill building requires complementary and enabling service sectors of telecommunications, financial services, and logistics.

The liberalization of trade in services can play a role in creating these complementary networked services that underpin greater use of IT. Increased cross-border trade in services can be positive for both industrial and developing countries. Industrial-country exporters of services, specifically the United States, gain from liberalized trade in services, since these are areas of comparative advantage. For many developing economies, increased trade flows and overall GDP come from improved domestic services. Extending the Information Technology Agreement and actively pursuing a more liberalized global environment for services through the

WTO Doha Development Round and other trade negotiations are part of the process of implementing domestic reforms that will have positive consequences for international competitiveness for both the United States and its trading partners.

Innovation and its diffusion and application are the foundation for productivity growth, but they are also a source of disruptive change. The pipeline of innovation and the ability to use innovation to transform business activities to raise living standards may be at risk in the United States because researchers and workers are increasingly scarce or not up to the challenge of change. These supply-side forces, along with the shifting geography of demand for technology products toward rapidly growing economies abroad, propel businesses to move both research and production there. If the demand for products and the supply of researchers and qualified workers are growing fastest in emerging markets, that is where the companies will go. The financial resources to support innovation, as well as enhance the crucial resource of researchers and a literate, numerate workforce, are crucial to maintain US leadership and rising living standards.

A proactive US policy agenda will promote innovation here and encourage and enable US workers and businesses to embrace and use IT to make the most of global opportunities in production, sales, and trade in both the manufacturing and services arenas. To have no policy agenda or strategy has both short- and long-term consequences. In the short term, a slowdown in productivity growth or poor matching of labor skills to evolving labor demands implies lackluster job creation and a US economy operating below its potential. In the longer term, if innovation flags, skill building is inadequate, and customers complacent, the United States will relinquish its economic leadership in the global economy.

A proactive agenda must meet innovation, transformation, and global challenges. Innovation creates a technological frontier, which pushes out the potential of the economy. Innovation increasingly will be global, but will the United States continue to be a leader? Transformation means that businesses must be able to change products and production techniques, and workers must have the desire and skills to welcome new job opportunities. But transformation also means business turbulence and job restructurings and losses, even as there is greater growth overall. Global competition comes as more countries use IT domestically for growth, rather than only as a source of export revenues. This, in turn, means that more countries could be customers and partners, if markets are open. A proactive agenda by IT firms and IT-using firms, in conjunction with policymakers, centered around these themes can meet the specific challenges of new ideas, new jobs, and new competition so as to deepen the benefits of the globalization of IT for the overall US economy. Failing to meet these challenges puts US economic success and global technological leadership at risk (figure 7.1).

Figure 7.1 The policy challenge

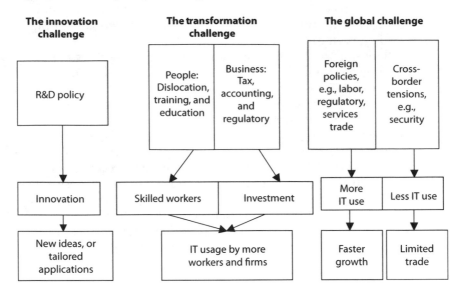

A Proactive Policy Agenda

The Innovation Challenge

Innovation pushes out the technology frontier and creates the products and applications that raise productivity. IT products and applications create and expand opportunities to use information technology, which creates new business and jobs, raising income and wealth by applying IT innovations to customer demands.

Innovation and its application are the foundation for productivity growth and the fundamental source of change. Research is now more global, and there are important gains to this globalization—good ideas are not constrained by national boundaries, and tailored products and applications often address national preferences and regulations. US data emphasize the importance of people—researchers—in the innovation intensity of US IT firms, and they point to the importance of having educated workers who can respond to flexible workplace practices. Not only the pipeline of innovation, but the ability to use innovation to transform business activities to raise living standards, are at risk to the extent that the "people part" of both innovation and application is scarce or not up to the challenge of change. Additional key requirements to meet the innovation challenge follow.

Keep the Innovation Pipeline Full with People and Funding

Whereas productivity gains can come simply by diffusing existing technology to new sectors and new economies, some challenges to diffusion will be met only by innovation. Moreover, it takes time after innovations are presented for business applications to spring up to meet customer needs. These issues may be particularly germane for the sectors and countries that are not currently intensive users of IT. Therefore, it is crucial that the innovation pipeline be kept full, even if the value of innovations is not immediately apparent.

A first requirement is to nurture researchers. IT software and services, the locus for innovations and their applications for use by non-IT sectors in the US economy, are much more research worker–intensive than other sectors of the US economy, including IT hardware.

A second requirement is funding for research and development. Private funding of R&D through venture or internal funds plays a very important role in innovation. But the economy-wide spillovers to innovation imply that government funding should complement private R&D. Questions of who bears risk, reaps reward, and directs research strategies need to be addressed when public-private-academic partnerships are launched. Intellectual property considerations need to be factored into the equation to balance innovator rights against benefits of broader usage.

Embrace the Benefits of the Globalization of Innovation

A globalized update to the adage "necessity is the mother of innovation" is that innovation will be promoted by the idiosyncratic needs of certain sectors, the unpredictable situations in some countries, and the concentration of intellectual resources in certain places. Since the geographical scope for innovation already extends beyond the United States, making sure that US firms can access these global technologies as well as sell their products abroad is important for continued productivity growth both here and in other countries. In addition, innovation as an activity, particularly applied innovation, can be fragmented, with some of the components of the activity done more cheaply abroad. Globalization of innovation reduces its price, leading to more widespread use of the new application and associated economic gains.

Also, vibrant consumers demanding new products at home are key to keeping innovation percolating at home. A complacent market is a poor environment for new ideas.

The Transformation Challenge

Achieving broad-based productivity growth demands more transformation in the domestic economy as well as greater engagement by US companies abroad and by foreign economies in global trade. What with the increased tradability of services, pressures for transformation will extend to more sectors of the US economy, to more countries, and to more workers. On top of that, continued innovation implies an ongoing and rapid pace of change.

The very rapid pace of technological change that opens new global production possibilities to firms highlights the issues of labor market dislocation and change. Overall, technological change and globalization put an even higher premium on more education and higher skills (measured by formal schooling, trade apprenticeships, or other metrics). Policies are particularly needed to address two types of job losses in the technologically volatile marketplace: permanent job loss and the depreciation of skills. Some of the key requirements to meet the transformation challenge follow.

Deepen Economic Transformation via More Widespread Use of IT

Global integration of the production of IT hardware significantly reduced prices and improved performance, which supported the first wave of productivity growth. IT services and software are a rising share of the computer "package" and key to making it "work" for the customer. Nascent global integration and standardization of elements of services and software production portend a rapid reduction in these prices along with improved operability and better tailoring to diverse needs.

Productivity gains from intensive use of IT are clear. But large segments of the US economy, particularly smaller firms, and much of the rest of the world have not yet integrated IT fully into their business operations and economies. The cheaper, improved, and tailored IT package of hardware, software, and services has the potential to extend the use of information technology to the sectors and businesses that have lagged in terms of productivity growth. This, in turn, has the potential to initiate a second wave of transformation and overall productivity growth. Reducing the price and improving the functionality of the productivity tools of IT services and software will support a deepening and more pervasive use of IT in the United States.

Institute New Policies for Permanent Job Loss

Successful transformation by businesses implies some permanent job loss. Whether dislocated by technology or trade, workers need to get back to work quickly to avoid a loss of specific job skills and familiarity with job requirements. Extended unemployment benefits (which provide more time for adjustment), training assistance, wage insurance, and portable and available social insurance (such as health and pensions) are all strategies to ease and promote the transition to a new job and career.

In particular, policies that create positive incentives to move to a new job increase the likelihood that the worker will learn the skills on the job that move wages upward on a new career path. For a period of time, wage insurance (Kletzer 2001, Kletzer and Rosen 2005) replaces a portion of the difference between the old wage at the lost job and the new wage at the new job. This policy acknowledges that a low rung on a new job ladder probably does not pay as much as the previous tenured job, which is now gone. But it creates the incentives, nonetheless, to move to the new job. Facilitating the redeployment of labor resources makes both the individual and the economy better off.

Institute New Policies to Address Skill Depreciation

For some skilled workers, particularly in science and technology, globalization and technology do not eliminate their job category altogether, but they may alter the career path by speeding skill depreciation and by removing certain "rungs" of the career ladder. Classic "market imperfections" argue for a "human capital" investment tax credit to promote skill upgrading within an organization and career path.

A human capital investment tax credit recognizes that technological skills take a long time to develop, yet depreciate quickly, and may be made uncompetitive by competition from other countries. A tax credit recognizes three realities of the marketplace for skills: free riders, incomplete information, and spillovers. First, firms that engage in substantial training of their own workers to move their skills up the ladder beyond the threat of international competition and to keep abreast of technological change face the disincentive of "free riding" by other firms that do not train. Second, "incomplete information" about the whole career ladder may dissuade students from getting into the career pipeline, as some first-rung jobs may no longer be available in the United States. Third, such a tax credit recognizes the "spillover" benefits to the economy as a whole of having a technologically trained workforce that diffuses to all sectors of the economy.

These rather familiar market imperfections are the rationale for the R&D tax credit and the investment tax credit for IT capital. Given the importance of innovation and skills in the competitive and globalized environment of the 21st century, a human capital investment tax credit offered to individuals, through firms, and implemented by educational institutions has even greater merit. Of course, workers must acknowledge the demands being put on them and rise to the challenge.

Retaining high-wage jobs in the United States held by the prime-aged, educated workforce, in part through the mechanism of the human capital investment tax credit, is not just altruism but is also in society's interest. This group of workers is key to intergenerational prosperity—they support fiscal transfers to the currently old and finance the education of the currently young. Keeping them employed at the frontier of their capabilities, as defined by the frontier of the economy, warrants society's and the government's support.

The Global Challenge

Meeting the US productivity challenge demands not only deeper global engagement by US IT firms but also commitment by foreign countries to open markets and create an environment favorable to more extensive use of IT by firms throughout their economies. Because China and India are both major IT producers and users, their policy choices are particularly important in this regard.

However, there are growing challenges to deepening and extending the successful global business model. That is, incorporating that model in more countries and extending it to include more information-intensive services sometimes collides with other issues important to policymakers, ranging from taxes to information privacy, digital rights management, and national security. Managing the tension between the global nature of the business model and the often domestic concerns of policymakers is key. Some of the steps needed to meet the global challenge follow.

Promote Globalization of IT Abroad to Extend Productivity Gains There and Here

The productivity experience of the United States has not been widely shared. Extending the productivity gains to the rest of the world is critical for the United States to enjoy continued productivity gains itself. Differences in patterns of investment and flexibility of domestic markets are important factors holding back the effective use of IT in many countries, industrial and developing alike. Rapid innovation and falling prices for information technology products make imported IT cheaper, but many countries still impose tariffs on these products. Tariffs on imported IT disproportionately reduce its use inside an economy, thus holding back productivity. In addition, tariffs on imported IT bias investment, and generally inhibit the development of the high-tech export sector that many countries desire. All told, market access for IT products and services, and an enabling environment abroad facilitated by liberalization of the services sector, are important for US firms and foreign countries alike.

Work Toward Interoperable Strategies that Reduce the Tension Between Countries' Domestic Policy Objectives

There is no one right approach to the role that a government will play in the increasingly interrelated world of fragmented and globalized production of services. Approaches to taxation, treatment of data, and information-based national security will not converge to one homogeneous approach because resources as well as societal values and priorities differ. However, if the domestic-focused policies ignore the impact on the global marketplace and business incentives, a country will forgo some of the gains of the next wave of globalization based on IT services and software.

A Plea for Data

This book presents a vast array of data from statistical agencies, international institutions, consultancies, and private firms to support analysis and policy discussion. However, available data have not kept pace with the rapid pace of change in the IT sector, its globalization, its adoption by businesses, and its impact on workers. Particular weakness in the data involve the more dramatic areas of change: the shift toward IT services and software in both production and demand, the globalization of R&D, the rise of the global company, and changing skills in occupations and industries.

A funded program is needed that focuses on collecting disaggregate data by product, industry, country, and occupation and that, importantly, provides the data in a more time fashion. Data cannot, in raw form, directly answer the most pressing questions and concerns about US businesses in the global economy or the impact of technological change and globalization on US workers. But analysis of more pertinent and timely data would significantly improve the understanding of the forces of globalization and technological change and thereby aid policy design.

Final Word

Investment in and use of information technology in the US economy have had important effects that have been magnified by the globalization of the sector and the competitive pressures on the entire economy that come from global engagement. The ensuing enhanced diffusion of IT has had the positive effects of increased productivity and GDP growth and reduced inflation.

Innovation lies at the heart of investment in and use of information technology. Some innovations are novel, some more applied. Some are supported by research funded publicly, some privately. Some are initiated here, and some abroad. All are complemented with professionals trained in technology, analysis, implementation, and communications and come ultimately from a population that demands "new and better."

The transformations that boost these gains also yield more rapid job churn in the economy and demand different job skills. Some workers respond easily to the educational and job challenges; others less so. Globalization-powered technological change may well have increased overall wage disparity in the United States.

Maximizing the benefits of the technological innovations and transformations that go hand-in-hand with deeper globalization is key to ensuring the continued positive impact of IT on the US economy. But so too is ensuring that the benefits of those innovations are more widely obtainable and completely shared across society. Failing to engage all resources implies forgoing some of the potential of the economy. The pace and economywide scope of technological change and globalization are quickening and broadening across business and society. Urgent attention to appropriate policies is crucial.

Appendix A
Methodology and Definitions

Attempts by statistical agencies to coherently capture rapid economic changes on a macro level are inevitably beset by the twin constraints of funding problems and issues with survey-respondent burden and disclosure. Comparisons of international datasets reveal that the statistical material provided by the US Department of Commerce's Bureau of Economic Analysis (BEA) on US multinational companies and foreign direct investment in the United States[1] is by far the best and most publicly accessible tool to describe the fundamental changes to production patterns, products traded, research and development, and geographic locations that economic globalization has brought to the information technology sector.

These BEA data form the nucleus of the statistical foundation of this book, and hence an overview of BEA definitions of key and frequently used statistical items and issues covered will greatly facilitate the reader's understanding of the text and of the extent to which the data coverage is valid.[2]

Definitions

Foreign versus US residency. The country of residence, not the country of citizenship, determines whether a direct investor or a business enter-

---

1. Principally financial and operating data on US multinationals from the BEA's annual surveys on US direct investment abroad and on foreign multinationals present in the United States through the BEA's annual survey of foreign direct investment.

2. This appendix is based largely on BEA (1994, 1995, and 2001) and www.bea.gov.

prise is US or foreign. A US person is any person who resides in, or is subject to the jurisdiction of, the United States, including the 50 states, District of Columbia, Puerto Rico, and all US territories and possessions, while "foreign" means that which is situated outside the United States. A person is considered a resident of the country in which he or she is located if the person resides or expects to reside in that country for one year or more, except if (1) the person resides outside his or her country of citizenship for business purposes for more than one year, yet intends to return within a reasonable time, or (2) the person resides outside his or her country of citizenship due to government employment, during which time the person is regarded as a resident of his or her country of citizenship regardless of the length of stay.

US parent. A US parent is a US legal person who has direct investment of 50 percent or greater, direct or indirect ownership interest in a foreign business enterprise. All foreign business enterprises owned by the US parent are excluded from the data reported under this heading.

Foreign parent. A foreign parent is the first person outside the United States in a US affiliate's ownership chain that has a direct investment interest of 50 percent or greater, direct or indirect ownership interest in the affiliate.

US majority-owned foreign affiliate (MOFA). A majority-owned foreign affiliate of a US firm is a foreign business enterprise that is directly or indirectly owned or controlled by one US person (or group of persons exercising influence as a single parent) to the extent of 50 percent or more of the voting securities for an incorporated business enterprise or an equivalent interest for an unincorporated business enterprise.

Majority-owned US affiliate of a foreign parent (MOUSA). The reciprocal ownership requirements (foreign parent, US-domiciled affiliate) are characteristic of a foreign affiliate in the United States, as are all other features in the classification of foreign majority-owned affiliates in the United States. The following description of the rules governing US-owned foreign affiliates can thus all be applied reciprocally to similar foreign affiliates in the United States.

Foreign affiliate. A foreign affiliate consists of operations and activities in a foreign country that a US person conducts. If such operations and activities are incorporated abroad, they are by definition considered a foreign affiliate. If operations and activities are unincorporated, yet legally or functionally separate from those of the US person, a case-by-case consideration of status is made.

The BEA lists the following characteristics as indicating foreign affiliate status of an unincorporated operation and activity:

- It pays foreign income taxes.

- It has a substantial physical presence abroad, as evidenced by plant and equipment or by employees that are permanently located abroad.

- It has separate financial records that would allow the preparation of financial statements, including a balance sheet and income statement.

- It takes title to the goods it sells and receives revenue from the sale, or it receives funds from customers for its own account for services it performs.

IT Industries in BEA Data

The US company data on which the BEA relies are proprietary in nature, and hence any data that might reveal the business details of any single company are suppressed by the BEA. This presents researchers using publicly available data with a trade-off: either attempt maximum industry-level detail, sacrificing geographic specificity, or vice versa. While the choice obviously depends on the individual project, this book has attempted to achieve the greatest degree of industry classification possible. We have tried to minimize the risk of measuring something that is in the data yet has nothing to do with developments in the IT sector (in statistical terms, a type II error).

All micro or firm-level data included in BEA surveys on multinational activities, be they US parents, US foreign affiliates abroad, or foreign-owned affiliates in the United States, are classified according to the primary industry/country of the affiliate or the primary industry of the US parent, with by far the majority of data classified according to the industry/country of the foreign affiliate. This does make an important difference in some industries, in which many foreign affiliates are predominantly wholesale outlets, as the activities of such affiliates will be classified as wholesale, if classified according to the primary activity of the foreign affiliate, irrespective of the relationship to the product sold to other industries. However, if classified according to the industry of the US parent, many affiliates otherwise classified as "wholesale trade" will now be classified according to the main activity of the US parent, which may or may not be wholesale trade.

This results in a downward bias in the data classified according to the industry of the foreign affiliate, as some foreign affiliates will be classified as wholesale, rather than in the industry of the products transacted. However, reporting data according to the industry of the US parent leads to a significant risk of double counting, as the same item will be recorded when leaving a foreign affiliate production plant and when sold to customers by a foreign affiliate wholesale operation. In each individual case, the particular characteristics of the data were taken into account before the decision was made to present data by either industry of the affiliate or industry of the US parent.

This book uses BEA data categorized according to two industry classification systems, the Standard Industrial Classification (SIC) established in 1987 and the North American Industry Classification System (NAICS) adopted in 1997 in an attempt to better capture the emergence and growth of the services sector and new and advanced technologies, as well as to offer better comparability with International Standard Industrial Classifications (ISIC revision 3). NAICS contains for the IT sector much more industry detail than the old SIC system.

Unfortunately, individual industry categories between the two classification systems are not all immediately comparable. Construction of time series spanning both SIC and NAICS data thus entails the detailed amalgamation of a number of different SIC and NAICS categories into what then becomes one coherent time series. For the purposes of this book, two major sectors of IT industries have been generated: (1) IT hardware (for 1989–98 covering SIC categories 357 and 367 and for 1999–2003 covering NAICS categories 3341 and 3344) and (2) IT services (for 1989–98 covering SIC category 737 and for 1999–2003 covering NAICS categories 514 and 5415). The detailed descriptions of each category as described by the US Census Bureau (at www.census.gov) are provided below. The selection of individual industries reflects the desire to achieve as comprehensive and precise coverage as possible of each sector, as well as the availability of detailed publicly accessible data.

IT Hardware

SIC 357: Computer and Office Equipment

This industry group includes establishments primarily engaged in manufacturing electronic computers; computer storage devices; computer terminals; computer peripheral equipment not elsewhere classified; calculating and accounting machines, except electronic computers; and office machines not elsewhere classified.

SIC 367: Electronic Components and Accessories

This industry group includes establishments primarily engaged in manufacturing electron tubes; printed circuit boards; semiconductors and related devices; electronic capacitors; electronic resistors; electronic coils, transformers, and other inductors; electronic connectors; and electronic components not elsewhere classified.

NAICS 3341: Computer and Peripheral Equipment Manufacturing

This industry comprises establishments primarily engaged in manufacturing and/or assembling electronic computers, such as mainframes, personal computers, workstations, laptops, and computer servers; and computer peripheral equipment, such as storage devices, printers, monitors, input/output devices, and terminals. Computers can be analog, digital, or hybrid. Digital computers, the most common type, are devices that do all of the following: (1) store the processing program or programs and the data immediately necessary for the execution of the program; (2) can be freely programmed in accordance with the requirements of the user; (3) perform arithmetical computations specified by the user; and (4) execute, without human intervention, a processing program that requires the computer to modify its execution by logical decision during the processing run. Analog computers are capable of simulating mathematical models and comprise at least analog, control, and programming elements.

NAICS 3344: Semiconductor and Other Electronic Component Manufacturing

This industry comprises establishments primarily engaged in manufacturing semiconductors and other components for electronic applications. Examples of products made by these establishments are capacitors, resistors, microprocessors, bare and loaded printed circuit boards, electron tubes, electronic connectors, and computer modems.

IT Services

SIC 737: Computer Programming, Data Processing, and Other Computer-Related Services

- Establishments primarily engaged in providing custom computer programming services on a contract or fee basis. These establishments often perform a variety of additional services, such as computer software design and analysis, modification of existing software, and training in the use of custom software.

- Establishments primarily engaged in designing and developing prepackaged software, including operating, utility, and applications programs. These establishments may also prepare software documentation for the user, install software for the user, and train the user in the use of the software.

- Establishments primarily engaged in developing or modifying computer software and packaging or bundling the software with hardware (computers and peripheral equipment) to create an integrated system for specific application. These establishments are involved in all phases of systems development, from design through installation.

- Establishments primarily engaged in providing computer processing and data preparation services. Service may consist of complete processing and preparation of reports from data supplied by the customer, or it may be specialized, such as data entry or making data processing equipment available on an hourly or timesharing basis.

- Establishments primarily engaged in providing online information retrieval services on a contract or fee basis. The information generally involves a range of subjects and is taken from other primary sources. Establishments that collect and originate the data are classified in the industry associated with that activity.

- Establishments primarily engaged in providing onsite management and operation of computer and data processing facilities on a contract or fee basis.

- Establishments primarily engaged in renting or leasing (except finance) computers and related data processing equipment on the customer's site, whether or not also providing maintenance or support services. Establishments primarily engaged in both manufacturing and leasing computers and related data processing equipment are classified in Division D, manufacturing, and separate establishments owned by the manufacturer and primarily engaged in leasing are classified in wholesale trade.

- Establishments primarily engaged in the maintenance and repair of computers and computer peripheral equipment.

- Establishments primarily engaged in providing computer-related services, not elsewhere classified, such as computer consulting, disk and diskette conversion, and tape recertification.

NAICS 514: Information Services and Data Processing Services

Industries in the Information Services and Data Processing Services subsector group establishments that provide, store, and process information, and that provide access to information. The main components of the subsector are news syndicates, libraries, archives, online information service providers, and data processors.

NAICS 5415: Computer Systems Design and Related Services

This industry comprises establishments primarily engaged in providing expertise in the field of information technologies through one or more of the following activities: (1) writing, modifying, testing, and supporting software to meet the needs of a particular customer; (2) planning and designing computer systems that integrate computer hardware, software, and communication technologies; (3) onsite management and operation of clients' computer systems and/or data processing facilities; and (4) other professional and technical computer-related advice and services.

Cross-Border Trade

Throughout the book there are frequent comparisons between data originating only from US multinational IT companies, and data referring to total US cross-border IT trade. A major difference between data from affiliates and data for US cross-border trade is that cross-border trade is classified by the type of goods or services actually transacted, rather than by the industrial classification of the US parent or foreign-affiliate transactor. Therefore these comparisons necessitate selection of the suitable, comparable cross-border trade data categories for IT hardware and services to match the classification of US multinational data.

Cross-Border IT Hardware Trade

For the purposes of this book, cross-border US exports and imports of IT hardware (goods) are the sum of lines C48 "Computers, Peripherals and Parts" and C49 "Semiconductors" (Exports) and line C116 "Computers, Peripherals and Parts" and C117 "Semiconductors" (Imports) in table 2 ("US Trade in Goods") in the US International Transactions Accounts Data tables, respectively (see www.bea.gov). These two lines correspond to US Export/Import-End-Use-Categories 21301 "Computer Accessories, Peripherals and Parts" and 21320 "Semiconductors and Related Devices," in that order (see http://reportweb.usitc.gov).

Cross-Border IT Services Trade

US cross-border trade in IT software services is represented in categories 2 and 3 from the tables of unaffiliated trade in "Business, Professional and Technical Services," covering "Computer and Data Processing Services" as well as "Database and Other Information Services" (see table at www.bea.gov).

Some Statistical Caveats

Valuation and Timing

The BEA data are collected through annual surveys, and therefore all data are in current US dollars. This means that the valuation of foreign affiliate operations may reflect movements in exchange rates, rather than real changes. In addition, intercompany valuations of assets may not be conducted at market exchange rates, which will further introduce an element of uncertainty. However, there is no reason to believe that this represents a systematic data bias, and as such a risk to the validity of conclusions.

Respondents to BEA surveys are required to submit data for the company fiscal year ending in the calendar year of the survey. This means that comprehensive financial and operating data from BEA surveys are not directly comparable to calendar year estimates of transactions between foreign affiliates and their US parents that appear in the US International Transactions Accounts or with the calendar year estimates of the US direct investment position abroad. The BEA adjusts the data for calendar year presentation according to the size, number, and timing of their financial years of US parents and foreign affiliates (for 1994 data, see www.bea. gov). Yet, as with exchange rate valuation, there is no reason to expect this problem to introduce systematic bias into our longer time series, and this issue thus presents no complications for the inferences drawn from the data.

Company Reclassifications

Despite attempting to match our data as carefully as possible with the industry that is the subject of this book, it is impossible to detect variation in the aggregate macro data arising from reclassifications of individual firms from one primary industry class into a different class as the activities of the firm change. A specific case is the reclassification of IBM from a "hardware" to a "software and services" firm.

Appendix figure A.1 shows the revenue streams from the different business segments of IBM. Suppose IBM described its different business segments in its annual reports according to the SIC or NAICS classifications used by the BEA. If so, IBM and any affiliates with similar revenue distribution would have been classified in 1991 as an IT hardware company, as hardware was its primary industry of business. However, in light of the change in activities, by 2001, IBM would have been classified as an IT services company, as services were now its primary industry of business.

Due to the rules of confidentiality covering BEA data, it is impossible to discern the classification of individual companies and thus researchers using public data cannot control for such reclassifications. One must

Figure A.1   IBM revenues by business segment, 1991–2004

percent

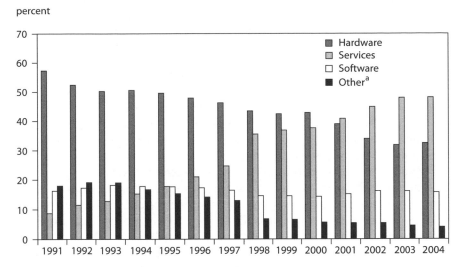

a. Content varies throughout the period but includes segments such as maintenance, rentals, financing, and enterprise investment.

Note: Due to a change in reporting segments from 1997–98, a break in the time series for "other" is present between these two years. This, however, does not affect the main conclusions of this table.

Source: Company 10-K filings.

maintain the assumption of stability in BEA business enterprise classification over time. Yet in the IT sector, characterized by the rapid transformation of firms, this may constitute a data weakness. On the other hand, many firms have multiple activities and yet are assigned to one classification of BEA data, and this variation may to some degree make up the weakness of classifying all of a company's data according to its primary industry of activity. Reclassification of some IT hardware companies into IT services companies, for instance, will reflect an industry trend, which might otherwise go unnoticed in the aggregate data until IT services became the primary industry of activity for most IT companies.

Cross-Border Trade Data

While the concepts and definitions underlying the data collected in surveys on trade in goods are nearly identical to those used for the data on total US trade in goods compiled by the US Census Bureau, the BEA flags two issues clouding comparisons. First, in the surveys, US trade in goods data are requested on a "shipped" basis—that is, on the basis of when, where, and to (or by) whom the goods were shipped—in order for them to be comparable with the data on total US trade. However, most survey respondents keep their accounting records on a "charged" basis—that is, on the basis of when, where, and to (or by) whom the goods were charged. Second, additional differences between the BEA and Census Bureau trade data may result from the data coming from two sources. The BEA data are based on company records, whereas the Census Bureau data are compiled from export and import documents filed by the shipper with the US Customs Service on individual transactions. The timing, valuation, origin or destination, shipper, and product involved in a given export or import transaction may be recorded differently on company records than on customs export and import documents.

To make completely accurate product-by-product comparisons of deliveries through the two different channels, cross-border trade and foreign affiliate sales, particular data on the type of product sold by a foreign affiliate would have to be collected. Unfortunately, no such data exist—principally due to concerns over the undue burden such data collection would present to respondents (Whichard and Borga 2002). But while this methodological difference clearly presents a limitation on valid data comparisons, it does not constitute a significant analytical obstacle when focusing, as does this book, on development trends over time in the IT industry.

Annual Wage Data

Data on total employment and total compensation costs are collected in the BEA annual surveys and are used in this book to deduce an estimate of average wages for IT industry parents and foreign affiliates. This is not an exact science, and two concerns warrant caution. First, for the employment data, a part-time employee is counted the same as a full-time employee. Thus, compensation per employee may vary across parents or affiliates simply because of differences in the share of part-time workers in total employment. Second, compensation per employee may be distorted by data for businesses or business segments acquired or sold during the year. To some extent this is akin to a stock-and-flow problem, as compensation paid is spread out over the year, while employment stock is taken at year-end.

Keeping these issues in mind, however, does not prevent discerning comparative differences between greatly disparate entities, as is done in this book. Nor does it prevent time-trend determination.

Ownership Overlaps

For reasons of data consistency and respondent burden, the above-mentioned definitions of ownership of US parent companies, US MOFAs, and MOUSAs are not mutually exclusive. As such, it is possible that a degree of overlap exists, for instance, in the case of a majority-owned US affiliate that itself holds majority-owned foreign affiliates. Financial and operational data for value added, which may be shifted around geographically for tax optimization purposes by multinational companies, are at particular risk of being materially affected by this statistical overlap.

References

Acemoglu, Daron. 2002. Technical Change, Inequality, and the Labor Market. *Journal of Economic Literature* 40 (March): 7–72.

Ahmad, Nadim, Francois Lequiller, Pascal Marianna, Dirk Pilat, Paul Schreyer, and Anita Wölfl. 2003. *Comparing Labour Productivity Growth in the OECD Area: The Role of Measurement.* OECD STI Working Papers 2003/14. Paris: Organization for Economic Cooperation and Development, Directorate for Science, Technology and Industry.

Aizcorbe, Ana. 2001. Price Measures for Semiconductor Devices. Federal Reserve Board of Governors, Washington. Photocopy (January).

Aizcorbe, Ana. 2002. *Why Are Semiconductor Prices Falling So Fast? Industry Estimates and Implications for Productivity Measurement.* Finance and Economics Discussion Series Paper 2002-20. Washington: Federal Reserve Board (April).

Aizcorbe, Ana. 2005. *Moore's Law, Competition and Intel's Productivity in the Mid-1990s.* BEA Working Paper 2005-08. Washington: Bureau of Economic Analysis.

Aizcorbe, Ana, Kenneth Flamm, and Anjum Khurshid. 2002. *The Role of Semiconductor Inputs in IT Hardware Price Decline: Computers vs. Communications.* Finance and Economics Discussion Series Working Paper 2002-37 (June). Washington: Federal Reserve Board, Division of Research and Statistics and Monetary Affairs.

Atrostic, B. K., and Sang Nguyen. 2005. *Computer Input, Computer Networks, and Productivity.* CES Discussion Paper 05-01. Washington: Center for Economic Studies, US Census Bureau.

Autor, David H., Lawrence Katz, and Alan Krueger. 1997. *Computing Inequality: Have Computers Changed the Labor Market?* NBER Working Paper 5956. Cambridge, MA: National Bureau of Economic Research.

Autor, David H., Frank Levy, and Richard J. Murnane. 2001. *The Skill Content of Recent Technological Change: An Empirical Exploration.* NBER Working Paper 8337. Cambridge, MA: National Bureau of Economic Research.

Autor, David H., Frank Levy, and Richard J. Murnane. 2002. Upstairs-Downstairs: How Introducing Computer Technology Changed Skills and Pay on Two Floors of Cabot Bank. *Regional Review* Q2: 22–30. Boston, MA: Federal Reserve Bank of Boston.

Baily, Martin N., and Jens Gersback. 1995. Efficiency in Manufacturing and the Need for Global Competition. *Brookings Papers on Economic Activity: Microeconomics.* Washington: Brookings Institution.

Baily, Martin N., and Jacob Funk Kirkegaard. 2004. *Transforming the European Economy*. Washington: Institute for International Economics.

Baily, Martin N., and Robert Z. Lawrence. 2004. What Happened to the Great US Job Machine? The Role of Trade and Electronic Offshoring. *Brookings Papers on Economic Activity*, no. 2 (Fall): 201–60.

Bair, Jennifer, and Gary Gereffi. 2001. Local Clusters in Global Chains: The Causes and Consequences of Export Dynamism in Torreon's Blue Jeans Industry. *World Development* 29, no. 1: 1885–903.

Bardhan, Ashok Deo, and Dwight Jaffee. 2005. *Innovation, R&D, and Offshoring*. Research Report 1005. Berkeley, CA: Fisher Center for Real Estate and Urban Economics, University of California (October).

Bardhan, Ashok Deo, and C. Kroll. 2003. The New Wave of Outsourcing: BPO, BSO and the US Economy. *Quarterly Report* (Fall). Berkeley, CA: Fisher Center for Real Estate and Urban Economics, University of California.

Baygan, Gunseli, and Catherine L. Mann. 1999. Technological Sophistication and Labor Productivity in the OECD. Institute for International Economics, Washington. Photocopy.

Bayoumi, Tamim, and Markus Haacker. 2002. *It's Not What You Make, It's How You Use IT: Measuring the Welfare Benefits of the IT Revolution Across Countries*. IMF Working Paper 02/117. Washington: International Monetary Fund.

Bayoumi, Tamim, David Coe, and Elhanan Helpman. 1996. *R&D Spillovers and Global Growth*. NBER Working Paper 5628. Cambridge, MA: National Bureau of Economic Research.

BEA (Bureau of Economic Analysis). 1994. *Methodology of the 1994 Benchmark Survey of US Direct Investment Abroad*. Washington. Available at www.bea.gov (accessed October 1, 2005).

BEA (Bureau of Economic Analysis). 1995. *A Guide to BEA Statistics on US Multinational Companies*. Washington. Available at www.bea.gov (accessed October 1, 2005).

BEA (Bureau of Economic Analysis). 2000. *Recognition of Business and Government Expenditures for Software as Investment: Methodology and Quantitative Impacts, 1959–98*. Washington.

BEA (Bureau of Economic Analysis). 2001. *Foreign Direct Investment in the United States: Final Results of 1997 Benchmark Survey*. Washington. Available at www.bea.gov (accessed October 1, 2005).

BEA (Bureau of Economic Analysis). 2005. *Survey of Current Business* 85, no. 10 (October). Washington: Department of Commerce.

Bernard, Andrew B., and J. Bradford Jensen. 1997. Exporters, Skill Upgrading, and the Wage Gap. *Journal of International Economics* (February): 3–31.

Bernard, Andrew B., J. Bradford Jensen, and Peter K. Schott. 2002. *Survival of the Best Fit: Competition from Low Wage Countries and the (Uneven) Growth of US Manufacturing Plants*. NBER Working Paper 9170. Cambridge, MA: National Bureau of Economic Research.

Bernard, Andrew B., J. Bradford Jensen, and Peter K. Schott. 2003. *Falling Trade Costs, Heterogeneous Firms, and Industry Dynamics*. NBER Working Paper 9639. Cambridge, MA: National Bureau of Economic Research.

Bernard, Andrew B., J. Bradford Jensen, and Peter K. Schott. 2005. *Importers, Exporters, and Multinationals: A Portrait of Firms in the U.S. That Trade Goods*. Working Paper 05-10. Washington: Institute for International Economics.

Black, Sandra E., and Lisa M. Lynch. 2001. How to Compete: The Impact of Workplace Practices and information Technology on Productivity. *Review of Economics and Statistics* 83, no. 3 (August): 434–45.

Black, Sandra E., and Lisa M. Lynch. 2003. The New Economy and the Organization of Work. In *The Handbook of the New Economy*, ed. Derek Jones. New York: Academic Press.

Black, Sandra E., and Lisa M. Lynch. 2004. What's Driving the New Economy? The Benefits of Workplace Innovation. *Economic Journal* (February).

Black, Sandra E., and Lisa M. Lynch. Forthcoming. Measuring Organizational Capital in the New Economy. In *Measuring Capital in the New Economy*, ed. Carol Corrado, John Haltiwanger, and Dan Sichel. Chicago, IL: University of Chicago Press.

Blonigen, Bruce. 2005. A Review of the Empirical Literature on FDI Determinants. University of Oregon. Photocopy (April).

BLS (Bureau of Labor Statistics). 2002. Employee Tenure in 2002. Statement released on September 19, 2002. Washington. Available at www.bls.gov (accessed October 1, 2005).

BLS (Bureau of Labor Statistics). 2004. Employee Tenure in 2004. Statement released on September 19, 2004. Washington. Available at www.bls.gov (accessed October 1, 2005).

BLS (Bureau of Labor Statistics). 2005a. *Occupational Outlook Handbook,* 2004–05 ed. Washington. Available at www.bls.gov (accessed October 1, 2005).

BLS (Bureau of Labor Statistics). 2005b. *Employment Statistics from BLS Household and Payroll Surveys: Summary of Recent Trends.* Washington. Available at www.bls.gov (accessed October 1, 2005).

BLS (Bureau of Labor Statistics). 2006. *Occupational Outlook Handbook,* 2006–07 ed. Washington. Available at www.bls.gov (accessed April 24, 2006).

Boning, Brent, Casey Ichniowski, and Kathryn Shaw. 2001. *Opportunity Counts: Teams and the Effectiveness of Production Incentives.* NBER Working Paper 8306. Cambridge, MA: National Bureau of Economic Research.

Bora, Bijit. 2004. *Information Technology Agreement and World Trade.* WTO Discussion Paper. Geneva: World Trade Organization (November).

Bora, Bijit, and Xiupeng Liu. 2004. The Impact of the Information Technology Agreement on World Trade. World Trade Organization, Geneva. Photocopy (October).

Borga, Maria, and Michael Mann. 2003. US International Services. *Survey of Current Business* (October). Washington: Bureau of Economic Analysis.

Borga, Maria, and Michael Mann. 2004. US International Services Cross-Border Trade in 2003 and Sales Through Affiliates in 2002. *Survey of Current Business* (October). Washington: Bureau of Economic Analysis.

Bound, John, and George Johnson. 1992. Changes in the Structure of Wages in the 1980s: An Evaluation of Alternative Explanations. *American Economic Review* 82, no. 3 (June): 371–92.

Bradbury, Katherine. 2005. *Additional Slack in the Economy: The Poor Recovery in Labor Force Participation During this Business Cycle.* Public Policy Briefs 05–2. Boston, MA: Federal Reserve Bank of Boston.

Bresnahan, Timothy, Erik Brynjolffsson, and Loren Hitt. 2002. Information Technology, Workplace Organization, and the Demand for Skilled Labor: Firm-Level Evidence. *Quarterly Journal of Economics* 117, no 1: 339–76.

Brown, Drusilla K., Alan V. Deardorff, and Robert M. Stern. 2001. Impacts on NAFTA Members of Multilateral and Regional Trading Arrangements and Initiatives and Harmonization of NAFTA's External Tariffs. Paper presented at the Industry Canada Conference on North American Linkages, June.

Brynjolffsson, Erik, and Lorin Hitt. 2000. Beyond Computation: Information Technology, Organization Transformation, and Business Performance. *The Journal of Economic Perspectives* 14, no. 4 (Fall).

Brynjolffsson, Erik, and Chris F. Kemerer. 1996. Network Externalities in Microcomputer Software: An Econometric Analysis of the Spreadsheet Market. *Management Science* 42, no. 12 (December).

Buckley, Patricia, and Sabrina Montes. 2002. Main Street in the Digital Age: How Small and Medium-Sized Businesses Are Using the Tools of the New Economy. US Department of Commerce, Economics and Statistics Administration. Photocopy (February).

Card, David, and Thomas Lemieux. 2000. *Can Falling Supply Explain the Rising Return to College for Younger Men? A Cohort-Based Analysis.* NBER Working Paper 7655. Cambridge, MA: National Bureau of Economic Research.

Clausing, Kimberly A. 1998. *The Impact of Transfer Pricing on Intrafirm Trade.* NBER Working Paper 6688. Cambridge, MA: National Bureau of Economic Research.

Coe, David, and Elhanan Helpman. 1995. International R&D Spillovers. *European Economic Review* 39, no. 5: 859–87.

Crafts, Nicholas F. R. 2004. *Social Savings as a Measure of the Contribution of a New Technology to Economic Growth*. Working Paper in Large-Scale Technological Change 06/04. London School of Economics (July).

Daveri, Francesco. 2002. *The New Economy in Europe*. WIDER Discussion Paper 2002/70. Helsinki, Finland: United Nations University World Institute for Development Economics Research.

Dedrick, Jason, Vijay Gurbaxani, and Kenneth L. Kraemer. 2002. *Information Technology and Economic Performance: A Critical Review of the Empirical Evidence*. Center for Research on Information Technology and Organizations, University of California, Irvine. Photocopy (November).

Dee, Philippa, and Kevin Hanslow. 2001. Multilateral Liberalization of Services Trade. In *Services in the International Economy*, ed. Robert M. Stern. Ann Arbor, MI: University of Michigan Press.

Deloitte Research. 2003. The Cusp of a Revolution—How Offshoring will Transform the Financial Services Industry (February). Available at www.deloitte.com (accessed May 2, 2006).

Desai, Mihir A., James R. Hines. 2002. *Expectations and Expatriations: Tracing the Causes and Consequences of Corporate Inversion*. NBER Working Paper 9057. Cambridge, MA: National Bureau of Economic Research.

Desai, Mihir A., C. Fritz Foley, and James R. Hines. 2002. *Chains of Ownership, Regional Tax Competition, and Foreign Direct Investment*. NBER Working Paper 9224. Cambridge, MA: National Bureau of Economic Research.

Deutsche Bundesbank. 2001. *Problems of International Comparisons of Growth—A Supplementary Analysis*. Monthly Report (May). Frankfurt.

Dunne, Timothy, Lucia Foster, John Haltiwanger, and Kenneth Troske. 2000. *Wage and Productivity Dispersion in US Manufacturing: The Role of Computer Investment*. NBER Working Paper 7465. Cambridge, MA: National Bureau of Economic Research.

Eaton, Jonathan, and Samuel Kortum. 1996. Trade in Ideas: Patenting and Productivity in the OECD. *Journal of International Economics* 40: 251–78.

ESA (Economics and Statistics Administration). 2002. *Digital Economy 2002*. Washington: US Department of Commerce.

Electronic Trend Publications. 2004. *The Worldwide Electronics Manufacturing Services Market*, 1st ed. (July). Available at www.electronictrendpubs.com.

Elmeskov, Jorgen, and Stefano Scarpetta. 2000. New Sources for Economic Growth in Europe? Paper presented at The New Millennium—Time for an Economic Paradigm, Oesterreichische National Bank, Vienna. Photocopy (June).

Figura, Andrew. 2003. *The Effect of Restructuring on Unemployment*. Washington: Federal Reserve Board of Governors (October 27).

Flamm, Kenneth. 1997. More for Less: The Economic Impact of Semiconductors. In Celebration of the 50th Anniversary of the Invention of the Transistor. Semiconductor Industry Association. Photocopy (December).

Foster, Lucia, John Haltiwanger, and C. J. Krizan. 2002. *The Link between Aggregate and Micro Productivity Growth: Evidence from Retail Trade*. NBER Working Paper 9120. Cambridge, MA: National Bureau of Economic Research.

Fraumeni, Barbara, and Sumiye Okubo. 2005. R&D in the National Income and Product Accounts: A First Look at Its Effect on GDP. In *Measuring Capital in the New Economy*, ed. Carol Corrado, John Haltiwanger, and Daniel Sichel. Chicago, IL: The University of Chicago Press.

GAO (General Accounting Office). 2000. H-1B Foreign Workers: Better Controls Needed to Help Employers and Protect Workers. GAO/HEHS-00-157. Washington.

Gereffi, Gary. 2001. Beyond the Producer-Driven/Buyer-Driven Dichotomy: The Evolution of Global Value Chains in the Internet Era. *IDS Bulletin* 32, no. 3 (July): 30–40.

Goldin, Claudia, and Lawrence F. Katz. 2001. Decreasing (and Then Increasing) Inequality in America: A Tale of Two Half-Centuries. In *The Causes and Consequences of Increasing Income Inequality*, ed. F. Welch. Chicago, IL: The University of Chicago Press.

Griffith, Rachel, Stephen Redding, and J. Van Reenan. 2000. *Mapping the Two Faces of R&D: Productivity Growth in a Panel of OECD Industries*. Institute for Fiscal Studies Working Paper 02/00. London: Institute for Fiscal Studies.

Groshen, Erica, and Simon Potter. 2003. Has Structural Change Contributed to a Jobless Recovery? *Current Issues in Economics and Finance* 9, no. 8 (August). New York: Federal Reserve Bank of New York.

Grimm, Bruce T., Brent R. Moulton, and David B. Wasshausen. 2002. Information Processing Equipment and Software in the National Accounts. Bureau of Economic Analysis, Washington. Photocopy (April).

Gruen, David. 2001. Australia's Strong Productivity Growth: Will It Be Sustained? *RBA Bulletin* (February). Sydney: Reserve Bank of Australia.

Gust, Christopher, and Jaime Marquez. 2000. Productivity Developments Abroad. *Federal Reserve Bulletin* (October). Washington: Federal Reserve Board.

Gust, Christopher, and Jaime Marquez. 2002. *International Comparison of Productivity Growth: The Role of Information Technology and Regulatory Practices*. International Finance Discussion Papers 727 (May). Washington: Federal Reserve Board.

Haacker, Markus, and James Morsink. 2002. *You Say You Want a Revolution: Information Technology and Growth*. IMF Working Paper 02/70 (April). Washington: International Monetary Fund.

Haskel, J. E., S. C. Pereira, and M. S. Slaughter. 2002. *Does Inward Foreign Direct Investment Boost the Productivity of Domestic Firms?* NBER Working Paper 724 (Jan). Cambridge, MA: National Bureau of Economic Research.

Helpman, Elhanan, Marc J. Melitz, and Stephen R. Yeaple. 2003. *Export vs. FDI*. NBER Working Paper 9439. Cambridge, MA: National Bureau of Economic Research.

Hines, James R. 1996. Altered States: Taxes and the Location of Foreign Direct Investment in America. *American Economic Review* 86, no. 5: 1076–94.

Hines, James R. 1997. Tax Policy and the Activities of Multinational Corporations. In *Fiscal Policy: Lessons from Economic Research*, ed. A. J. Auerbach. Cambridge, MA: MIT Press.

Hines, James R. 2000. International Taxation. *NBER Reporter* (Spring). Cambridge, MA: National Bureau of Economic Research.

Ichniowski, Casey, Kathryn Shaw, and Gabrielle Prennushi. 1997. The Effects of Human Resource Management Practices on Productivity. *American Economic Review* 87, no. 3: 291–313.

INS (US Immigration and Naturalization Service). 2000a. *Characteristics of Specialty Occupation Workers (H-1B): May 1998 to July 1999*. Washington.

INS (US Immigration and Naturalization Service). 2000b. *Leading Employers of Specialty Occupation Workers (H-1B): October 1999 to February 2000*. Washington.

INS (US Immigration and Naturalization Service). 2002a. *Characteristics of Specialty Occupation Workers (H-1B): Fiscal Year 2000*. Washington.

INS (US Immigration and Naturalization Service). 2002b. *Characteristics of Specialty Occupation Workers (H-1B): Fiscal Year 2001*. Washington.

Intel Corporation. 2004. *Technology and Research at Intel: Architectural Innovation for the Future*. Available at ftp://download.intel.com/technology/techresearch/innovations (accessed October 1, 2005).

Jensen, J. Bradford, and Lori Kletzer. 2005. *Tradable Services: Understanding the Scope and Impact of Services Offshoring*. Institute for International Economics. Working Paper 05–9. Washington: Institute for International Economics.

Jensen, J. Bradford, and Nathan Musick. 1996. *Trade, Technology, and Plant Performance*. ESA/OPD 96-4. Washington: US Department of Commerce Economics and Statistics Administration.

Jorgenson, Dale, Mun S. Ho, and Kevin J. Stiroh. 2002. Projecting Productivity Growth: Lessons from the US Growth Resurgence. Paper prepared at the Conference on Technology, Growth, and the Labor Market, Federal Reserve Bank of Atlanta, March 14.

Katz, Lawrence F., and David H. Autor. 1999. Changes in the Wage Structure and Earnings Inequality. In *Handbook of Labor Economics* 3A, ed. O. Ashenfelter and D. Card. Amsterdam: North-Holland Press.

Katz, Lawrence F., and Kevin M. Murphy. 1992 Changes in Relative Wages, 1963–1987: Supply and Demand Factors. *Quarterly Journal of Economics* 107, no. 1 (February): 35–78.

Keller, Walter. 2001a. *International Technology Diffusion*. NBER Working Paper 8573. Cambridge, MA: National Bureau of Economic Research.

Keller, Walter. 2001b. *Knowledge Spillover at the World's Technology Frontier*. CEPR Working Paper 2815. Washington: Center for Economic Policy and Research.

Keller, Walter, and Stephen R. Yeaple. 2002. Multinational Enterprises, International Trade, and Productivity Growth: Firm-Level Evidence from the United States. Photocopy (September).

Kirkegaard, Jacob Funk. 2004. Outsourcing—Stains on the White Collar? Institute for International Economics, Washington. Photocopy (February).

Kirkegaard, Jacob Funk. 2005. *Importing Skills: Foreign High-Skilled Workers on H-1B and L-1 Visas in the United States*. Institute for International Economics Working Paper 05-15. Washington: Institute for International Economics.

Kletzer, Lori G. 2001. *A Prescription to Relieve Worker Anxiety*. International Economics Policy Brief 01-2 (March). Washington: Institute for International Economics.

Kletzer, Lori G., and Howard Rosen. 2005. Easing the Adjustment Burden on US Workers. In *The United States and the World Economy: Foreign Economic Policy for the Next Decade*, by C. Fred Bergsten and the Institute for International Economics. Washington: Washington: Institute for International Economics.

Knight, Sarah Cleeland. 2003. The Institutional Determinants of Internet Adoption: A Focus on Asia and Latin America. Research paper for Georgetown University. Photocopy (July).

Kraemer, Kenneth L., and Jason Dedrick. 2000. Information Technology and Economic Development: Results and Policy Implications of Cross-Country Studies. In *Information Technology, Productivity, and Economic Growth International Evidence and Implications for Economic Development*, ed. M. Pohjola. Oxford: Oxford University Press.

Krueger, Alan. 1993. How Computers Have Changed the Wage Structure: Evidence from Micro Data. *Quarterly Journal of Economics*: 33–60.

Landefeld, J. Steven, and Bruce T. Grimm. 2000. A Note on the Impact of Hedonics and Computers on Real GDP. *Survey of Current Business* (December). Washington: Bureau of Economic Analysis.

Lardy, Nicholas. 2005. China: The Great Economic Challenge? In *The United States and the World Economy: Foreign Economic Policy for the Next Decade*, by C. Fred Bergsten and the Institute for International Economics. Washington: Institute for International Economics.

Lee, Y. S., and Seo H. Wan. 2001. Contribution of Information and Communication Technology to Total Factor Productivity and Externality Effects in 38 Countries. *Korea Telecommunications Policy Review* (in Korean).

Levy, Frank, and Richard J. Murnane. 1992. U.S. Earnings Levels and Earnings Inequality: A Review of Recent Trends and Proposed Explanations. *Journal of Economic Literature* 30 (September): 1333–81.

Levy, Frank, and Richard J. Murnane. 2004. *The New Division of Labor: How Computers Are Creating the Next Job Market*. Princeton, NJ: Princeton University Press.

Lewis III, Howard, and J. David Richardson. 2001. *Why Globalization Really Matters!* Washington: Institute for International Economics.

Mann, Catherine L. 1994. US International Transactions in 1993. *Federal Reserve Bulletin* (May): 365–78.

Mann, Catherine L. 1997. Computers and Semiconductors in the United States: Linking the World in Global Trade. In *Korea's Economy 1997*, volume 13. Washington: Korea Economic Institute of America.

Mann, Catherine L. 1998. Globalization and Productivity Growth in the United States and Germany. In *Globalization, Technological Change, and Labor Markets*, ed. Stanley Black. Boston, MA: Kluwer Academic Publishers.

Mann, Catherine L. 2000. Electronic Commerce in Developing Countries: Issues for Domestic Policy and WTO Negotiations. In *Services in the International Economy*, ed. Robert Stern. Ann Arbor, MI: University of Michigan Press.

Mann, Catherine L. 2001. International Internet Governance: Oh, What a Tangled Web We Could Weave! *Georgetown Journal of International Affairs* (Summer/Fall).

Mann, Catherine L. 2002. Balance and Overlap in the Global Electronic Marketplace: The UCITA Example. *Washington University Journal of Law and Policy* (Summer).

Mann, Catherine L. 2004. The US Current Account, New Economy Services, and Implications for Sustainability. *Review of International Economics* 12, no. 2 (May).

Mann, Catherine L. 2005. Globalization, Information Technology, and US Economic Performance. Paper presented at Globalization: Prospects and Problems, Conference in Honor of Jagdish Bhagwati's 70th Birthday, University of Florida, Gainesville, January 28–30.

Mann, Catherine L., and Sarah Cleeland Knight. 2000. Electronic Commerce in the World Trade Organization. In *The WTO after Seattle*, ed. Jeffrey Schott. Washington: Institute for International Economics.

Mann, Catherine L., and Katharina Plueck. 2005. *The US Trade Deficit: A Disaggregated Perspective*. Working Paper 05–11. Washington: Institute for International Economics.

Mann, Catherine L., and Daniel H. Rosen. 2001. *The New Economy and APEC*. Singapore and Washington: APEC Secretariat and the Institute for International Economics.

Mann, Catherine L., Sue E. Eckert, and Sarah Cleeland Knight. 2000. *Global Electronic Commerce: A Policy Primer*. Washington: Institute for International Economics.

Marquez, Jaime. 2005. *Estimating Elasticities for US Trade in Services*. International Finance Discussion Paper 2005-836. Washington: Federal Reserve Board of Governors (July).

Mataloni, Raymond J. 2005. US Multinational Companies: Operations 2003. *Survey of Current Business* (July). Washington: Bureau of Economic Analysis.

McKinsey Global Institute. 2001. *US Productivity Growth 1995–2000*. Washington.

McKinsey Global Institute. 2002. *How IT Enables Productivity Growth*. Washington.

McKinsey Global Institute. 2005. The Emerging Global Labor Market: Part II—The Supply of Offshore Talent in Services. Washington. Photocopy (June).

Mishel, Lawrence, and Jared Bernstein. 2003. Wage Inequality and the New Economy in the US: Does IT-led Growth Generate Wage Inequality? *Canadian Public Policy* 29 (Special Supplement): 204–21.

Moran, Theodore H. 1999. *Foreign Direct Investment and Development: The New Policy Agenda for Developing Countries and Economies in Transition*. Washington: Institute for International Economics.

Moran, Theodore H. 2001. *Parental Supervision: The New Paradigm for Foreign Direct Investment and Development*. POLICY ANALYSES IN INTERNATIONAL ECONOMICS 64. Washington: Institute for International Economics.

Morisi, Teresa L. 1996. Commercial Banking Transformed by Computer Technology. *Monthly Labor Review* (August): 30–36.

Mun, Sung-Bae, and M. Ishaq Nadiri. 2002. *Information Technology Externalities: Empirical Evidence from 42 US Industries*. NBER Working Paper 9272. Cambridge, MA: National Bureau of Economic Research.

Nardone, T., M. Bowler, J. Kropf, K. Kirkland, and S. Wetrogan. 2003. Examining the Discrepancy in Employment Growth between the CPS and the CES. Paper presented to the Federal Economic Statistics Advisory Committee, October 17.

Navaretti, Giorgio Barba, and David G. Tarr. 2000. International Knowledge Flows and Economic Performance: A Review of the Evidence. *World Bank Economic Review* 14, no. 1: 1–15.

Nephew, Erin, Jennifer Koncz, Maria Borga, and Michael Mann. 2005. US International Services Cross-Border Trade in 2004 and Sales Through Affiliates in 2003. *Survey of Current Business* (October). Washington: Bureau of Economic Analysis.

OECD (Organization for Economic Cooperation and Development). 2000. *Literacy in the Information Age: Final Report of the International Adult Literacy Survey.* Paris.

OECD (Organization for Economic Cooperation and Development). 2002a. *Information Technology Outlook: ICTs and the Information Economy.* Paris.

OECD (Organization for Economic Cooperation and Development). 2002b. *Measuring the Information Economy.* Paris.

OECD (Organization for Economic Cooperation and Development). 2003. *The Source of Economic Growth in OECD Countries.* Paris.

OECD (Organization for Economic Cooperation and Development). 2004a. *Information Technology Outlook 2004.* Paris..

OECD (Organization for Economic Cooperation and Development). 2004b. *Trends in International Migration 2004.* Paris.

OECD (Organization for Economic Cooperation and Development). 2004c. *Main Science and Technology Indicators (MSTI),* 2004/2nd ed. Paris.

OECD (Organization for Economic Cooperation and Development). 2005a. *OECD Education at a Glance 2005.* Paris.

OECD (Organization for Economic Cooperation and Development). 2005b. *Learning a Living: First Results of the Adult Literacy and Life Skills Survey.* Paris.

Oliner, Stephen, and Daniel Sichel. 2000. The Resurgence of Growth in the Late 1990s: Is Information Technology the Story? *Journal of Economic Perspectives* 14, no. 4: 3–22.

Oliner, Stephen, and Daniel Sichel. 2002. Information Technology and Productivity: What Are We Now and Where Are We Going? *Economic Review.* Atlanta, GA: Federal Reserve Bank of Atlanta.

Parham, Dean. 2002. Australia: Getting the Most from ICTs. Conference paper for the Communications Research Forum, Productivity Commission, Government of Australia, October.

Pohjola, Matt. 2001. Information Technology and Economic Growth: A Cross-Country Analysis. In *Information Technology, Productivity, and Economic Growth,* ed. Matt Pohjola. Oxford: Oxford University Press.

Samuelson, Paul A. 2004. Where Ricardo and Mill Rebut and Confirm Arguments of Mainstream Economists Against Globalization. *Journal of Economic Perspectives* 18, no. 3 (Summer): 135–46.

Scarpetta, Stefano, Andrea Bassanini, Dirk Pilat, and Paul Schreyer. 2000. *Economic Growth in the OECD Area: Recent Trends at the Aggregate and Sectoral Level.* Economics Department Working Paper 248. Paris: Organization for Economic Cooperation and Development.

Schott, Peter K. 2001. *Do Rich and Poor Countries Specialize in a Different Mix of Goods? Evidence from Product-Level US Trade Data.* NBER Working Paper 8492. Cambridge, MA: National Bureau of Economic Research.

Schott, Peter K. 2004. Across-Product Versus Within-Product Specialization in International Trade. *Quarterly Journal of Economics* 119, no. 2 (May): 647–78.

Schreyer, Paul. 2001. *Measuring Productivity: Measurement of Aggregate and Industry-Level Productivity Growth: OE Manual.* Paris: OE Publications.

Schultze, Charles L. 1999. Downsized and Out? Job Security and American Workers. *Brookings Review* (Fall). Washington: Brookings Institution.

Schultze, Charles L. 2004. *Offshoring, Import Competition, and the Jobless Recovery.* Brookings Institution Policy Brief 136. Washington: Brookings Institution.

Shapiro, Carl, and Hal Varian. 1999. A *Strategic Guide to the Network Economy*. Boston, MA: Harvard Business School Press.

Slaughter, Matthew. 2003. Mainstay VI: Technology, Trade, and Investment: The Public Opinion Disconnect. Emergency Committee for American Trade. Photocopy (January).

Stiroh, Kevin. 2001. *Information Technology and the US Productivity Revival: What Do the Industry Data Say?* Staff Reports 115 (January). New York: Federal Reserve Bank of New York.

Stiroh, Kevin. 2002. Information Technology and the U.S. Productivity Revival: A Review of the Evidence. Summary paper and update of a presentation at the New Economies, Hedonic Measures, and International Comparability session of the 2001 Conference of the National Association of Business Economists, September.

Solow, Robert. 1957. Technical Change and the Aggregate Production Function. *Review of Economics and Statistics* 63: 275–82.

Triplett, Jack. 2004. *Handbook on Hedonic Indexes and Quality Adjustments In Price Indexes: Special Application to Information Technology Products*. OECD STI Working Paper 2004/9. Paris: Organization for Economic Cooperation and Development, Directorate of Science, Technology and Industry.

UNCTAD (UN Conference on Trade and Development). 2002. *Manual of Statistics on International Trade in Services*. New York, Geneva, Paris, and Brussels: UNCTAD, European Commission, International Monetary Fund, Organization for Economic Cooperation and Development, and World Trade Organization.

UNDP (UN Development Programme). 2001. *Human Development Report 2001: Making New Technologies Work for Human Development*. New York: Oxford University Press.

US Census Bureau. 1997. *Bridge Between NAICS and SIC*. Washington. Available at www.census.gov (accessed September 30, 2005).

USCIS (US Citizenship and Immigration Services). 2003. *Characteristics of Specialty Occupation Workers (H-1B): Fiscal Year 2002*. Washington.

USCIS (US Citizenship and Immigration Services). 2004a. *Characteristics of Specialty Occupation Workers (H-1B): Fiscal Year 2003*. Washington.

USCIS (US Citizenship and Immigration Services). 2004b. *Yearbook of Immigration Statistics*. Washington.

USCIS (US Citizenship and Immigration Services). 2005. Allocation of Additional H-1B Visas Created by the H-1B Reform Act of 2004. *Federal Register* 70, no. 86 (May 5).

Valletta, Rob, and Geoffrey MacDonald. 2004. *The Computer Evolution*. Economic Letter 2004–19 (July 23). San Francisco: Federal Reserve Bank of San Francisco.

van Ark, Bart. 2005. Does the European Union Need to Revive Productivity Growth? Groningen Growth and Development Centre Research Memorandum GD-75. Groningen, The Netherlands: University of Groningen.

van Ark, Bart, R. Inklaar, and R. H. McGuckin. 2003. "Changing Gear" Productivity, ICT and Service Industries: Europe and the United States. In *The Industrial Dynamics of the New Digital Economy*, ed. Jens Frøslev Christensen and Peter Maskell. Cheltenham, UK: Edward Elgar.

Vickery, Graham, and Desiree van Welsum. 2005. Potential Offshoring of ICT-Intensive Using Occupations. April 2005 Report to Working Party on the Information Economy. Paris: Organization for Economic Cooperation and Development.

Waverman, Leonard, Meloria Meschi, and Melvyn Fuss. 2005. The Impact of Telecoms on Economic Growth in Developing Countries. In *Africa: The Impact of Mobile Phones*. Moving the Debate Forward, Vodafone Policy Paper Series 2 (March).

Whichard, Obie, and Maria Borga. 2002. Selected Issues in the Measurement of US International Services. *Survey of Current Business* (June): 3638. Washington: Bureau of Economic Analysis.

Wilson, Daniel J. 2004. *IT and Beyond: The Contribution of Heterogeneous Capital to Productivity*. Working Paper 2004-23. San Francisco: Federal Reserve Bank of San Francisco.

Wilson, John S., Catherine L. Mann, and Tsunehiro Otsuki. 2003. Trade Facilitation and Economic Development: A New Approach to Measuring the Impact. *World Bank Economic Review* 7, no. 3. Washington: World Bank.

Wilson, John S., Catherine L. Mann, and Tsunehiro Otsuki. 2005. Assessing the Benefits of Trade Facilitation: A Global Perspective. *World Economy*: 841–71.

WITSA (World Information Technology and Services Alliance). 2002. *Digital Planet*. Arlington, VA.

WITSA (World Information Technology and Services Alliance). 2004. *Digital Planet*. Arlington, VA.

Zeile, William J. 2005. US Affiliates of Foreign Companies Operations in 2003. *Survey of Current Business* (August). Washington: Bureau of Economic Analysis.

Index

foreign residency, definition of, 201
foreign specialist workers. *See* H-1B visa
    holders
foreign students, in US, 185
foreign workers, competition from, 126,
    133, 178, 179*b*–80*b*, 180, 185, 193
Foxconn, 51*t*
free riders, 197
functional integration, and globalization
    of services, 106
functional skills, of US workforce, 181,
    183*f*, 183–84
funding
    for innovation, 195
    for R&D, 168, 168*n*
F-1 visa, 146, 146*n*

GDP elasticity, and IT investment, 5
GDP growth, and rising importance of IT,
    76–78
General Agreement on Trade in Services
    (GATS), 118
General Atlantic Partners, 113*b*
General Electric, 113*b*–14*b*
General Electric Capital Information
    Services (GECIS), 113*b*–14*b*
geographical location. *See also*
    outsourcing; *specific location*
    and diffusion of innovation, 193
    of electronics manufacturing services
        companies, 48–49, 50*t*–51*t*
    of hardware production, 34–35, 36*f*,
        48–49
    of intellectual property rights, 177, 177*n*
    of R&D activities, 166–68, 169*f*, 170*f*,
        171, 172*t*, 185
    of semiconductor production, 121*b*
    of services production, 115–16, 121*b*
    and tradability of services occupations,
        136–37
    of US multinational firms, and
        production factors, 34–35, 35*f*, 48–49
global companies. *See also* foreign-owned
    firms; multinational firms (US-
    owned); *specific firm*
    classification and ranking of, 58–60,
        59*t*–60*t*
    reclassification of, 208–209, 209*f*
    rise of, 52–55, 53*t*–54*t*
globalization
    accelerating pace of, 2–3, 98
    policy agenda for, 191–200
    relation of IT to, 1–10

global marketplace
    expansion of, 12–27
    integration of US firms into, 27–38
    sales by US firms in, 27–29, 28*f*
global production network
    electronics manufacturing, 48
    integrated, costs and technology as
        drivers of, 33–38
    for IT hardware, 32*t*, 32–33
government, role in IT globalization
    promotion, 198–200
government funding, for R&D, 168, 168*n*,
    195
Greenspan, Alan, 131
GSM Association, 83*b*

hardware, 3
    asset values, 40–42
    classification systems for, 204–205
    contract manufacturers of, role for, 46–49
    definition of, 4*b*
    income elasticity of, 7
    intensity, 74, 75*t*
    intrafirm trade in, 99–101, 100*n*
    markets for, expansion of, 13, 15*t*
    mergers and acquisitions activity,
        39–40, 39*f*
    price elasticity of, 7
    price of
        effect of globalization on, 62–65
        effect of supply on, 54–55
        as part of overall IT package, 68,
            69*b*–70*b*
        and product pricing difficulties, 124
    production of, 11
        capital intensity in, 33, 34*f*, 35, 35*f*
        cost savings and technology in, 33
        fragmentation of, effect on
            competitiveness, 97
        geographical location of, 34–35, 36*f*,
            48–49
        global network for, 32*t*, 32–33
        labor costs with, 33–35
        by US multinational firms, 30, 30*f*, 32,
            32*t*
    research intensity in, 163–64, 166
    shift to services and software from,
        28–29, 31, 40*b*, 55, 74, 163, 177, 208
    top global companies, 53*t*–54*t*, 54
    trade in
        data collection on, 199, 207
        pattern of, 99–103, 100*f*
    venture financing in, 187*f*, 188

H-1B visa holders, 142–43
  characteristics of, 143*n*, 143–44, 144*b*
  corporate users of, 153, 154*t*
  national origin of, 151, 151*n*, 153, 154*t*
  number of, 143, 145*f*, 145–47, 146*n*,
    147*t*–50*t*, 152, 153*n*
  top US-located employers, 153, 154*t*
  transfer of visa status by, 146, 146*n*
  wages paid to, 152–57, 156*b*–57*b*
headquarters services, 112, 112*f*, 114, 121*b*
health sector, IT investment in, 83, 88
Hewlett-Packard, 173*b*
Hong Kong, performance in global
  markets, 54
human capital. *See also* tax credits, human
    capital investment
  importance of, 194–95
  and innovation, 178–85
  investment in, 197–98

IBM
  affiliate operations, 114*b*
  headquarters services, 112
  patents granted, 170, 171*t*
  reclassification of, 208–209, 209*f*
  R&D activities, 173*b*
  shift from hardware to services in, 40*b*,
    58*n*, 208–209, 209*f*
immigration. *See* US visa holders
Immigration Act of 1990, 151*n*
imports. *See also* trade patterns
  arm's length, 99–100, 113*b*
  competition for, and labor productivity,
    81
  effect on prices, 90
  global IT, 19, 21*t*, 23*t*
  of intellectual property, 176
incentive-based compensation system,
    and labor productivity, 78
income disparity, effect of IT globalization
    on, 192
income elasticity
  definition of, 5
  and IT investment, 5–7
India
  engineers from, 179*b*–80*b*
  environment of innovation in, 192
  IT spending in, 17, 18, 26
  performance in global markets, 52
  policy agenda, 198
  services industry in, 113*b*
  US students from, 185
  US trade in services with, valuation of,
    123

US visa holders from, 143–44, 151,
    151*n*, 153, 154*t*
  venture financing in, 186
  wages paid in, versus wages for US
    visa holders, 157
Indigo N.V., 173*b*
Indonesia, social savings, 92
industrial countries. *See also specific
    country*
  and globalization of services, 116
  IT experiences of
    comparison of, 92–95, 94*t*
    lessons for developing countries
      from, 95
inflation, and prices, 79
information exchange, and IT
    investment, 7
"51 Information" (NAICS), 122
information technology
  change accelerated by, 1–2
  definition of, 3–5, 4*b*
  diffusion of
    effect on labor market, 125, 132
    throughout US economy, 74, 75*t*–76*t*,
      199–200
    and US productivity growth, 74–89,
      199–200
  economic characteristics of, 5
  effect on US economy, 2, 74–75
    versus other countries, 89–95
  focus on, 1–10
  globalization of
    implications for prices, 62–70
    productivity growth linked to,
      promotion of, 198
  global production patterns,
    fragmentation of, 19–27, 20*t*–23*t*,
      32
    and competitiveness, 97
    and employment, 37
  markets for, expansion of, 13, 14*t*–16*t*
  mergers and acquisitions in, 13, 38–42,
    43*t*–45*t*
  production of, employment in, 126
  as related to communications, 3
  role in productivity growth, 191
  role in transforming US workplaces
    and businesses, 76–78, 105, 199–200
    and labor market, 126
    and policy agenda, 192, 195–98
  spending on (*See* spending)
  two-way trade in, importance of,
    19, 31
  uptake of, constraints on, 88–89

usage of
and benefits of globalization, 192,
199–200
cost reduction through, 85, 86f, 87–88,
88t
versus production, 90
and wage dispersion, 138
Information Technology Agreement
(1997), 2, 19, 24b–26b, 192
effects of, 25b–26b
information technology–enabled services
(ITES), 27n, 106
information technology firms. *See* foreign-
owned firms; global companies;
multinational firms (US-owned);
specific firm
information technology hardware. *See*
hardware
information technology investment. *See*
investment
information technology networks, role in
productivity enhancement, 87
information technology occupations
data on, 138–42, 139t–41t, 152, 199
educational demands for, 180–84
growth of, 137
types of, 126, 127b–28b
unemployment rate dynamics, 132,
132f, 143, 164
information technology package, overall
price of, 68, 69b–70b
and product pricing difficulties, 124
information technology products. *See also*
hardware; services; software
global exports of, 12
global markets for, linkages between
US firms and, 11–60
global spending on, 12
international trade data on, collection
of, challenges in, 122–24, 199
marketplace for
expansion of, 12–27
measures of, 12
prices of, and globalized production, 11
US cross-border trade in, 98–103
US market for, 11
information technology professionals
cross-border movement of, 142–57
foreign, US visas for (*See* United States
visa holders)
information technology services. *See*
services
information technology software. *See*
software

innovation. *See also* research and
development; technological change
adjustment to, policy agenda for, 191
cross-border transfer of, effect on
tradability, 161
disruption caused by, avoidance of, 193
effect on prices, 162
foreign, purchasing of, 171, 173b
funding for, 195
globalization of, 159–89
embracing, 195
example of, 175b
and globalization of venture financing,
185–88, 186f, 187f
human capital and, 178–85
macroeconomic effects of, 191
measures of, 168, 169f
promotion of, policy agenda for, 193
research-capital intensity of, 164, 164t
and research employment, 184–85
role in economic development, 159,
199–200
and R&D, 160–62
insurance, cross-border trade in, 107n
"integrating" skills, 142
Intel Corporation, 64, 121b, 171
intellectual property
in manufacturing, 177
ownership of, benefits of, 176, 177f
internal company information technology
spending, definition of, 4b
International Association for the
Evaluation of Educational
Achievement (IEA), 184n
International Monetary Fund, 123
Internet
adoption of, 2
economic impact of, 8
and outsourcing of services, 107
top global companies, 53t, 54
venture financing in, 187f, 188
intrafirm trade, 99
in business and professional services,
112, 112f
data collection on, 123–24, 199
within foreign-owned firms, 99,
101–103
in hardware, 99–101, 100n
in intellectual property, 176
in R&D, 162, 177, 178f
in services, 103–104, 104f
in software, 99
within US multinational firms, 99–103,
102f

intrafirm transfers, of IT professionals, US visas for. *See* L-1 visa holders
investment, 2. *See also* venture financing
  and benefits of IT globalization, 192
  in communications equipment, 13
  diffusion of, into US economy, 62
  economic effects of, 5–7
  effect on labor market, 125
  focus on software in, 71–74
  in human capital, 197–98
  importance of communications equipment in, 71, 72f
  and job churn rates, 130, 131f
  and labor productivity, 78, 92, 93b, 94–95
  link between workers and, 78
  network externalities, 7–10
  rate of return to, 7–10
  in semiconductor production, effect on prices, 63
  in services, 115
  and skill-biased technological change, 133–34
  and transactional linkages, 85, 86f
  uneven sectoral diffusion of, 81–89, 84f
  in US economy, macroeconomic overview of, 70–74
  waves of, and NIPA data, 71, 72f
Ireland, social savings, 90, 91n, 91f
ITA. *See* Information Technology Agreement (1997)
ITES. *See* information technology–enabled services (ITES)

Japan
  performance in global markets, 52, 54
  semiconductor market in, 56, 56f, 57t
  share of global IT exports, 19
  social savings, 92
job churn, 128–31, 129f, 131f, 199
job loss. *See also* unemployment rate
  permanent, policies for, 196–97
Job Openings and Labor Turnover Survey (JOLTS), 127b
job tenure, effect of technological change on, 129–30, 130n

Korea, 19, 25, 54, 92

labor. *See also* employee(s); employment; workforce
  in business and professional services, effect of globalization on, 135–42
  data collection on, 127b–28b, 138–42, 139t–41t, 199, 210
  demand for, effect of automation on, 136
  effect of business cycle on, 131–33, 132f
  effect of globalization on, 125–58, 191, 196
    in services industry, 116
  effect of innovation on, 178–85, 196
  effect of outsourcing on, 126, 133, 136, 136n
  occupation data, 138–42, 139t–41t, 199
  restructuring of, 126
  skilled (*See* skilled labor)
labor condition application (LCA), 152–53
labor costs. *See also* wage differentials; wage premium
  in hardware production, 33–36
  in services, 33–35, 68
  in software, 68
labor intensity, of R&D, 164, 164t
labor productivity, 131
  globalization, technology and, 80–81, 131
  and IT investment, 78, 92, 93b, 94–95
  and wage dispersion, 133
Lenovo, 40b
license fees, for intellectual property, 176–77, 177f
licensure
  effect on IT uptake, 88
  effect on services trade, 117
literacy
  document, 181, 183f
  prose, 181
L-1 visa holders, 142–43
  characteristics of, 143–44, 144b
  number of, 143, 144f, 153n
  wages paid to, 152–57

macroeconomic benefits
  of globalization, 191, 194
    proactive policy agenda for, 193, 194f
  of labor restructuring, 126
  of R&D, 175–78, 177f
  of services trade liberalization, 118
majority-owned foreign affiliates (MOFAs)
  definition of, 202
  foreign production by, 29, 30f, 34, 35f
  and ownership overlaps, 211
  and pattern of trade in hardware, 99, 101n–102n, 101–103
  trade in intellectual property, 176

versus communications, 13, 14*t*–15*t*
goods versus software and services, 17–19, 18*f*
internal company, definition of, 4*b*
and multinational firm sales, 27, 28*f*
versus software and services, 17–19, 18*f*
R&D, 164–66, 165*t*, 167*f*, 167
spillovers. *See* network externalities
Standard Industrial Classification (SIC), 204–207
State Employment Security Agency (SESA), 156*b*
supply-side forces, and diffusion of innovation, 193

Taiwan, 54, 91*n*
tariffs, on IT products, 2, 24*b*, 198
and IT usage, 90
task content, and wage premiums, 134–35
tax credits, human capital investment, 197–98
technological change. *See also* innovation
and accelerated globalization, 98
adjustment to, policy agenda for, 191
and cross-border trade replacement, 136
disruption caused by, avoidance of, 193
as driver of production, 33
and education profiles, 180–84
and globalization of services, 106–107
and job tenure, 129–30
and labor market, 125, 196
macroeconomic effects of, 191
and outsourcing, 106–107
and prices, 162
in semiconductor production, effect on prices, 63–64
skill-biased, and investment, 133
technology, and labor productivity, 80–81
technology bubble
effect on IT professional unemployment rate, 143
and global sales by US firms, 27
and IT expenditures, 13, 19
and job churn rates, 130, 131*f*
technology frontier, created by innovation, 161, 193, 194
technology risk, in IT occupations, 132–33
telecommunications
costs of, and outsourcing of services, 107
cross-border trade in, 107, 107*n*, 111
telecommunications carriers, as top global companies, 60

telecommunications networks, as leaders in IT intensity, 85
terms of trade, effect on prices, 90
Thailand, 91*n*
Thomson VentureXpert, 40, 42, 186
total factor productivity (TFP) growth, and diffusion of IT, 78, 90, 91*f*, 93*b*
tradability
effect of IT on, 97
of services, 106, 116–17, 161, 196
of services occupations, 136–37
and transfer of innovations, 161
trade
exposure to, and technology spillovers, 161
growth in, and services trade, 107, 111*f*–12*f*
intrafirm (*See* intrafirm trade)
linked to productivity, relevance of technology to, 80–81
trade balance, 98–104
effect of R&D on, 176–78, 177*f*
in services, 103, 107, 110*f*–11*f*, 116
trade deficit, effect of trade liberalization on, 98
trade facilitation
and liberalization of IT trade, 98
role of services in, 119–20, 119*t*
trade liberalization, 98
effect on services trade, 118*t*, 118–20
policy agenda for, 192–93
promotion of, 198
trade negotiations, over services trade, potential for, 117–21
trade patterns
in hardware, 99–103, 100*f*
imbalances in, 20*t*–2323*t*, 26
intrafirm, 99–103, 102*f*
in services, 99, 103–104, 104*f*
in software, 99
trade surplus, intellectual property, 176–77, 177*f*
training
software, 68
workforce, 196
and labor productivity, 78
transactional linkages, and IT investment, 85, 86*f*
transaction costs
effect of IT on, 2
and globalization of services, 105–106
transfer pricing, by multinational firms, 124
Trends in International Mathematics and Science Study (TIMSS), 184, 184*n*

wage insurance, 196–97
wage premium, 133–34, 152
   and labor productivity, 80
   and labor tradability, 137
welfare gains, from services trade
   liberalization, 119
wireless services, 82*b*–83*b*
Wolfson Microelectronics, 175*b*
work design, and labor productivity, 78
workforce. *See also* employee(s);
    employment; labor
   development of, policy agenda for, 193
   educational attainment of, 180, 181, 182*f*
   functional skills of, 181, 183*f*, 183–84

workforce training, 196
   and labor productivity, 78
workplaces, IT transformation of, 76–78,
    105, 199–200
   and labor market, 126
   and policy agenda, 192, 195–98
World Trade Organization (WTO)
   Information Technology Agreement,
    24*b*–26*b*, 192–93
   trade database, 114*n*

Y2K glitches
   effect on IT employment, 132–33
   software repair to avoid, 73, 73*n*

Other Publications from the Institute for International Economics

WORKING PAPERS

BOOKS

Subsidies in International Trade*
Gary Clyde Hufbauer and Joanna Shelton Erb
1984   ISBN 0-88132-004-8
**International Debt: Systemic Risk and Policy
Response***   William R. Cline
1984   ISBN 0-88132-015-3
**Trade Protection in the United States: 31 Case
Studies***   Gary Clyde Hufbauer, Diane E. Berliner,
and Kimberly Ann Elliott
1986   ISBN 0-88132-040-4
**Toward Renewed Economic Growth in Latin
America*** Bela Balassa, Gerardo M. Bueno, Pedro-
Pablo Kuczynski, and Mario Henrique Simonsen
1986   ISBN 0-88132-045-5
Capital Flight and Third World Debt*
Donald R. Lessard and John Williamson, editors
1987   ISBN 0-88132-053-6
**The Canada-United States Free Trade Agreement:
The Global Impact***
Jeffrey J. Schott and Murray G. Smith, editors
1988   ISBN 0-88132-073-0
World Agricultural Trade: Building a Consensus*
William M. Miner and Dale E. Hathaway, editors
1988   ISBN 0-88132-071-3
Japan in the World Economy*
Bela Balassa and Marcus Noland
1988   ISBN 0-88132-041-2
**America in the World Economy: A Strategy for
the 1990s***   C. Fred Bergsten
1988   ISBN 0-88132-089-7
**Managing the Dollar: From the Plaza to the
Louvre***   Yoichi Funabashi
1988, 2d. ed. 1989   ISBN 0-88132-097-8
**United States External Adjustment and the World
Economy***   William R. Cline
May 1989   ISBN 0-88132-048-X
Free Trade Areas and U.S. Trade Policy*
Jeffrey J. Schott, editor
May *1989*   ISBN 0-88132-094-3
**Dollar Politics: Exchange Rate Policymaking in
the United States***
I. M. Destler and C. Randall Henning
September 1989   ISBN 0-88132-079-X
**Latin American Adjustment: How Much Has
Happened?***   John Williamson, editor
April 1990   ISBN 0-88132-125-7
**The Future of World Trade in Textiles and
Apparel***   William R. Cline
1987, 2d ed. June *1999*   ISBN 0-88132-110-9
**Completing the Uruguay Round: A Results-
Oriented Approach to the GATT Trade
Negotiations***   Jeffrey J. Schott, editor
September 1990   ISBN 0-88132-130-3

Economic Sanctions Reconsidered (2 volumes)
Economic Sanctions Reconsidered:
Supplemental Case Histories
Gary Clyde Hufbauer, Jeffrey J. Schott, and
Kimberly Ann Elliott
1985, 2d ed. Dec. 1990   ISBN cloth 0-88132-115-X
                              ISBN paper 0-88132-105-2
**Economic Sanctions Reconsidered: History and
Current Policy**   Gary Clyde Hufbauer,
Jeffrey J. Schott, and Kimberly Ann Elliott
December 1990   ISBN cloth 0-88132-140-0
                              ISBN paper 0-88132-136-2
**Pacific Basin Developing Countries: Prospects for
Economic Sanctions Reconsidered: History
and Current Policy**   Gary Clyde Hufbauer,
Jeffrey J. Schott, and Kimberly Ann Elliott
December 1990   ISBN cloth 0-88132-140-0
                              ISBN paper 0-88132-136-2
**Pacific Basin Developing Countries: Prospects
for the Future***   Marcus Noland
January 1991   ISBN cloth 0-88132-141-9
                              ISBN paper 0-88132-081-1
Currency Convertibility in Eastern Europe*
John Williamson, editor
October 1991   ISBN 0-88132-128-1
**International Adjustment and Financing: The
Lessons of 1985-1991*** C. Fred Bergsten, editor
January 1992   ISBN 0-88132-112-5
**North American Free Trade: Issues and
Recommendations***
Gary Clyde Hufbauer and Jeffrey J. Schott
April 1992   ISBN 0-88132-120-6
Narrowing the U.S. Current Account Deficit*
Alan J. Lenz/*June 1992*   ISBN 0-88132-103-6
The Economics of Global Warming
William R. Cline/*June 1992*   ISBN 0-88132-132-X
**US Taxation of International Income: Blueprint
for Reform***   Gary Clyde Hufbauer,
assisted by Joanna M. van Rooij
October 1992   ISBN 0-88132-134-6
**Who's Bashing Whom? Trade Conflict in High-
Technology Industries** Laura D'Andrea Tyson
November 1992   ISBN 0-88132-106-0
Korea in the World Economy* Il SaKong
January 1993   ISBN 0-88132-183-4
**Pacific Dynamism and the International
Economic System***
C. Fred Bergsten and Marcus Noland, editors
May 1993   ISBN 0-88132-196-6
Economic Consequences of Soviet Disintegration*
John Williamson, editor
May 1993   ISBN 0-88132-190-7
**Reconcilable Differences? United States-Japan
Economic Conflict***
C. Fred Bergsten and Marcus Noland
June 1993   ISBN 0-88132-129-X

Reforming Korea's Industrial Conglomerates
Edward M. Graham
January 2003   ISBN 0-88132-337-3
**Industrial Policy in an Era of Globalization:
Lessons from Asia**
Marcus Noland and Howard Pack
March 2003   ISBN 0-88132-350-0
Reintegrating India with the World Economy
T. N. Srinivasan and Suresh D. Tendulkar
March 2003   ISBN 0-88132-280-6
**After the Washington Consensus:
Restarting Growth and Reform
in Latin America**   Pedro-Pablo Kuczynski
and John Williamson, editors
March 2003   ISBN 0-88132-347-0
**The Decline of US Labor Unions and
the Role of Trade**   Robert E. Baldwin
June 2003   ISBN 0-88132-341-1
**Can Labor Standards Improve
under Globalization?**
Kimberly Ann Elliott and Richard B. Freeman
June 2003   ISBN 0-88132-332-2
**Crimes and Punishments? Retaliation
under the WTO**   Robert Z. Lawrence
October 2003   ISBN 0-88132-359-4
Inflation Targeting in the World Economy
Edwin M. Truman
October 2003   ISBN 0-88132-345-4
**Foreign Direct Investment and Tax
Competition**   John H. Mutti
November 2003   ISBN 0-88132-352-7
**Has Globalization Gone Far Enough?
The Costs of Fragmented Markets**
Scott Bradford and Robert Z. Lawrence
February 2004   ISBN 0-88132-349-7
**Food Regulation and Trade:
Toward a Safe and Open Global System**
Tim Josling, Donna Roberts, and David Orden
March 2004   ISBN 0-88132-346-2
**Controlling Currency Mismatches in
Emerging Markets**
Morris Goldstein and Philip Turner
April 2004   ISBN 0-88132-360-8
**Free Trade Agreements: US Strategies
and Priorities**   Jeffrey J. Schott, editor
April 2004   ISBN 0-88132-361-6
Trade Policy and Global Poverty
William R. Cline
June 2004   ISBN 0-88132-365-9
**Bailouts or Bail-ins? Responding
to Financial Crises in Emerging Economies**
Nouriel Roubini and Brad Setser
August 2004   ISBN 0-88132-371-3
Transforming the European Economy
Martin Neil Baily and Jacob Kirkegaard
September 2004   ISBN 0-88132-343-8

**Chasing Dirty Money: The Fight Against
Money Laundering**
Peter Reuter and Edwin M. Truman
November 2004   ISBN 0-88132-370-5
**The United States and the World Economy:
Foreign Economic Policy for the Next Decade**
C. Fred Bergsten
January 2005   ISBN 0-88132-380-2
**Does Foreign Direct Investment Promote
Development ?**   Theodore Moran, Edward
M. Graham, and Magnus Blomström, editors
April 2005   ISBN 0-88132-381-0
American Trade Politics, 4th ed.
I. M. Destler
June 2005   ISBN 0-88132-382-9
**Why Does Immigration Divide America?
Public Finance and Political Opposition
to Open Borders**   Gordon Hanson
August 2005   ISBN 0-88132-400-0
Reforming the US Corporate Tax
Gary Clyde Hufbauer and Paul L. E. Grieco
September 2005   ISBN 0-88132-384-5
The United States as a Debtor Nation
William R. Cline
September 2005   ISBN 0-88132-399-3
**NAFTA Revisited: Achievements
and Challenges**
Gary Clyde Hufbauer and Jeffrey J. Schott,
assisted by Paul L. E. Grieco and Yee Wong
October 2005   ISBN 0-88132-334-9
**US National Security and Foreign Direct
Investment**
Edward M. Graham and David M. Marchick
May 2006   ISBN 0-88132-391-8
        ISBN 978-0-88132-391-7
**Accelerating the Globalization of America:
The Role for Information Technology**
Catherine L. Mann, assisted by Jacob Kirkegaard
June 2006   ISBN 0-88132-390-X
        ISBN 978-0-88132-390-0

SPECIAL REPORTS

1   **Promoting World Recovery: A Statement
        on Global Economic Strategy***
        by 26 Economists from Fourteen Countries
        December 1982   ISBN 0-88132-013-7
2   **Prospects for Adjustment in Argentina,
        Brazil, and Mexico: Responding to the
        Debt Crisis***   John Williamson, editor
        June 1983   ISBN 0-88132-016-1
3   **Inflation and Indexation: Argentina, Brazil,
        and Israel***   John Williamson, editor
        March 1985   ISBN 0-88132-037-4

DISTRIBUTORS OUTSIDE THE UNITED STATES

Australia, New Zealand, and Papua New Guinea
D. A. Information Services
648 Whitehorse Road
Mitcham, Victoria 3132, Australia
Tel: 61-3-9210-7777
Fax: 61-3-9210-7788
Email: service@dadirect.com.au
www.dadirect.com.au

India, Bangladesh, Nepal, and Sri Lanka
Viva Books Private Limited
Mr. Vinod Vasishtha
4737/23 Ansari Road
Daryaganj, New Delhi 110002
India
Tel: 91-11-4224-2200
Fax: 91-11-4224-2240
Email: viva@vivagroupindia.net
www.vivagroupindia.com

Mexico, Central America, South America, and Puerto Rico
US PubRep, Inc.
311 Dean Drive
Rockville, MD 20851
Tel: 301-838-9276
Fax: 301-838-9278
Email: c.falk@ieee.org
www.uspubrep.com

Southeast Asia (*Brunei, Burma, Cambodia, Indonesia, Malaysia, the Philippines, Singapore, Taiwan, Thailand, and Vietnam*)
APAC Publishers Services PTE Ltd.
70 Bendemeer Road #05-03
Hiap Huat House
Singapore 333940
Tel: 65-6844-7333
Fax: 65-6747-8916
Email: service@apacmedia.com.sg

Canada
Renouf Bookstore
5369 Canotek Road, Unit 1
Ottawa, Ontario KlJ 9J3, Canada
Tel: 613-745-2665
Fax: 613-745-7660
www.renoufbooks.com

Japan
United Publishers Services Ltd.
1-32-5, Higashi-shinagawa
Shinagawa-ku, Tokyo 140-0002
Japan
Tel: 81-3-5479-7251
Fax: 81-3-5479-7307
Email: purchasing@ups.co.jp
For trade accounts only. Individuals will find IIE books in leading Tokyo bookstores.

Middle East
MERIC
2 Bahgat Ali Street, El Masry Towers
Tower D, Apt. 24
Zamalek, Cairo
Egypt
Tel. 20-2-7633824
Fax: 20-2-7369355
Email: mahmoud_fouda@mericonline.com
www.mericonline.com

United Kingdom, Europe (*including Russia and Turkey*), Africa, and Israel
The Eurospan Group
c/o Turpin Distribution
Pegasus Drive
Stratton Business Park
Biggleswade, Bedfordshire
SG18 8TQ
United Kingdom
Tel: 44 (0) 1767-604972
Fax: 44 (0) 1767-601640
Email: eurospan@turpin-distribution.com
www.eurospangroup.com/bookstore

**Visit our Web site at:
www.iie.com
E-mail orders to:
IIE mail@PressWarehouse.com**